19010

THE WORLD OF THE TALMUD

Here is a rich and [...] on to the world of the T[...] studies and debates [...] d Babylonian academ[...] efore 200 B.C. to the ye[...]

In this b[...] n of *Pirke Abot* (The Wisdom of th[...] one of the treatises of the Talmud, Judah Gold[...] has illuminated for the modern reader the interpretation of the Bible and the development of Jewish law and tradition which concerned the Rabbis who made the study of the Talmud their major preoccupation.

Pirke Abot is a collection of the sayings of the Synagogue Fathers, maxims which summarized the anguish, ecstasy and understanding they had experienced in their penetrating study and practice of the Law. The earliest sages quoted are men who lived sometime between the latter half of the fifth and the third century before the Common Era. The latest are descendants of Rabbi Judah the Prince, who lived in the third century of the Common Era. Their maxims record their reflections on what constitutes God-fearing, civilized conduct and thought.

Included in this edition, too, are the first English translations of many of the Classical Commentaries on *Pirke Abot* made by generations of Talmud scholars, whose close study and interpretation of the teachings of their predecessors made the ancient Wisdom of the Fathers a fresh testament for the Sons.

Judah Goldin, Professor of Hebrew Literature at the University of Pennsylvania, has been Dean and Associate Professor of Agada at the Seminary College, the Jewish Theological Seminary of America, a visiting Professor of Jewish Literature and History at Duke University and an Associate Professor of Religion at the University of Iowa. He is the author of *The Period of The Talmud* and the translator of *The Fathers According to Rabbi Nathan.*

The illumination on the front cover of this edition is a detail from The Rothschild manuscript XXIV and is reproduced by the courtesy of the Collection of the Bezalel National Museum, Jerusalem.

Library
Oakland S.U.M.

SIGNET and MENTOR Books You'll Want to Read

(0451)

☐ **WHAT THE GREAT RELIGIONS BELIEVE by Joseph Gaer.** An enlightening account of the world's historic religions—Hinduism, Jainism, Christianity, Islam, Zoroastrianism, Confucianism, Judaism, Zen Buddhism, and others—with selections from their sacred literature. Bibliography. (119789—$2.95)

☐ **THE GOSPEL ACCORDING TO ZEN: Beyond the Death of God edited by Robert Sohl and Audrey Carr.** This unusual book brings together the most enlightening parables, riddles and poems of East and West, to explore and illuminate the beliefs behind religion. (621840—$2.95)

☐ **THE MEANING OF THE DEAD SEA SCROLLS by A. Powell Davies.** A fascinating interpretation of one of the most important archaeological discoveries of recent times, ancient documents which revolutionized religious teachings and beliefs. (620976—$1.95)

☐ **THE SERMON ON THE MOUNT According to Vedanta by Swami Prabhavananda.** A fascinating and superbly enlightening Hindu reading of the central gospel of Christianity by the renowned author of books on Indian religious philosophy. (622383—$3.95)

Buy them at your local bookstore or use this convenient coupon for ordering.

THE NEW AMERICAN LIBRARY, INC.,
P.O. Box 999, Bergenfield, New Jersey 07621

Please send me the books I have checked above. I am enclosing $_____
(please add $1.00 to this order to cover postage and handling). Send check or money order—no cash or C.O.D.'s. Prices and numbers are subject to change without notice.

Name_____

Address_____

City _____ State _____ Zip Code _____

Allow 4-6 weeks for delivery.
This offer is subject to withdrawal without notice.

the Living Talmud

THE WISDOM
OF THE FATHERS

and Its Classical

Commentaries

selected and translated

with an Essay by

Judah Goldin

A MENTOR BOOK from
NEW AMERICAN LIBRARY

© 1957 BY JUDAH GOLDIN
COPYRIGHT, 1955, BY YALE UNIVERSITY PRESS

All rights reserved

A publication under the auspices of
The Jewish Theological Seminary of America
LOUIS FINKELSTEIN
Chancellor and President of the Faculties
SAUL LIEBERMAN
Dean of the Rabbinical School and Professor of Talmud

*This book is also available in a hardcover edition
published by The University of Chicago Press.*

 MENTOR TRADEMARK REG. U.S. PAT. OFF. AND FOREIGN COUNTRIES
REGISTERED TRADEMARK—MARCA REGISTRADA
HECHO EN WINNIPEG, CANADA

SIGNET, SIGNET CLASSIC, MENTOR, PLUME, MERIDIAN AND NAL
BOOKS *are published by New American Library,
1633 Broadway, New York, New York 10019*

FIRST MENTOR PRINTING, SEPTEMBER, 1957

11   12   13   14   15   16   17   18   19

Printed in Canada

To my mother and more than brother Harry

הרבה צער נצטערו עמי בתורה

and to the memory of my father

Contents

In Praise of Wisdom

"Give thy ears, hear what is said," declared the Egyptian Amen-em-opet, "give thy heart to understand them. To put them in thy heart is worth while, [but] it is damaging to him who neglects them. Let them rest in the casket of thy belly, that they may be a key in thy heart." An author of the Biblical Book of Proverbs was to echo this thought: "Incline thine ear, and hear the words of the wise, and apply thy heart unto my knowledge. For it is a pleasant thing if thou keep them within thee; let them be established altogether upon thy lips." And he goes on: "That thy trust may be in the Lord, I have made them known to thee this day, even to thee."

About two hundred years before the Common Era, Jesus the son of Sirach was to say: "My son, if thou wilt, thou shalt be instructed; and if thou wilt yield thy soul, thou shalt be prudent. If thou love to hear, thou shalt receive; and if thou incline thine ear, thou shalt be wise. Stand thou in the multitude of the elders; and whoso is wise, cleave thou unto him. Be willing to listen to every godly discourse; and let not the proverbs of understanding escape thee. If thou seest a man of understanding, get thee betimes unto him, and let thy foot wear out the steps of his doors. Let thy mind dwell upon the ordinances of the Lord, and meditate continually in his commandments: he shall establish thine heart, and thy desire of wisdom shall be given unto thee."

Not long thereafter a distinguished citizen of Zeredah, Yose ben Joezer, had this to say: "Let thy house be a meeting-place for the Sages, and sit in the very dust at their feet, and thirstily drink in their words."

There is no need to assume that there is always direct borrowing whenever we encounter coincident thoughts and expressions. For everywhere Wisdom has been pursued, and courted, and praised, perhaps even a little more than she deserved. Indeed, one who knew her well once confessed: "For in much wisdom is much vexation; and he that increaseth

9

knowledge increaseth sorrow." But he may have been in a bad mood then.

In each age many of those who have reflected on their experiences have been tempted to summarize what they learned. And if they knew how to turn a phrase to telling effect, they put their reflections into maxims. To us they sound like quotations; to them the maxims were a personal, keenly felt response to the anguish and sufferings they had endured, the despondence and ecstasies they had lived through, and finally the understanding they had arrived at.

How is the original heartbeat to be heard? *"Let these words which I command thee this day, be upon thy heart* (Deuteronomy 6:6), that is, let them not be in thy sight like some antiquated decree which no man takes seriously, but rather like some recently promulgated one to which everybody hastens eagerly"* (Sifre Deuteronomy, 33, ed. Finkelstein, p. 59).

Pirke Abot, the *Wisdom of the Fathers,* is a collection of maxims, sayings of the Synagogue Fathers from the Men of the Great Assembly (sometime between the latter half of the fifth and the third centuries B.C.) down through descendants of Rabbi Judah the Prince in the third century of the Common Era. These maxims are a record of the Father's preoccupations, their emphases and values, and their epigrammatic formulation of reflections on what constitutes God-fearing, civilized conduct and thought.

Pirke Abot is one of the treatises of the Talmud, that enormous archive of the studies, and debates, and dialogues in the Palestinian and Babylonian academies, all devoted to the interpretation of the Bible and the development of Jewish law and tradition. As one of the Talmudic treatises, *Pirke Abot* came to be studied and commented on with that thoroughness which has always characterized study of the Talmud—that is to say, teachers and sages undertook not only to explain the patent meaning of its terms, but to derive implications from these sayings, to make clear the permanent relevance of the teachings of the Talmudic Fathers. In every generation therefore Talmud students took up the text of *Pirke Abot,* commented on it sentence by sentence and clause by clause, drew upon the interpretations of their predecessors and added something of their own. In this way they made the ancient Wisdom of the Fathers a fresh testament for the Sons. And thus, the text of *Pirke Abot* and the classical commentaries on it became an active constituent of the legacy of the living Talmud.

I

On the Talmud

I

This is the way the Babylonian Talmud begins:

FROM WHAT TIME IN THE EVENING MAY THE *Shema*[1]
BE RECITED? FROM THE TIME THE PRIESTS[2] MAY BEGIN
TO EAT OF THEIR HEAVE-OFFERING, UNTIL THE END OF
THE FIRST WATCH[3]. . . .

"On what basis does the Tanna set forth with the
statement[4], FROM WHAT TIME? Besides, why does he
first state it in terms of evening? He should first state it
in terms of morning!"

"For the Tanna the basis is Scripture, where it is written,
[*And thou shalt rehearse them . . .*] *when thou liest
down and when thou risest up* (Deuteronomy 6:7). And
this is the meaning of his statement in the Mishna: When
is it that recitation of the *Shema* at lying-down-time may
take place? FROM THE TIME THE PRIESTS MAY BEGIN
TO EAT OF THEIR HEAVE-OFFERING.— If you wish, say
this: The Tanna has taken his cue from the idiom in the
account of the creation of the world, where it is written,

[1] The fundamental prayer of Judaism beginning with the words
Shema Yisrael, "Hear, O Israel: the Lord our God, the Lord is one.
And thou shalt love the Lord thy God with all thy heart, and with
all thy soul, and with all thy might," consisting of Deuteronomy
6:4–9, 11:13–21, and Numbers 15:37–41.

[2] Who had become ritually unclean (Leviticus 22:4–7); even
after the necessary immersion they had to wait for sunset before
they could eat consecrated foods or heave-offering (Numbers
18:8–20).

[3] I.e., the fourth hour of the night, according to Rabbi Eliezer, who
maintains that the night is divided into three parts ("watches").

[4] "Statement," "state" are intended here as technical terms to
suggest the verb *teni*, from which the noun *tanna* is derived.

13

And [first] there was evening and [then] there was morning, one day" (Genesis 1:5).

"In that case, what about the sequel, which states, IN THE MORNING TWO BENEDICTIONS ARE READ BEFORE THE *Shema* AND ONE AFTER IT, AND IN THE EVENING TWO BENEDICTIONS ARE READ BEFORE AND TWO AFTER? Why not the clause about the evening first?"

"The Tanna opened the discussion with 'evening' and then moved on to the statement of 'morning' [FROM WHAT TIME IN THE MORNING MAY THE *Shema* BE RECITED]; so long as he was on the 'morning' subject, he went on to details of morning matters, and then reverted to details of evening matters."

Notice, no dramatis personae described or even named, no word about the time and place of the give-and-take. A statement is quoted, and immediately one plunges into the questions and answers which were exchanged in the academy as the scholars tried to understand and explain a "text." The heart of the matter—*explication de texte*—is what counts; it alone, hardly anything else.

It would be untrue to say that the Talmud never identifies the individuals who engage in debate. There are hundreds of dialogues recalled and who says what is carefully recorded. Thus, on certain issues Hillel said one thing, Shammai another; the School of Hillel held one view, the School of Shammai another. Later Rabbi Eliezer ben Hyrcanus says this, Rabbi Joshua ben Hananiah that; Rabbi Akiba insists that *this* is the law, while Rabbi Ishmael disagrees. So too with Rabbi Judah and Rabbi Meir, and later still in the third century Rabbi Johanan and Rabbi Simeon ben Lakish, or in Babylonia, Rab and Samuel, and in the fourth century Abbaye and Raba, and so on. Men are quoted by name even when there is no controversy. And yet the fact remains that the texture of the Talmudic substance is that of anonymity. The principal thing is the discussion, the line of argument, the nature of the reasoning employed and the logic of contention.

So too, it is not true that we never know where and when some decisions were reached. Some, we are informed, were arrived at in Jamnia or Usha in Palestine, some in Sura and Pumbedita in Babylonia. The location may be reported even more precisely, as the upper story of Hananiah ben Hezekiah ben Gorion's house. Nor is there never a reference to time. But again, the fact is that the chief preoccupation of the

Talmud, of the compilers of the Talmud, is with the content and direction of the discussion itself.

Finally, it is a serious, if not gross, oversimplification to say that for the Talmud nothing but exegesis counts, as though *pesak halakah*—determining what the law is—were immaterial, as though purely scholastic exercise, with no concern for practice and behavior, were the only aim of life. "One in whom there are no good works, though he studied much Torah, to what may he be likened? To a tree which stands in the desert, whose branches are numerous but whose roots are few: even if [only one] wind blows against it, it uproots it and sweeps it down . . . he is like a person who builds first with bricks and afterwards with stones: even when a little water gathers, it overthrows him immediately . . . he is like lime poured over bricks: even though a little rain falls on it, it softens immediately and is washed away . . . he is like a cup that has no base: as soon as the cup is filled it overturns, and whatever was in it spills . . . he is like a horse that has no bridle: when one mounts it, it throws him off headlong." Or even more to the point: "On one occasion when Rabbi Tarfon, Rabbi Yose the Galilean, and Rabbi Akiba were assembled in . . . Lydda, the following question was raised before them: Which is the more important, is study the more important, or is practice the more important? Rabbi Tarfon spoke up and said: 'Practice is the more important.' Rabbi Akiba spoke up and said: 'Study is the more important.' Whereupon they all spoke up and said: 'Study is the more important, for study leads to practice.'" Study, interpretation, debate are the discipline for living; without them no right action is likely; and with this the Talmud is very much concerned. Similarly, Talmudic discussion does seek to arrive at a conclusive outcome, so that it may be said at last—despite conflicting views—"Such and such is the law" (*Halakah ke-Reb Peloni*, or *Hilketa ke-Reb Peloni*).

What do we mean then by "only exegesis of the text counts"? This: That the Talmud is not a code or catechism, laying down in summary, categorical form what man's obligations are. It is on the contrary the record of a process, the actual process by means of which the law is made clear. Hence the tensions it preserves—views in conflict, argument advancing and withdrawing, contradictions harmonized only with acutest dialectic, diverse subjects made to reveal underlying unifying principles, the movement of the mind from theme to theme, and the succession of generations of scholars seeking for the new developments and insights sanctioned by the old. This process involved analysis and interpretation of the Scriptures, and of the rules derived from scriptural exegesis and the Oral Tradition, and organized later on into a kind of code-textbook by the Patriarch Rabbi Judah and his colleagues, about the year 200 of the regular calendar. This code-textbook is called the Mishna; and it is specifically the Mishna which the Talmud undertakes to explain, so that we may know what it means and what are its legitimate implications.

Let us return to the first page of the Babylonian Talmud, the first page of the first chapter of the first treatise of the Talmud. That treatise is called *Berakot,* that is, it is devoted primarily to the theme of benedictions and statutory prayers a Jew must recite. The Mishna opens with "From what time in the evening may the *Shema* be recited." But—protests the Amora, the Talmudic sage—this is hardly putting first things first! Before the Tanna, the sage of the Mishna, asks "From what time . . . may the *Shema* be recited," does he not in the first place have to establish that there *is* an obligation to recite the *Shema* daily? For where will you find in so many words that such an obligation exists? Moreover, if we are to discuss the times for reciting the *Shema,* why begin with the evening duty? Would it not be more natural to start with the morning duty?

To which a second Amora, a second Talmudic sage, replies: The author of the Mishnaic statement, the Tanna, opens the Mishna with "From what time . . . may the *Shema* be recited," because the obligation as such to recite the *Shema* he finds in the Biblical injunction [*And thou shalt speak of —rehearse—these words . . .*] *when thou liest down and when thou risest up;* hence the Tanna may proceed at once to attempt to fix the *time* for such recitation; and since in the Biblical idiom "lying down" is put first and only then "rising up," the Tanna adopts the same order: he raises the question as regards the evening duty first.

There is, however, says the Talmud, another explanation possible as to why the Tanna speaks first of the evening and then of the morning obligation. He takes as his cue the account of the creation of the world, where the order of the words in the verse is first evening, then morning: *And [first] there was evening and [then] there was morning.*

If this is the reason—retorts an Amora—why evening obligations are discussed first, why does a subsequent Mishna in our chapter read thus: "In the morning two benedictions

. . . and in the evening . . . two after," listing morning obligations first, and then evening obligations? Here too, evening
obligations should be stated first!

To which comes the following reply: The Tanna of our
Mishna began with a discussion of the evening duty and
followed that with a discussion of the morning duty (FROM
WHAT TIME IN THE MORNING MAY THE *Shema* BE RECITED);
once having taken up the morning theme, he continues with
it; and having disposed of it, he returns to the laws relating
to recitation of the evening *Shema*.

The Talmud is hardly done with the exposition of that one
statement of our Mishna. For example, one surely wonders
why the question "From what time in the evening may the
Shema be recited" is answered obliquely, "From the time the
priests may begin to eat of their heave-offerings." After all,
we do know when priests who had been ritually unclean and
had undergone the necessary immersion may begin to eat of
their heave-offerings; that is, when the stars appear. Why not
say so directly then? The evening *Shema* may be recited when
the stars appear!

And there is more to our Mishna than the first statement.
But the Talmudic passage we have cited and reviewed may
serve as an example of the Talmudic method. Briefly—what
a grotesque adverb for a Talmudic discussion!—the Talmud
takes each statement of the Mishna and subjects it to the
closest kind of scrutiny and analysis. And just as the Tannaim
(plural of Tanna), the Sages whose teachings are contained in
the Mishna and its cognate works—in other words, the Sages
of the first two centuries of our era—just as the Tannaim meticulously examined and explored and explained the Biblical
terms and commands, so the Amoraim (plural of Amora),
the Sages whose teachings and investigations are contained in
the Talmud—in other words, the Sages of Babylonia and
Palestine from about 200 to 500 of our era—so the Amoraim
examined and explored and explained the Mishnaic terms and
regulations. No word, no rule of the Mishna is trivial.

II

Such is the presumption and conviction of the Amoraim,
the men whose sayings and citations and views and debates
constitute the Talmud. It is an inevitable presumption and
conviction, considering who these men were, what was the

theme of their work, and what the tradition they inherited.

First then, the men. They were scholars and jurists, and like all genuine scholars and students of the law knew that texts are to be taken seriously, not with half a mind. The terms of a statement are not immaterial, above all if the law is to avoid ambiguity and misapplication. If, for example, therefore, the Mishna declares, "A MAN MAY BETROTH A WOMAN BY HIS OWN ACT OR BY THAT OF HIS AGENT," the Talmud is quite right to raise the question "If one can betroth a woman by the act of his agent, is it even necessary to state that he can do so personally"; why then the superfluous "by his own act"? Or again, if the Mishna says, "A MAN MAY GIVE HIS DAUGHTER IN BETROTHAL WHILE SHE IS A *Na'arah*" (the six months after she has become twelve years and a day old), the emphasis of the Talmud is very much to the point: "Only when she is a *na'arah*, but not while a minor: this supports Rab. For Rab Judah said in Rab's name—some say in Rabbi Eleazar's name: One may not give his daughter in betrothal while she is a minor, [but must wait] until she grows up and says, 'I want So-and-so.' " It is this very seriousness towards terms which makes Talmudic exegesis so detailed and exacting, makes it scholastic, perceptive, and finally comprehensive.

As to the theme—it is, after all, all of life. Concretely, the contents of the Mishna are distributed over sixty-three—originally, sixty—treatises. These treatises are organized under six divisions, or orders. *Seeds* (*Zeraim*) is devoted to laws and cases of an agricultural society, to the discussion of charity and priestly gifts and first-fruit offerings, which are spoken of in Scripture in an agricultural context; the order as a whole is introduced by the treatise *Berakot* (Benedictions and Prayers), perhaps, as Maimonides writes in the Introduction to his great Commentary on the Mishna, because man must first learn how properly to express his gratitude for what he enjoys in this world, since everything belongs to God.

The second order is *Specially Appointed Days* (*Moed*) and it deals with those laws which grow out of institutions like the Sabbath, holy days, fast days and their observance. *Women* (*Nashim*), the third order, has to do with all kinds of problems affecting relations between men and women, marriage and divorce regulations, and some subjects which by association can be brought within this framework. Then comes the fourth order, *Damages* (*Nezikin*), on civil and criminal law, on courts and judicial procedure; but there is also a tractate on regulations governing the legal (commercial and social) re-

lationship with idol-worshippers, and another treatise, a kind
of archive document, recording traditions attested to by Sages
in the Academy. It is in this order, by the way, that *Pirke
Abot* is included. The bulk of the fifth order, *Holy Things
(Kodashim)*, is about sacrifices and the temple ritual, and one of
its treatises, *Non-sacred Things (Hullin)*, takes up specifically
the rules pertaining to the slaughter of animals not intended
for sacrifice, and the eating of animal food. Finally, there are
the treatises of the sixth order, called euphemistically *Purities
(Toharot)*. These treat of the difficult laws related to cere-
monial impurity.

But even this itemization of the orders hardly captures the
rich variety and flexibility of subject matter incorporated in
the Mishna. A problem will be raised and, let us say, in
examining it some formula or principle will be stated. By
association a number of laws will be cited, not because they
are immediately germane to the theme of the treatise, but
because they are examples of the general principle, and these
examples will reflect an additional aspect of life. Thus, for
instance, in the fourth chapter of the treatise *Bills of Divorcement (Gittin)* rules governing withdrawal of a bill of
divorcement are cited. On this subject an ordinance by Rabban
Gamaliel the Elder is reported, and his motive for this
ordinance is given, namely, *"mi-pene tikkun ha-olam,"* in the
interests of maintaining good order in society. Thereupon other
ordinances based on the same motive, and not only by Gamaliel,
and not only on divorce matters, are introduced, and these in
turn prove the springboard for the citation of ordinances
"mi-pene darke shalom," for the sake of peaceful relationships
in society. So that in a treatise devoted to divorce laws, one
suddenly finds (in the fifth chapter) the following:

> THESE THINGS THEY[1] SAID IN THE INTERESTS OF PEACE:
>   A PRIEST READS FIRST,[2] AFTER HIM A LEVITE, AND
> AFTER HIM AN ISRAELITE—IN THE INTERESTS OF PEACE.
>   AN *erub*[3] IS PUT IN THE SAME HOUSE WHERE IT WAS
> PUT OF OLD—IN THE INTERESTS OF PEACE.

[1] The earlier generations of Sages.
[2] At the public reading of the Law.
[3] A legal expedient for circumventing certain difficulties created
by the Sabbath regulations. The *erub* referred to in our Mishna—
before the Sabbath depositing food prepared from joint contributions
in one of the dwellings of a courtyard—gives the tenants of the courtyard unrestricted access to each other's premises, and they may "carry
burdens" from one private domain to another, an activity otherwise
forbidden on the Sabbath.

THE CISTERN NEAREST THE WATERCOURSE IS TO BE FILLED FIRST—IN THE INTERESTS OF PEACE.

[TO TAKE WHAT'S IN THE] HUNTING, FOWLING, OR FISHING TRAPS[1] [OTHERS HAVE LAID] IS CONSIDERED ROBBERY—IN THE INTERESTS OF PEACE. RABBI YOSE SAYS: THAT'S ROBBERY IN THE FULL SENSE OF THE WORD.

[TO TAKE AWAY FROM] A DEAF-MUTE, IDIOT, OR MINOR[2] WHAT HE HAS FOUND IS CONSIDERED ROBBERY —IN THE INTERESTS OF PEACE. RABBI YOSE SAYS: THAT'S ROBBERY IN THE FULL SENSE OF THE WORD.

WHEN A POOR MAN IS PICKING OLIVES ON TOP OF THE TREE, IT'S ROBBERY [TO SNATCH UP] WHAT FALLS DOWN[3]—IN THE INTERESTS OF PEACE. RABBI YOSE SAYS: THAT'S ROBBERY IN THE FULL SENSE OF THE WORD.

THE POOR OF THE HEATHEN ARE NOT TO BE HELD BACK FROM THE HARVEST GLEANINGS,[4] THE FORGOTTEN SHEAF,[5] AND *Peah*[6]—IN THE INTERESTS OF PEACE.

All of which is hardly reminiscent of divorce, but nevertheless suggestive of the elasticity of the Mishnaic structure and illustrative of some of its preoccupations.

Now, the Talmud,* as commentary on the Mishna, takes on a similar, and even greater, elasticity. In discussion not only will assorted subjects be juxtaposed, in order dialecti-

---

[1] Although the one who laid such a trap—i.e., a trap which is not a "receptacle" in the full sense of the word—has, strictly speaking, not acquired ownership of his catch until it has actually come into his possession.

[2] Although legally they cannot acquire ownership.

[3] Although he is legally not the owner until he has "taken hold" of it.

[4] Leviticus 19:9 f., 23:22.

[5] Deuteronomy 24:19.

[6] Leviticus 19:9 f., 23:22. Although Scripture fixes no specific amount, the Sages declared (Mishna Peah 2:1): "Not less than one sixtieth part [of the harvest] should be given as *Peah*. And though they have said that no measure is fixed for *Peah*, it is always determined by the size of the field, the number of the poor, and the abundance of the yield."

* In the Babylonian Talmud there is no Talmud for the treatises of *Zeraim* (except for *Berakot*), *Shekalim* in *Moed*, *Eduyot* and *Abot* in *Nezikin*, *Middot* and *Kinnim* in *Kodashim* (and for *Tamid* there is a Talmud only in part), the treatises of *Toharot* (except for *Niddah*). In the Palestinian Talmud there is no Talmud for *Eduyot* and *Abot* in *Nezikin* and for the treatises in *Kodashim* and *Toharot* (there is a partial Talmud for *Niddah*). The Talmud for *Shabbat* is not complete; so too in the case of *Makkot*.

cally to arrive at common, underlying principles; but very
often, a discussion having been terminated, another will be
reported immediately thereafter only because in the first discussion some statement was made, or some authority referred
to, about which or whom there is more to be said. In this
way, little by little themes of social and private, urban and
rural, civil, criminal, ritual, public and domestic character are
introduced and explored, so that virtually nothing of human
experience is overlooked.

Studying Talmud therefore ("reading Talmud" would be
a comical expression!) one moves from argument to counter-
argument and from subject to subject in rapid—and complex
or subtle—transitions. Two elements, however, remain constant: the texture of the material is almost entirely scholastic,
cases, precedents, principles are invoked and intersect with the
give-and-take of dialogue and debate. And all of this is
governed by a kind of eager reaching out towards the divine
imperative. Everything is discussed and argued in a mood of
conviction that the discussion is an attempt to fulfill God's
commandment. *"The words of the wise are as goads, and
as nails well-fastened are those that sit together in groups;
they are given from one shepherd* (Ecclesiastes 12:11):
Even as a goad directs the beast along the furrows, so the
words of the Torah direct man along the paths of life. Perhaps
even as the goad is withdrawn, so also the words of the
Torah may be withdrawn? The verse says, *And as nails well-
fastened:* even as the well-fastened is not removable, so are
the words of the Torah not removable.

"Those that sit together in groups are the scholars who come
into [the academy] and sit in groups: some forbid and others
permit, some declare a thing unclean and others declare it
clean, some pronounce a thing unfit and others pronounce it
fit. Lest anyone say to thee: [In that event] I shall sit back
and not study, Scripture declares, *They are given from one
shepherd:* one God created them, one leader gave them, the
Master of all things uttered them! Thou too, therefore, make
thine ear like a hopper and take in the words of them that forbid and the words of them that permit, the words of them that
declare unclean and the words of them that declare clean, the
words of them that pronounce unfit and the words of them
that pronounce fit."

Scholastic debate, then, is a discipline for "the ways of
life." There is no denying that in argument scholars will also

resort to farfetched, unrealistic notions—so that sometimes one begins to wonder, is this an earnest religious exercise or no more than intellectual athletics for its own sake and delight; is it sensitivity to real problems or nothing more than schoolmen's lingo? An oversimplifying answer to this question would only increase confusion. Willy-nilly intellectual effort presses on to the extremes of argument; and like the Hellenistic rhetor the Talmudic rabbi did not shun *disputatio in utramque partem.* Sometimes the Talmud itself registers protest against extravagant supposition: "Are we talking about fools!" But there are times too when the very high purpose of Talmudic law demands the capacity for ingenious and fantastic interpretation. If a man, said the Palestinian Rabbi Johanan of the third century, could not come up with a hundred arguments for declaring a reptile ritually clean—though Scripture, Leviticus 11:29, categorically declares it unclean!—he would lack the skill necessary to open capital case trials with reasons for acquittal—an absolute requirement in capital judicial procedure: "Capital cases must begin with reasons for acquittal and may not begin with reasons for conviction."

In short, there are in Talmudic literature artificial interpretations, and this literature is filled with controversy and debate and casuistry over minutest details. But this is how one arrives at an understanding of the words of "the Master of all things"; in any event, this was the method and these were the themes of the Amoraim who quite rightly saw themselves as continuing a long tradition.

The beginnings of that tradition cannot be pinned down with precision. The view that along with the revelation of the Written Torah was a revelation of an Oral Torah, that is, that interpretations of and deductions from the Scriptures must have accompanied the Scriptures themselves, has at least this to recommend it: no written text, particularly if it is meant as a guide for conduct, can in and of itself be complete; it must have some form of oral commentary associated with it. This much however is clear: from the fifth century B.C. onward there was a conscious effort on the part of teachers to expound the canonical books of the Torah, to make clear its meaning and its applicability. *"To explore the Torah of the Lord and put it into practice, and to teach in Israel statutes and ordinances"* (Ezra 7:10) was not only the program of Ezra but of the colleagues whom he attracted to himself, the

Soferim, "Scribes," as we call them, but, literally, the "Men of the Book." It was the Soferim who made what was implicit in the Book of the Torah of God explicit and intelligible (compare the idiom in Nehemiah 8:8), and under their tutelage too, as times required, enactments and decrees were issued. Such teaching and legislating as the Soferim conducted through their schools and councils were carried on orally, in order carefully to distinguish between what was the Written Torah, *Scripture,* and the body of exegesis, interpretation *by* [*word of*] *mouth,* Oral Torah.

The activity of the Soferim, and the results of their activity, became the heritage of the later sages who continued study, instruction, and legislation along the lines the Soferim had drawn. These latter sages, roughly from about 200 B.C. through the second century of the regular calendar—especially those of the first two centuries of the Common Era—were the creators of the Mishna. What did their intellectual and spiritual work consist of? They interpreted the Scriptures; a number of their interpretations indeed were acute commentary of the plain meaning of the Biblical text, its difficult and rare words, its legal injunctions, its homiletical intent. This exegetical activity is known as *Midrash,* i.e., the investigation and explanation of the Scriptural content. There were recognized hermeneutic principles governing exegetical method, and for the terminology of some of these principles the Rabbis did not hesitate to appropriate what they could use from their Greek counterparts. By means of exegesis, they strove to find Scriptural support for laws and regulations which were operative in their society. When conditions warranted or demanded it, they created enactments (*takkanot*) or preventive measures (*gezerot*). In the course of time, as the material of these oral teachings and enactments accumulated, distinguished masters undertook to put the substance of the law into some systematic and logical form, in other words, into a Mishna.

Of the famous sages in this chain of authorities, *Pirke Abot* lists many in its first chapter. Among the most influential men in the first century were Hillel and Rabban Johanan ben Zakkai. In the development of the Mishna, the greatest contribution seems to have been made by Rabbi Akiba—who died a martyr's death in the Hadrianic persecutions of the second century. "To what might Rabbi Akiba be likened," the Talmudic sources say; "to a laborer who took up his basket and set forth. When he found wheat, he put some in the basket; when he found barley, he put that in; spelt, he put that in; lentils, he put them in. Upon returning home he sorted out the wheat by itself, the barley by itself, the beans by themselves, the lentils by themselves. This is how Rabbi Akiba acted; and he arranged the whole Torah in rings." Put into our own idiom, the parable tells us that Rabbi Akiba did two things with the mass of interpretations and traditions he inherited: first, he organized them in a systematic way, according to proper subject matter; second, he converted case laws into general rules.

To the body of this Mishna Rabbi Akiba's disciples attached additional comments, those of their master and of his contemporaries. His disciples thus prepared Mishnayot (plural of Mishna) for their own use, each of these versions based on Rabbi Akiba's work. The multiplication of versions, however, could easily have led to considerable confusion, due to variants and divergences of transmission—the notes of no two students have ever corresponded to the lectures of their professor or to one another! As a result, toward the end of the second or the beginning of the third century, Rabbi Judah the Prince and his colleagues assembled and collated the traditions of the different colleges where versions of Rabbi Akiba's Mishna were being expounded, and published an authoritative edition of the Mishna. Henceforth there was to be only that one Mishna, the work redacted by Rabbi Judah the Prince and his collaborators. All previous editions were displaced; all material finally excluded from the authoritative Mishna was committed to "extraneous" compilations (*Baraitot*).

This does not mean that the Mishna was put into written form. Individual copies no doubt were kept by individual men, for their own use and for their own notes; but these enjoyed no authority. When we say that an authoritative Mishna was published, we mean oral publication, that is, particular men (they are also called Tannaim), noted for their memory ("basket full of books," the Talmud loves to call them), memorized the "canonical" text,* and they were the living text referred to in the academies,* as the Mishna was

* To us it no doubt seems that an oral text would be less trustworthy than a written one. This was not necessarily the case with the ancients. There is an interesting passage in the *Phaedrus* which is quite illuminating in this connection. Plato has Socrates say the following: "I heard, then, that at Naucratis, in Egypt, was one of

now adopted as the text for further study and interpretation.

All this activity of more than four hundred years, which culminated in the redaction of the Mishna (for hereafter it was *the* Mishna) was localized in the Palestinian academies. But by the end of the second and beginning of the third centuries an important center of creative Jewish life had developed in the east too, in Babylonia. Leading scholars and academies in Babylonia now took the initiative to carry on the tradition of study and law. Thus it happened that when the Mishna was adopted as the recognized source of the Oral Law, there were two centers where it was to be studied and commented on, Palestine and Babylonia. In each country there were scholars and schools interpreting the Mishna, to be sure with a good deal of contact between the two countries, nevertheless each with its own instruction and its own application, as local conditions and needs required. So it came to be that a Palestinian Talmud and a Babylonian Talmud developed in the succeeding centuries, the Palestinian Talmud drawn up about 400 and the Babylonian Talmud about 500 of the

the ancient gods of that country, the one whose sacred bird is called the ibis, and the name of the god himself was Theuth. He it was who invented numbers and arithmetic and geometry and astronomy, also draughts and dice, and, most important of all, letters. Now the king of all Egypt at that time was the god Thamus, who lived in the great city of the upper region, which the Greeks call the Egyptian Thebes, and they call the god himself Ammon. To him came Theuth to show his inventions, saying that they ought to be imparted to the other Egyptians. But Thamus asked what use there was in each, and as Theuth enumerated their uses, expressed praise or blame, according as he approved or disapproved. The story goes that Thamus said many things to Theuth in praise or blame of the various arts, which it would take too long to repeat; but when they came to the letters, 'This invention, O king,' said Theuth, 'will make the Egyptians wiser and will improve their memories; for it is an elixir of memory and wisdom that I have discovered.' But Thamus replied, 'Most ingenious Theuth, one man has the ability to beget arts, but the ability to judge of their usefulness or harmfulness to their users belongs to another; and now you, who are the father of letters, have been led by your affection to ascribe to them a power the opposite of that which they really possess. For this invention will produce forgetfulness in the minds of those who learn to use it, because they will not practise their memory. Their trust in writing, produced by external characters which are no part of themselves, will discourage the use of their own memory within them. You have invented an elixir not of memory, but of reminding; and you offer your pupils the appearance of wisdom, not true wisdom, for they will read many things without instruction and will therefore seem to know many things, when they are for the most part ignorant and hard to get along with, since they are not wise, but only appear wise' " (Fowler translation, *Phaedrus*, 274C–275A).

Common Era.* And the creators of the Talmud are known as Amoraim (Expositors). Their work was the study and interpretation of the Mishna, derivation of laws which were implicit in either its cases or views, or rules which might legitimately be drawn from them to fit new circumstances, in brief, treating the Mishna in a way comparable to the way the Tannaim, the creators of the Mishna, had treated Scripture and earlier traditions. Talmud (sometimes it is called Gemara) in other words is the exegetical and dialectical activity which makes the Mishna meaning clear and relevant to the generations after the compilation of the Mishna.

III

When one enters the world of the Talmud, one enters a world unlike any other. Not because nowhere else is there so serious a concern with law: no civilized culture has ever been without legalism and casuistry: these are the basic stuff of well-ordered existence and relationships. Not because the Talmud is only a record of Halakah, law and legal argumentation. There is, after all, a wealth of Hagada (or Agada), non-legal material, in the Talmud—legends, folklore, ethical and "philosophical" and theosophical and theological speculation, homilies, parables, prayers, gnomic sayings, historical reminiscence, old wives' tales too: in other words, that large, unbounded expression of the human imagination reacting to the universe, in anguish, in wonder responding to the here and now and to what was and to what will be in the end of time. Taken crumb by crumb, one could perhaps find parallels in

* The "final" compilation of the Palestinian and Babylonian Talmud was achieved in stages, rather than in one act. For example, the earliest part of the Palestinian Talmud was redacted in Caesarea, and was rather elementary in character. Later other parts were redacted, with concentration on those treatises that would be of immediate, practical value. In the case of the Babylonian Talmud there seems to have been more carefully planned editorial activity; and the post-Amoraic scholars not only arranged the discussions in this Talmud but also added occasional comments of their own. Among other things, the reason the Babylonian Talmud overshadowed the Palestinian—so that in a sense it came to be *the* Talmud—was that in the centuries after the compilation of the Talmud, the heads of the Babylonian academies pressed hard for its adoption by various Jewish communities; and the political triumph and expansion of Islam put the Babylonian scholars at an advantage. Bagdad became a most dynamic center, attracting to its academies students from everywhere; in turn wherever they settled they brought and taught the Babylonian Talmud.

many places to this particular law or the other particular saying or proverb or tale. What makes the Talmudic substance *sui generis* is (a) its non-"literary" quality, and (b) its unabashed conviction that if human character is to be refined and be given a divine dimension, then nothing is so far-reaching a *paideia* as Halakah. Obviously some comment is called for here.

The non-"literary" quality of Talmudic substance does not mean that in the Talmud there is an indifference to forms of expression or an aloofness to the requirements even of literary grace. The very seriousness towards terms, the very striving toward precision, is proof to the contrary. And there is frequently a compactness or sharpness to Talmudic passages and sentences that reveals genuine alertness to style and verbal effect. But we must never forget that the Talmud is not a literary treatise or literary composition brought into being by an author—who selects a subject, prepares an introduction, goes on to a beginning, middle, and conclusion, neatly (ideally speaking of course) organizes all he wants to say and artistically moves either his characters or his ideas so that they appear with the proper lights and shadows. In a literary work, you see things; in the Talmud, you hear voices. Here is a kind of transcript of the very words exchanged in the academy or in a vineyard or on a journey or in a court session. The scene, the protagonists, the beginning, middle, end, you must supply as, on the basis of the conversations, you try to picture what it was all like and how it developed. The Talmudic rabbis were not writers of books, but teachers, by word of mouth creating and expanding the Oral Torah. We do not so much read what these great sages said as hear them in their sessions —but there are no prepared speeches. What there is is intellect reacting to intellect.

How disembodied this all seems! As though a mechanical brain conference were in progress. Anything but that. Why? Not only because the Sages themselves would have shuddered at dehumanizing activity; tall talk of any kind unrelated to human life, fancy definition utterly abstracted from experience, was simply not their medium of discourse or ambition. What keeps even the pages of the Talmud, the record itself, alive is the concreteness of the arguments, the cases, the vividness of illustrations and even of hypothetical examples; and what adds to the vitality is the injection of agadic reflections into the midst of halakic proceedings. "IF ONE SET OFF A FIRE," says the Mishna, "AND IT CONSUMED WOOD OR

STONES OR EARTH, HE IS LIABLE, FOR IT IS SAID, *If fire break out, and catch in thorns, and then shocks of corn, or the standing corn, or the field are consumed; he that kindled the fire shall surely make restitution"* (Exodus 22:5).

Raba now raises the following question: "Was it really necessary for the Merciful One to have written [in His Torah] *thorns, shocks of corn, standing corn,* and *field?"* What purpose is served by this multiplication of words? To which the Talmud replies:

"Necessary indeed! For if the Merciful One had written [only] *thorns,* I might have thought: only as regards thorns has the Merciful One imposed liability, because in their case fire is a common occurrence and negligence is therefore common too;[1] but in the case of shocks of corn, since fire is not a common occurrence, and therefore negligence is not common either, I might have said there should be no liability.[2]

"Again, if the Merciful One had written [only] *shocks of corn,* I might have thought: only as regards shocks of corn has the Merciful One imposed liability, because in their case the loss is considerable; but in the case of thorns, since the loss is slight, I might have said there should be no liability."

"What need is there to list *standing corn?"*

"[To teach that] just as standing corn is something out in the open, so [only to] whatever is out in the open [does our law apply]."[3] . . .

"What need is there to list *field?"*

"To include [in this law the case of fire] scorching a neighbor's plowed field, and blacking his stones."

"Then the Merciful One should have written [only] *field,* and the other terms would have been unnecessary!"[4]

"Necessary indeed! For if the Merciful One had written *field* [only], I might have thought: only what is *in* the field is included [in the law], nothing else.[5] Now [the verse] has taught us [otherwise]."

And with hardly a pause the Talmud now proceeds to report:

Said Rabbi Samuel bar Nahmani in the name of Rabbi

---

[1] Therefore a person should be held liable because he was presumably neglectful.
[2] Because this was probably an accident.
[3] Hidden articles would, therefore, not be included.
[4] Since *field* includes everything.
[5] The earth itself, for example.

Jonathan: Calamity never comes upon the world unless
there are wicked in the world, and it begins always with the
righteous, as it is said, *If fire break out, and catch in thorns:*
when does fire break out? Only when thorns are available.[1]
"And it always begins with the righteous," as it is said,
And the shocks of corn have been consumed: it is not said,
And then it will consume the shocks of corn, but, *And the
shocks of corn have been consumed,* the shocks of corn
have already been consumed.

Rab Joseph taught: What is the meaning of the verse,
*And none of you shall go out of the door of his house until
the morning?* (Exodus 12:22). Once permission has been
given to the Destroyer, he does not distinguish between
righteous and wicked. Moreover, he begins first only with
the righteous, as it is said, *And I will cut off from thee
[first] the righteous and [then] the wicked* (Ezekiel 21:8).
Rab Joseph burst into tears: "Of such worthlessness are
they!"[2]

Said Abbaye to him: "It is to their advantage! As it is
written, *Verily, the righteous is taken away from before the
evil to come*" (Isaiah 57:1).

Rab Judah said in the name of Rab: A man should
always enter [a city] while "it is good"[3] and depart while
"it is good," as it is said, *And none of you shall go out of
the door of his house until the morning. . . .*

Rab Ammi and Rab Assi were sitting in the presence
of Rabbi Isaac Nafha. Said one to him: "Sir, would you
please make some halakic comment." And the other said
to him: "Sir, would you please make some agadic comment."

Rabbi Isaac began to make an agadic comment, and the
former would not let him go on. He began to make a
halakic comment, and the latter would not let him go on.
Said Rabbi Isaac to them: "I will tell you a parable; to what
may this be likened? To a man who has two wives, one
young and one old. The young one keeps pulling out his
white hairs and the old one keeps pulling out the black
hairs. Thus between them he becomes bald! —In that case,"
he continued, "I shall tell you something which may satisfy
both of you equally:

[1] *Thorns* is taken as a metaphor for the wicked and *shocks of
corn* as a metaphor for the righteous.
[2] The righteous, since they are the first to be destroyed.
[3] I. e., while there is bright sunlight. The expression "while
it is good" is appropriated from Genesis 1:4, "And God saw the
light, that it was good."

"*If a fire break out, and catch in thorns*—of its own it broke out!—*He that kindled the fire shall surely make restitution:* Said the Holy One, blessed be He: 'I am under obligation to make restitution for the fire which I kindled —it was I that set Zion afire, as it is said, *And He kindled a fire in Zion, which hath devoured the foundations thereof* (Lamentations 4:11); and it is I who will rebuild it in the future with fire, as it is said, *For I . . . will be unto her a wall of fire round about, and I will be the glory in the midst of her*' (Zechariah 2:9).

"As for the halakic comment— The verse (*If a fire break out*) opens with [an expression describing] damages caused by a person's property, but it closes with [an expression describing] the damage as caused by himself, (*he that kindled the fire*)—to teach you: The fire one kindles is like the arrow he shoots." [1]

There is then a good deal of Agada in the Talmud, and it serves not only as a relief for exacting, single-minded halakic discourse but also as wit, and as a reminder of the ideals which the Law was to help one realize. But of course, frequent as are these alternations of halakah and agada, what is most representative of the Talmud is the undistracted halakic discourse. Here most lucidly is revealed the non-"literary" quality and the pre-eminence attributed to Halakah. The following (slightly condensed) passage may serve as an example:

The Mishna states: "IF SOMEONE BLOWS THE *shofar*[2] IN A CISTERN, IN A CELLAR, OR IN A BARREL, IF ONE HEARD THE SOUND OF THE *shofar*, HE HAS FULFILLED HIS OBLIGATION; BUT IF HE HEARD THE ECHO, HE HAS NOT FULFILLED HIS OBLIGATION."* Then it adds: "AND ALSO, IF ONE

---

[1] That is, we do not say that the fire spreading from one's domain is after all traveling by its own momentum or independent of his act; since the person kindled the fire, we regard it as though he personally were carrying the fire causing damage far and wide, even as we say, he who shoots an arrow is regarded as personally bringing destruction, regardless of how far the arrow flies.

[2] The ram's horn sounded in the services on Rosh Hashana, the New Year. On the requirement to hear the sound of the *shofar*, see Leviticus 23:24 and Numbers 29:1.

* I add a note at this point for I do not want to interrupt the Talmudic discussion with data the Talmud itself apparently feels is not immediately to the point. The fact is our Mishna is not describing anything preposterous or farfetched at all. During the Hadrianic persecutions, it was death to be caught carrying out a number of religious practices. Pious Jews who were eager to carry out the commandment to hear the sound of the *shofar* would secretly and in the most out of the way places go to fulfill the commandment. They

WAS PASSING BEHIND A SYNAGOGUE, OR IF HIS HOUSE WAS
NEAR A SYNAGOGUE, AND HE HEARD THE SOUND OF THE
shofar, OR THE READING OF THE *megillah,*[1] IF ONE SET HIS
MIND TO IT, HE HAS FULFILLED HIS OBLIGATION; IF ONE
HAS NOT, HE HAS NOT FULFILLED HIS OBLIGATION—EVEN
THOUGH THE ONE HEARD AND THE OTHER HEARD, THE
ONE SET HIS MIND TO IT, BUT THE OTHER DID NOT SET
HIS MIND TO IT."

The subject to be explored, then, is "intention," or, to be
exact, whether in the carrying out of a religious duty it is
necessary to intend to carry out the duty or not; may the
"mechanical act" by itself suffice?

The Talmud says:

The following was sent to Samuel's father: If one were
coerced[2] into eating *maza,*[3] he has fulfilled his obligation. . . .

"This implies: if one blows the *shofar* simply to make
music,[4] he has fulfilled his obligation."

"But, of course! The one is like the other!"

"You might have argued: there it is a case of the
Merciful One having prescribed: Eat *maza,* and after all
he has eaten it. In our case, however, it is written, *A keeping in mind of the sound of the blast* (Leviticus 23:24)
—and our man is merely puttering about! So, we have been
taught [that nonetheless he has fulfilled his obligation]."

Evidently Raba thinks Religious Acts do not require
Intention.

Someone objected: "IF ONE WAS READING [THE *Shema*[5]
VERSES] IN THE TORAH AND THE TIME ARRIVED FOR
RECITING THE *shema,* IF HE SET HIS MIND TO IT, HE
HAS FULFILLED HIS OBLIGATION; OTHERWISE, HE HAS
NOT FULFILLED HIS OBLIGATION. Does this not mean,
set his mind on fulfilling his obligation?"

"No. [It might mean, intend] to read."

" 'To read?' But he is reading!"

---

would hide underground, in caves, in vats, and there enact their
religious faith. And even in these circumstances they worried lest
they had not properly carried out their obligations!—To none of
this the Talmud here refers, as though calamity had no right to
intrude on the deliberations of a legitimate problem.

[1] The Book of Esther, read on the festival of Purim.

[2] As Rab Ashi specifies in the Talmud, coerced by hostile
individuals.

[3] Unleavened bread which *must* be eaten on the first evening of
Passover. Passover week no leavened foods may be eaten.

[4] In other words, not intending to carry out the commandment.

[5] See above, p. 13, n. 1.

"It's a case of reading to spell out."[1]

"Come now, listen: IF ONE WAS PASSING BEHIND A SYNAGOGUE, OR IF HIS HOUSE WAS NEAR A SYNAGOGUE, AND HE HEARD THE SOUND OF THE *shofar*, OR THE READING OF THE *megillah*, IF ONE SET HIS MIND TO IT, HE HAS FULFILLED HIS OBLIGATION; IF ONE HAS NOT, HE HAS NOT FULFILLED HIS OBLIGATION. Does not this mean, if he set his mind to fulfill his obligation?"

"No. [It might mean, set his mind] on hearing."

" 'On hearing?' But he is hearing!"

"He may be thinking, it's only an ass braying."[2]

Someone objected: " 'If the listener [to the *shofar*] set his mind to it but not the one sounding it, or if the one sounding it did but the listener did not set his mind to it, the obligation has not been fulfilled. Both the listener [to the *shofar*] and the one sounding it must set their minds to it.' Very well then: 'If the one sounding it did but the listener did not set his mind to it' [is conceivable]—he thinks it's only an ass braying. But, 'If the listener set his mind to it but not the one sounding it'—how can you have an instance of that? Would it not be in the case of one who blows the *shofar* simply to make music?"

"Perhaps he's making barking noises."[3]

Said Abbaye to Raba: "But now then, one who sleeps in the *Sukkah*[4] on the eighth day should be flogged."[5]

He replied: "[No,] for I say there's no such thing as transgressing religious commandments except at the time they're scheduled [to be carried out]."[6]

Rab Shimon bar Abba objected: " 'How do we know that a priest who mounts the platform[7] may not say—Because the Torah has given me permission to bless Israel, I will

---

[1] That is, you can hardly call it even reading, since he is simply sounding out syllables and words for purposes of correct spelling.

[2] In other words, he is hardly aware that these are *shofar* sounds.

[3] He may be making sounds, but not sounding the notes as is legally required.

[4] The booth in which one is to dwell during the Feast of Booths (Sukkot). See Leviticus 23:42–43, "Ye shall dwell in booths *seven* days . . . ."

[5] For he is adding to the requirements of the commandment, and this goes contrary to the warning of Deuteronomy 4:2, "Ye shall not *add* unto the word which I command you . . . ."

[6] And on "the eighth day" the *Sukkah* obligation is past.

[7] To recite the priestly (threefold) benediction, Numbers 6:24–26, "The Lord bless thee, and keep thee. The Lord make His face to shine upon thee, and be gracious unto thee. The Lord lift up His countenance upon thee, and give thee peace."

add some blessing on my own, for instance, *The Lord, the God of your fathers, make you [a thousand times] so many more [as ye are]?* (Deuteronomy 1:11)—Because it says, *Ye shall not add unto the word [which I command you]'* (Deuteronomy 4:2). Now, in this case, once he had made the [prescribed] benediction, the scheduled time is past; and yet it is stated that [if he added a blessing on his own] he has transgressed!"

"Know with what we are dealing here? He hadn't yet finished [the prescribed benediction]."

"But there is a statement, 'He has finished!' "

"It means, finished one of its blessings."[1]

"But there is a statement, 'he has finished all its blessings!' "

"The situation here is different—since if another congregation should happen along, he might once again pronounce the [prescribed] benediction, the entire day is considered the time [for the priestly benediction]." . . .

Finally Raba said: "To fulfill a religious obligation, Intention is not required; [to be held guilty] of transgressing [a commandment] at the time scheduled [for it to be carried out], Intention is not required; Intention is required [to be held guilty of transgressing a commandment] at a time not scheduled for it."

Rabbi Zera said to his attendant: "Set your mind to it and blow the *shofar* for me."[2]

Evidently he thinks Intention is required of the one who sounds [the *shofar*].

Some objected: "IF ONE WAS PASSING BEHIND A SYN-AGOGUE, OR IF HIS HOUSE WAS NEAR A SYNAGOGUE, AND HE HEARD THE SOUND OF THE *shofar*, OR THE READING OF THE *megillah*, IF ONE SET HIS MIND TO IT, HE HAS FULFILLED HIS OBLIGATION; IF ONE HAS NOT, HE HAS NOT FULFILLED HIS OBLIGATION. Now, supposing he did set his mind to it, what then? He [the one sounding the *shofar*] could not have had him in mind!"

"We are dealing here with the congregational appointee, who has in mind everyone [who might hear]."

"Come now, listen: 'If the listener [to the *shofar*] set his mind to it but not the one sounding it, or if the one sounding it did but the listener did not set his mind to it,

[1] "The Lord bless thee, and keep thee."
[2] In other words, be sure you have in mind as you blow the *shofar* that I am to fulfill my obligation to hear the *shofar* sounded.

the obligation has not been fulfilled. Both the listener [to the *shofar*] and the one sounding it must set their minds to it.' [No doubt] this statement intends an equation of the one sounding [the *shofar*] and the one listening, [thus:] even as the listener listens for himself,[1] so the one sounding [the *shofar*] sounds it for himself. Yet the statement has it that the obligation has been fulfilled!"[2]

"There is a difference between the Tannaim [on this point]. For it is stated: 'The listener listens for himself, and the one sounding [the *shofar*] simply sounds it.[3] Said Rabbi Yose: When does this pertain? When [the one sounding the *shofar* is] a congregational appointee; but when he is some private individual, the obligation has not been fulfilled unless both the listener [to the *shofar*] and the one sounding it have set their minds to it.' "

The problem is hardly disposed of once for all. The post-Talmudic commentators come back to it, further analyzing the Talmudic reasoning in order to be able to arrive at a decision. The casuistry does not come to an end because the issue is not a dead one—is an act sufficient unto itself, or is it incomplete without an accompanying conscious intention? Or may some acts require intention and others not?

IV

"He who every day studies Halakah may be sure that he will be a member of the world to come." All Israel, of course, has a share in the world to come, as the Mishna elsewhere declares. But the Talmudic sages had made up their minds that all Israel—not merely some small elite—was to study Halakah: and live it, *halakah le-maaseh*. And that is why the post-Talmudic rabbis—the heads of the academies in Palestine and Babylonia after the sixth century, the commentators and codifiers of the Law in Asia, Africa and Europe after the decline of the Babylonian academies—could make of the

---

[1] That is, bears no one else in mind.

[2] Why then did Rabbi Zera insist that his attendant have him, Rabbi Zera, in mind? The printed text has "the obligation has not been fulfilled." The question of the Talmud rises from its interpretation of the sentence "Both the listener [to the *shofar*] and the one sounding it must set their minds to it," in the cited statement.

[3] That is, he is not consciously sounding the *shofar* to help a particular listener fulfill *his* obligation.

Talmud *the* central source for Jewish study, thought, and practice, without any really serious dissent. I do not mean to underestimate or to dismiss such protest movements as Karaism, the truly formidable revolt against Talmudic authority, allegedly to return directly to the Scriptures themselves. Significantly enough, no sooner had the founder of Karaism sounded the Back to Scripture alarm, than exegesis began, Talmudic hermeneutic rules, and extensions of these rules, being used to the full. And in these circles too preoccupation with the Law became at once a leading intellectual and spiritual enterprise—though whenever possible the Karaites did all they could to adopt old sectarian examples, in order to avoid reaching conclusions of the accepted Halakah. Anti-Talmudism—at least in Jewish history—is not necessarily antinomianism. It may be no more than the ambition to substitute one's own Talmud for *the* Talmud.

Or again: even the eighteenth-century pietistic movement known as Hasidism did not dislodge the Talmud from its central position, though Hasidism did awaken other forms of expression, which had no doubt been neglected because of the almost exclusive preoccupation with the Talmud, particularly with its Halakah.

For better or worse, the emphasis put on Halakah and halakic study by the Talmudic sages was a permanent one, so that even Kabbalists or philosophers—let alone homilists and poets and moralists—though they may have chafed inwardly, if they did, had to acknowledge the sovereign role of the Talmud. Unless one were ready to become a schismatic he had to come to terms with Talmudic Halakah.

Perhaps, after all, the centrality of Halakah within Judaism is not as surprising as on first thought it may seem. The Talmudic sages knew that once, long before their time, the people of Israel had been exiled from their land; the Sages knew too how in their own time Jews scattered in far-off countries sustained their identity and resisted submergence by the surrounding Hellenistic and Parthian cultures, only through being involved in the routine of contemplation and practice ordered by the Halakah. Moreover, there was hardly a decade in the seven hundred years from the beginning of the second century B.C.—with the possible exception of some years during the eighty years of Hasmonean ascendancy—when there was a sense of national security. The possibility that the people might be driven again into exile, the subjection, even in the Holy Land, to powers utterly hostile to Jewish values,

fixed deeply in the rabbinic consciousness the realization that
the Land by itself could not guarantee the survival of the
people as exemplars of a particular way of life. Could mere
sermonizing do it? And visions of pleromas and aeons, or
broodings on heaven and hell, could they? But life lived in
accordance with the Halakah could: the Temple, for example,
might go up in flames, but the study of the laws of sacrifice
and priestly gifts could go on anywhere—even outside Jerusalem, even outside the Holy Land—and the subject would
keep the memory of the cult and service fresh and the prayer
for restoration strong.

Of course, this is not intended to deny that quite a number
of Talmudic rabbis were also deeply preoccupied with mystical
themes and speculations—indeed more deeply preoccupied
with such themes than is generally assumed. A story like the
one about Ben Azzai, Ben Zoma, Akiba, and Elisha ben
Abuyah entering the orchard-Paradise (*pardes*); the very
prohibition by the Mishna of public discussion of the mystical
subjects of Creation and the Chariot; allusions to the possible
"misuse" of the Divine Name; the reference to Rabban
Johanan ben Zakkai's academy as "the Great House, because
there the praises of the Holy One, blessed be He, are re-
hearsed"—these, and other evidence too, are distinct signs
that the Talmudic masters and the Talmudic academies were
anything but sealed off from the kind of esoteric lore and deliberations that have engaged mystics and gnostics of all sorts
everywhere.

But none of this can blur what is no less distinct than
these signs, namely, that the focus of the Talmud is on the
Law, that, in a sense Law—its study and practice—was the
Talmudic *mystique*. For this indeed is what the Rabbis of
the Talmud hoped: that they could supply the exercises which
would become second nature in the World to Come, that
gracious time when the righteous will be crowned and nourished by the divine splendor, as are the ministering angels.
What, in the final analysis, is the Talmud if not the choreog-
raphy for life in the Messianic Age? So, on that prodigious
faith, one begins *now* to act out that life. *"Bless the Lord, ye
angels of His, ye mighty in strength* (Psalm 103:20). Whom
is the verse talking about? Said Rabbi Isaac: The verse is
talking about those who observe the law of the Sabbatical
Year (Leviticus 25:2–7). Ordinarily a person is ready to carry
out a commandment of one day's duration, of one week, of
one month. But for a whole year long! And here's someone

looking on as his field is neglected, his vineyard uncultivated, and paying tribute and holding his peace! Have you anything more heroic than that!" And there were saints who were ready to go even beyond this—and had to be restrained.

V

The treatise *Abot,* that is, [*The Wisdom of*] *the Fathers*—or, as it is frequently called, *Pirke Abot, The Chapters* [*of the Wisdom*] *of the Fathers*—may not convey the flavor of Talmudic *shakla ve-tarya,* the typical halakic give-and-take of the Talmud—for unlike all the other sixty-two Talmudic treatises, it is devoted entirely to Agada: here there is no dialectic and debate, no fixing of laws; the content here is in the form of maxims and epigrams—a kind of Talmudic Book of Proverbs—which the Tannaite Sages either coined or were fond of quoting. In other words, *Abot* will not reveal the Sages as the creators of the Halakah. On the other hand, it makes articulate and vivid what their values were, what ideals they strove to inculcate in their disciples and in the folk at large, and what gave them the right to insist that their teachings were the explicit and legitimate expression of the Biblical intention. "Moses received Torah from [Him who revealed Himself at] Sinai, and handed it on to Joshua, and Joshua to the Elders, and the Elders to the Prophets, and the Prophets handed it on to the Men of the Great Assembly . . . Simeon the Righteous was one of the last members of the Great Assembly . . . Antigonus of Soko took over from Simeon the Righteous . . . Yose ben Joezer of Zeredah and Yose ben Johanan of Jerusalem took over from them . . . Joshua ben Perahyah and Nittai the Arbelite took over from them . . . Judah ben Tabbai and Simeon ben Shetah took over from them . . . Shemaiah and Abtalyon took over from them . . . Hillel and Shammai took over from them . . . Rabban Johanan ben Zakkai took over from Hillel and Shammai. He used to say . . . Rabban Johanan ben Zakkai had five disciples . . . And each of them used to say . . ." And so the chain of tradition, beginning at Sinai, extends link by link down through the generations authorizing the teachers of the Law to expound the Torah and to establish the right course. "*According to the law which they shall teach thee, and according to the judgment which they shall tell thee, thou shalt do; thou shalt not turn aside from the word which they shall declare unto thee, to the right hand, nor to the left"* (Deuteronomy 17:11).

And what were the values and ideals of these teachers? *Abot* tells us: Be deliberate in judgment, raise many disciples, make a hedge about the Torah; the pillars of the good life are the Torah, worship, and acts of *pietas;* one must worship God with no thought of rations in return; one's house ought to be a place where the sages congregate, eagerly one ought to heed what they say; the poor ought always to find a welcome in one's house, idle chatter with women should be avoided like the plague; one should get himself a teacher and colleague to study with, should judge every man as one would himself want to be judged, favorably; evil associations are fatal, there is always a final reckoning; testimony must be scrupulously examined; honest labor, rather than power and courting government favors; scholars must weigh their words; love peace, love all men and draw them to the Torah; neglecting to study is deadly; if I do not look out for myself, no one else will, but if I look out for myself only, what kind of man am I; and if there's something to be done, now is the time to do it; study of the Torah must be a fixed, not haphazard or dilletante, occupation; what counts is deed and not speech; all men must be received with a cheerful countenance; on truth and justice and peace is the world established.

There is more, much more of the same and other kinds of reflection in *Abot*—on the relation of good works to study, on how one is to respect his fellow man and his fellow man's property, on the kind of talk that ought to take place at table, on the dangers incurred when one allows himself to be distracted from study or when he yields to frivolity, on freedom and determinism; the significance of the fact that not by one but by ten utterances was the world created; the kinds of men there are, and the kinds of dispositions, in the world.

And even this paraphrase has hardly summarized all that *Abot* has to say. But it can hint at the standards of behavior and thought the Sages wanted to fix and make the insignia of Israel.

Abot is now included in the fourth order, *Nezikin,* of the Talmud. Maimonides says (in part) that it was included in the order where matters of civil and criminal law and courts and judges are discussed because the ethical conduct described by *Abot* is above all to be exemplified by the sages and judges —and if they do not, who else will? Interestingly enough, in the Munich manuscript of the Talmud—the only manuscript we have of the whole Talmud, written in 1343—*Abot* comes at the end of all six orders. Apparently then, it may have served as a peroration of the "proceedings" of the Oral Law as a whole. Whether it did or did not, its teachings were certainly what the Talmud hoped to stamp onto the character of those who would study it. הַאי מָאן דְּבָעֵי לְמֶהֱוֵי חֲסִידָא ליקיים . . . מִילֵי דְאָבוֹת. "If one wishes to become a saint, let him carry out . . . the words of *Abot*."

II

The Wisdom of the Fathers

and Commentaries

ALL ISRAEL HAS A SHARE IN THE WORLD TO COME, AS IT IS SAID, *Thy people also shall be all righteous, they shall inherit the land for ever; the branch of my planting, the work of my hands, wherein I glory* (Isaiah 60:21).

The text of the *Wisdom of the Fathers* is divided into its traditional paragraphs, or *Mishnayot,* and each paragraph (or *Mishna*) is followed by relevant selections from the classical commentators, whose names are given in parenthesis at the end of each comment. Biblical quotations appear throughout in italics.

Chapter 1

MOSES RECEIVED TORAH FROM SINAI AND HANDED IT ON TO JOSHUA, AND JOSHUA TO THE ELDERS, AND THE ELDERS TO THE PROPHETS, AND THE PROPHETS HANDED IT ON TO THE MEN OF THE GREAT ASSEMBLY.

THEY SAID THREE THINGS: BE DELIBERATE IN JUDGMENT, RAISE MANY DISCIPLES, AND MAKE A HEDGE ABOUT THE TORAH.

MOSES RECEIVED TORAH: Not from the mouth of an angel and not from the mouth of a seraph, but from the mouth of the King of kings of kings, the Holy One, blessed be He (ARNB).

The Torah which the Holy One, blessed be He, gave to Israel was given by the hands of Moses only, as it is said, *These are the statutes and ordinances and laws, which the Lord made between Him and the children of Israel in Mount Sinai by the hand of Moses* (Leviticus 26:46): Moses merited becoming God's messenger to the children of Israel (ARN).

TORAH: Moses received the whole Torah, both the written and the oral one (Vitry).

It is written, *And I will give thee the tables of stone, and the law and the commandment* (Exodus 24:12): *the law* refers to the Written Torah; *the commandment* refers to the Oral Torah. Thus all the commandments were given to Moses at Sinai along with their interpretations: what was written down is called the Written Torah, the [accompanying] interpretation is called the Oral Torah (Rabbi Jonah).

By "Talmud" is meant the Oral Torah, for it is the commentary on the Written Torah. Indeed, were it not for the interpretations which Moses received from the mouth of the Almighty, we could not know the true meaning of the Written Torah (Duran).

FROM SINAI: That is, from Him who revealed Himself at Sinai (Bertinoro).

The Creator, exalted be He, revealed Himself on Mount Sinai rather than on any of the other mountains which He created, because it is the smallest mountain of all. For when He resolved to give the Torah to Israel, all the mountains assembled and began boasting, one saying to the other, "I am taller than you, and it is on me that the Lord will give the Torah." When the Creator, exalted be He, saw how they were boasting . . . He said to them: *Why look ye askance, ye mountains of peaks, at the mountain which God hath desired for His abode* (Psalm 68:17)—that is, He said to Mount Tabor, Hermon, and Carmel, "Why are you provoking each other? I shall give the Torah only from Mount Sinai, because it is the smallest of the mountains and I love only him who is humble" (Rabbi David the Prince).

BE DELIBERATE IN JUDGMENT: This teaches that a man should take his time before rendering judgment; for whoever takes time rendering judgment is unruffled in judgment. . . . Another interpretation. This teaches that a man should be patient in his speech and not short-tempered in his speech, for whoever is short-tempered in his speech will forget what he has to say (ARN).

If some litigation has come before you one, two, and three times, and then it is brought before you a fourth time, do not render decision at once, as if to say, "I have already considered this once and twice before." Instead examine the problem meticulously once again—perhaps you will discover some factor you overlooked previously (Vitry).

"Be deliberate in judgment" applies especially to judgment in litigation, even more than to decisions in other areas, for this is a basic principle in knowing the Lord; as the prophet Jeremiah, may he rest in peace, said, *Let him that glorieth glory in this, that he understandeth, and knoweth Me, that I am the Lord who exercise mercy, justice, and righteousness, in the earth; for in these things I delight, saith the Lord* (Jeremiah 9:23). Now how can a man be wise enough to *understand* the Lord? This is impossible! But we know Him by exercising justice and righteousness, for the Lord is the author of these. And that is why it is said, *He judged the cause of the poor and needy; then it was well. Is this not to know Me? saith the Lord* (Jeremiah 22:16) (Rabbi Jonah).

RAISE MANY DISCIPLES: The School of Shammai says: One ought to teach only him who is talented and meek and of distinguished ancestry and rich. But the School of Hillel says:

One ought to teach every man, for there were many sinners in
Israel who were drawn to the study of Torah, and from them
descended righteous, pious, and worthy folk (ARN).

When the Sages of the Talmud (Hullin 133a) say that a
person ought not to teach an unworthy student, they mean
only one who is of bad character: such an individual one should
certainly alienate (Meiri).

MAKE A HEDGE ABOUT THE TORAH: A vineyard surrounded
by a fence is not like a vineyard without a fence; but no man
ought to make the fence more important than the thing fenced
in. For if then the fence falls, he will tear down everything
(ARNB).

"Make a hedge about the Torah" refers to the decrees and
enactments of the Sages—these keep a man far from transgression, as the Blessed One said, *Therefore shall ye keep what I
have given you to keep* (Leviticus 18:30), which the Talmud
(Yebamot 21a) interprets to mean: Add protection to what
I have already given you as protection (Maimonides).

It is a great and noble thing to make a hedge and fence
about the commandments; in that way one who fears the words
of the Lord will escape neglecting them. That is why he who
carries out the words of the Sages, which are a hedge to the
commandments of the Torah, gives evidence of greater love
of piety than he who simply carries out the commandment itself. For carrying out the commandments is not a sufficient
proof of piety (Rabbi Jonah).

A hedge is an important device for carrying out the requirements of the Torah, and every single generation is obliged to
make enactments in behalf of those matters which people have
begun to neglect and transgress. Indeed were it not for such
enactments the Torah would have been undone little by little
(Duran).

In the first chapter of *Abot de-Rabbi Natan,* by way of interpreting "make a hedge," it is said: Make a hedge about thy
words the way the Holy One, blessed be He, made a hedge
about His words. Now it seems to me that by this interpretation we are instructed as follows: Let every man take care that
what he says shall not be too difficult for his listeners to understand, especially when he speaks words of the Torah; let him
take care to speak of them only at the right time, in the right
idiom, in the right place, and under the right circumstances,
both as regards himself and as regards his listeners. There is
an Arabic saying about a certain sage who used to talk too

long and he was asked, "Why do you go on endlessly, talking so long?" He replied, "So that even the fools might understand." To which folks retorted, "By the time the fools understand, the wise will have been worn out" (Meiri).

SIMEON THE RIGHTEOUS WAS ONE OF THE LAST MEMBERS OF THE GREAT ASSEMBLY.

HE USED TO SAY: ON THREE THINGS THE AGE STANDS—ON THE TORAH, ON THE TEMPLE SERVICE, AND ON ACTS OF PIETY.*

HE USED TO SAY: That is, he was in the habit of saying. That is why the idiom "he used to say" is used, not, Simeon the Righteous "says" (Duran).

ON THREE THINGS THE AGE (*olam*) STANDS: That is to say, for the sake of these three things was the world (*olam*) created (Rabbi Jonah).

According to the physician Solomon ben Yaish these three things . . . constitute the foundation and base of the world (Nahmias).

ON THE TORAH: The study of Torah is more beloved by God than burnt offerings. For if a man studies Torah he comes to know the will of God, as it is said, *Then shalt thou understand the fear of the Lord, and find the will of God* (Proverbs 2:5). Hence, when a sage sits and interprets Holy Writ to the congregation, Scripture accounts it to him as though he had offered up fat and blood on the altar (ARN).

Rabbi Simeon says: More precious to God are words of the Torah than burnt offerings and sacrifices (ARNB).

The following is reported in the Talmud (Aboda Zara 3a): From the very outset the Holy One laid it down as a condition with the works of Creation: "If Israel will accept the Torah well and good; otherwise I shall reduce the universe to chaos again" (Vitry).

On one occasion when Rabbi Tarfon, Rabbi Yose the Galilean, and Rabbi Akiba were assembled in Lydda, the following question was taken up: Which is more important, study or practice? Rabbi Tarfon spoke up and said, "Practice." Rabbi Akiba spoke up and said, "Study." Whereupon they concluded:

---

* In a forthcoming monograph I am furnishing the evidence to justify this translation of Simeon's saying.

Study is more important, for study leads to practice (Sifre Deuteronomy, 41, quoted by Aknin).

This round world is suspended in space and has nothing to rest on except the breath of Torah study from the mouths of students—just as a man may keep something up in the air by the blowing of his breath (Duran).

ON THE TEMPLE SERVICE: So long as the Temple service is maintained, the world is a blessing to its inhabitants and the rains come down in season . . . But when the Temple service is not maintained, the world is not a blessing to its inhabitants and the rains do not come down in season. . . .

There is no service more beloved of the Holy One, blessed be He, than the Temple service (ARN).

Now that there is no Temple service in the world sustained by the Torah, by acts of lovingkindness, and by prayer—for prayer takes the place of Temple service (Vitry).

This stands to reason. For the whole world was created only for man's sake, and man was created only to serve the Lord, blessed be He. Jerusalem was chosen of all places, and Israel of all peoples, so that the Temple service might be carried out. And our Sages, of blessed memory, have taught us (see Menahot 110a) that when there is no Temple, he who studies the laws of sacrifices and offerings is regarded as though he had offered them up in fact . . . Sacrifices to God are a broken heart. That means that praying with a broken heart is more effective as atonement than offering animal sacrifices—for he who prays with a broken heart offers up his own fat and blood. And the same is true of one who fasts (Duran).

ON ACTS OF PIETY (*Gemilut Hasadim*): Once as Rabban Johanan ben Zakkai was coming forth from Jerusalem Rabbi Joshua followed after him and beheld the Temple in ruins. "Woe unto us," Rabbi Joshua cried, "that this, the place where the iniquities of Israel were atoned for, is laid waste!"

"My son," Rabban Johanan said to him, "be not grieved; we have another atonement as effective as this. And what is it? It is acts of lovingkindness (*gemilut hasadim*), as it is said, *For I desire mercy and not sacrifice*" (Hosea 6:6) (ARN).

Acts of lovingkindness are greater than charity. As the Sages have said (Sukkah 49b): Charity applies only to the living, acts of lovingkindness apply to the living and the dead. Charity is something a man does with his wealth, acts of lovingkindness he carries out with his wealth and by means of his own person. In acts of lovingkindness the poor man's feelings are spared:

for example when one lends a poor man funds to help him in his hour of need; whereas when one gives the poor man charity, the poor man inevitably feels some shame. Charity affects the poor only; acts of lovingkindness affect the rich also (Vitry).

Of the Book of Ruth, Rabbi Zeira said (Ruth Rabba 2:14): In this book there is no discussion of laws of uncleanness and cleanness, the prohibited and permitted. Why therefore was it written? To teach us how great is the reward for those who practice acts of lovingkindness (Duran).

———

ANTIGONUS OF SOKO TOOK OVER FROM SIMEON THE RIGHT-EOUS.

HE USED TO SAY: BE NOT LIKE SLAVES WHO SERVE THEIR MASTER FOR THE SAKE OF THEIR ALLOWANCE; BE RATHER LIKE SLAVES WHO SERVE THEIR MASTER WITH NO THOUGHT OF AN ALLOWANCE—AND LET THE FEAR OF HEAVEN BE UPON YOU.

BE NOT LIKE SLAVES WHO SERVE . . . FOR THE SAKE OF THEIR ALLOWANCE: Let no man say, "I shall serve my Creator so that He provide me with my needs." Whether He provides or not, let one serve his Creator out of love, simply because *The Lord my God commanded me* (Deuteronomy 4:5). And even when sufferings come upon a man, let him not allow himself to waver or question. Let him serve Him with love, as it is written, *Happy the man whom Thou chastisest, O Lord* (Psalm 94:12) (Vitry).

It is written, *And thou shalt love the Lord thy God with all thy heart, and with all thy soul, and with all thy might* (Deuteronomy 6:4)—regardless of the measure He metes out to you, magnify Him (Aknin).

What Antigonus says is this: Let not your service of God, in carrying out the commandments, be motivated by desire for reward—as is the case with a child who does not appreciate the value of wisdom and will not study until you have bribed him with trinkets or money; neither let your service be motivated by ambition for glory or profit. Such service is not service for its own sake. It is against such conduct that the Sages warned: Do not make the words of the Torah a crown for self glorification. One must study for the sake of wisdom and Torah. And so too we are urged in the service of the Creator, that when we carry out His commandments we do so for the sake of the commandment, solely out of love of the commandment —as is the case when a person loves someone and strives always to please his beloved. The reward will indeed come of itself (Meiri).

True service is the kind of service a slave renders his master because of his love for him, whether the latter rewards him or not (Duran).

Antigonus of Soko had two disciples who used to study his words. They taught them to their disciples, and their disciples to their disciples. These proceeded to examine the words closely and demanded: "Why did our ancestors see fit to say this thing? Is it possible that a laborer should do his work all day and not receive his reward in the evening? If our ancestors, forsooth, had known that there is another world and that there will be a resurrection of the dead, they would not have spoken in this manner." So they arose and withdrew from the Torah and split into two sects, the Sadducees and the Boethusians: Sadducees named after Zadok, Boethusians, after Boethus. And they used silver vessels and gold vessels all their lives—not because they were ostentatious; but the Sadducees said, "It is a tradition among the Pharisees to afflict themselves in this world; yet in the world to come they will have nothing" (ARN).

AND LET THE FEAR OF HEAVEN BE UPON YOU: One who worships out of love inherits the life of this world but not the life of the world to come; one who worships out of awe and fear inherits the life of this world and the life of the world to come (ARNB, manuscript reading).

"Let the fear of Heaven be upon you," along with love—that is to say, do not behave irreverently towards Him on high, like an importunate son who grows presumptuous because of the very love he feels (Vitry).

For all his insistence that one should serve the Lord out of love, Antigonus has not exempted us from the commandment to fear Him. Along with worshipping God out of love, he says, do not altogether neglect the element of fear, "let the fear of Heaven be upon you," for the commandment to fear Him is clearly stated in the Torah, as it is said, *Thou shalt fear the Lord thy God* (Deuteronomy 6:13) (Maimonides).

The ancients, of blessed memory, used to say that one who loves his fellow does not neglect his commandment, but carries it out; and that one who fears his fellow does not violate his orders. That is why a sense of fear is very important with regard to the negative commandments, and, needless to say, with regard to the statutes, the reasons for which have not been revealed to us (Aknin).

———

YOSE BEN JOEZER OF ZEREDAH AND YOSE BEN JOHANAN OF JERUSALEM TOOK OVER FROM THEM.

YOSE BEN JOEZER SAYS: LET THY HOUSE BE A MEETING-PLACE FOR THE SAGES, AND SIT IN THE VERY DUST AT THEIR FEET, AND THIRSTILY DRINK IN THEIR WORDS.

YOSE BEN JOEZER . . . AND YOSE BEN JOHANAN: All the Sages listed in this chapter from this point through Hillel and Shammai are known as the Pairs (Duran), and they were the heads of the Sanhedrin . . . one serving as *Nasi* and the other as *Ab Bet Din* (Vitry).

OF ZEREDAH . . . OF JERUSALEM: That is, of the distinguished sages and men of the city (Aknin).

TOOK OVER FROM THEM: From the Men of the Great Assembly (Vitry).

From Simeon the Righteous and Antigonus of Soko (Rabbi Jonah).

LET THY HOUSE BE A MEETING-PLACE FOR THE SAGES: This teaches that a man's house ought to be a center for the Sages, disciples, and disciples of the disciples—as it is when one says to his fellow, "I shall await thee at such and such a place" (ARN).

It is said, *The Lord hath blessed the house of Obed-edom, and all that pertaineth unto him, because of the ark of God* (II Samuel 6:12). Now is there not an inference to be drawn here? If a house was blessed because of the ark of God in which were no more than the two Tables of the Commandments, how much the more will be the blessing when Sages and their disciples come into a person's house.

Another interpretation. When a sage comes into your house do not treat him with disrespect. Moreover, do not sit down with him on the couch or bench. Instead, sit at his feet on the ground, and take in all his words with awe and fear, as you would if you were listening to him in the study house (ARNB).

AND SIT IN THE VERY DUST AT THEIR FEET: One ought not to be too proud to wait upon the scholars. Note the verse, *Elisha the son of Shaphat is here, who poured water on the hands of Elijah* (II Kings 3:11). The verse does not say, "who studied with Elijah," but *who poured water for Elijah*. This teaches that acting humbly in the presence of scholars is really an exaltation; for behold, Elisha's role was elevated, and he was exalted in the sight of three kings (Aknin).

This is an exhortation to us to attend upon the Sages, for attendance is even more instructive than study (Nahmias).

AND THIRSTILY DRINK IN THEIR WORDS: For so long as words of the Torah enter and find the chambers of the heart unoccupied, they make their home in the person—and the evil impulse can have no dominion over him and no one can drive away these words from him. A parable is told: to what may this be likened? To a king who was on a journey; he came upon a palace whose rooms were unoccupied, and entered and occupied them. No man can expel him from there. So too, so long as the words of the Torah upon entering find the chambers of the heart unoccupied, they make their home in it; the evil impulse can have no dominion there and no one can drive these words away (ARNB).

Receive the words of the sage in your mind with all your heart and with all your soul and empty your heart of all worldly distractions (Aknin).

The words of the Torah have been compared to water, and so drink in their words thirstily, as a weary soul turns to fresh water (Nahmias).

What were the beginnings of Rabbi Akiba?

It is said: Before he was forty years of age he had studied nothing. One time he stood by the mouth of a well. "Who hollowed out this stone?" he wondered. He was told: "It is the water which falls upon it every day, continually." . . . Thereupon Rabbi Akiba drew the inference with regard to himself: If what is soft wears down the hard, all the more shall the words of the Torah, which are as hard as iron, hollow out my heart which is flesh and blood! Forthwith he turned to the study of Torah.

He went together with his son and they appeared before an elementary teacher. Said Rabbi Akiba to him: "Master, teach me Torah."

Rabbi Akiba took hold of one end of the tablet and his son of the other end of the tablet. The teacher wrote down *aleph bet* for him and he learned it; *aleph taw*, and he learned it; the Book of Leviticus, and he learned it. He went on studying until he learned the whole Torah. Then he went and appeared before Rabbi Eliezer and Rabbi Joshua. "My masters," he said to them, "reveal the sense of Mishna to me."

When they told him one halakah he went off to be by himself. "This *aleph*," he wondered, "why was it written? That *bet*, why was it written? This thing, why was it said?" He came back and asked them—and reduced them to silence. . . .

Each day Rabbi Akiba would gather a bundle of straw; part he would sell to provide for his food and part for his clothing. His neighbors rose up in protest and said to him, "Akiba, thou art slaying us with the smoke! Sell the straw to us and with the money buy oil, and study by the light of a lamp."

"I fill many needs with it," he answered them; "first, I study by its light; then again, I keep warm by its heat; and finally, I sleep on it." . . .

At the age of forty he went to study Torah; at the end of thirteen years he taught Torah to multitudes.

It is said: Before he departed from the world he owned tables of silver and gold, and mounted his couch on ladders of gold. His wife used to go about in golden sandals and in a golden tiara.

"Master," his disciples said to him, "thou hast put us to shame by what thou hast done for her."

He said to them: "Many were the trials she endured for my sake, that I might study Torah."

What were the beginnings of Rabbi Eliezer ben Hyrcanus?

He was twenty-two years old and had not yet studied Torah. One time he resolved: "I will go and study Torah with Rabban Johanan ben Zakkai." Said his father Hyrcanus to him: "Not a taste of food shalt thou get before thou hast ploughed the entire furrow."

He rose early in the morning and ploughed the entire furrow [and then departed for Jerusalem].

It is told: That day was the eve of the Sabbath, and he went for the Sabbath meal to his father-in-law's. And some say: He tasted nothing from six hours before the eve of the Sabbath until six hours after the departure of the Sabbath.

As he was walking along the road he saw a stone; he picked it up and put it in his mouth.—And some say: It was cattle dung.—He went to spend the night at a hostel.

Then he went and appeared before Rabban Johanan ben Zakkai in Jerusalem—until a bad breath rose from his mouth. Said Rabban Johanan ben Zakkai to him: "Eliezer, my son, hast thou eaten at all today?"

Silence.

Rabban Johanan ben Zakkai asked him again.

Again silence.

Rabban Johanan ben Zakkai sent for the owners of his hostel and asked them: "Did Eliezer have anything to eat in your place?"

"We thought," they replied, "he was very likely eating with thee, master."

He said to them: "And I thought he was very likely eating with you! You and I, between us, left Rabbi Eliezer to perish!"

[Thereupon] Rabban Johanan said to him: "Even as a bad breath rose from thy mouth, so shall fame of thee travel for thy mastery of the Torah."

When Hyrcanus his father heard of him that he was studying Torah with Rabban Johanan ben Zakkai, he declared: "I shall go and ban my son Eliezer from my possessions."

It is told: That day Rabban Johanan ben Zakkai sat expounding in Jerusalem and all the magnates of Israel sat before him. When he heard that Hyrcanus was coming, he appointed guards and said to them, "If Hyrcanus comes, do not let him sit down."

Hyrcanus arrived and they would not let him sit down. But he pushed on ahead until he reached the place near Ben Sisit Hakkeset, Nakdimon ben Gorion, and Ben Kalba Sabua. He sat among them trembling.

It is told: On that day Rabban Johanan ben Zakkai fixed his gaze upon Rabbi Eliezer and said to him: "Deliver the exposition."

"I am unable to speak," Rabbi Eliezer pleaded.

Rabban Johanan pressed him to do it and the disciples pressed him to do it. So he arose and delivered a discourse upon things which no ear had ever before heard. As the words came from his mouth Rabban Johanan ben Zakkai rose to his feet and kissed him upon his head and exclaimed, "Rabbi Eliezer, master, thou hast taught me the truth!"

Before the time had come to recess, Hyrcanus his father rose to his feet and declared: "My masters, I came here only in order to ban my son Eliezer from my possessions. Now, all my possessions shall be given to Eliezer my son, and all his brothers are herewith disinherited and have naught of them" (ARN).

———

YOSE BEN JOHANAN OF JERUSALEM SAYS: LET THY HOUSE BE OPENED WIDE, AND LET THE POOR BE MEMBERS OF THY HOUSEHOLD; AND TALK NOT OVERMUCH WITH WOMEN— EVEN WITH ONE'S OWN WIFE, THE SAGES SAID, ALL THE MORE THEN WITH HIS FELLOW'S WIFE! HENCE THE SAGES SAID: SO LONG AS A MAN TALKS OVERMUCH WITH WOMEN HE BRINGS EVIL UPON HIMSELF, NEGLECTS THE STUDY OF TORAH, AND IN THE END GEHENNA IS HIS PORTION.

LET THY HOUSE BE OPENED WIDE: This teaches that a man's house should have a spacious entrance, on the north, south, east, and west like Job's, who made four doors to his house. And why did Job make four doors to his house? So that the poor would not be troubled to go all around the house: one coming from the north could enter in his stride, one coming from the south could enter in his stride, and so in all directions (ARN).

Yose ben Johanan comes to supplement what Yose ben Joezer said, namely that just as one's house must be a meeting-place for the Sages, so must it be opened wide for guests and for the poor (Duran).

LET THE POOR BE MEMBERS OF THY HOUSEHOLD: Do not multiply slaves and maidservants to serve you. Instead invite the poor to be members of your household, and let them serve you; then you will receive a reward for hiring them (Vitry).

The Sages used to speak disparagingly of the acquisition of slaves; but they used to praise him who gave employment to the poor by taking them on as servants (Maimonides).

Teach the members of thy household humility. For when one is humble and the members of his household are humble, if a poor man comes and stands in the doorway of the master of the house and inquires of them "Is your father within?" they answer: "Aye, come in, enter." Even before he has entered a table is set for him. When he enters and eats and drinks and offers a blessing up to Heaven, great delight of spirit is vouchsafed to the master of the house.

But when one is not humble and the members of his household are short-tempered, if a poor man comes and stands in the doorway and inquires of them: "Is your father within?" they answer: "No!" and rebuke him and drive him off in anger (ARN).

Yose ben Johanan of Jerusalem says: O man, I command you to keep your house wide open for acts of charity, so that whoever is in trouble may enter it and find relief. So too keep it open for widows and orphans, and let them be as precious in your sight as your own sons and as members of your own household. Know that if you have given the needy anything, you have not given them anything of your own but of what the Creator, blessed be He, gave you. For the poor and the widows and the orphans are brokenhearted and they cannot endure anger or rebuke and their tears flow freely (Rabbi David the Prince).

AND TALK NOT OVERMUCH WITH WOMEN: This refers to idle chatter (Vitry).

The word for "talk" in this passage refers to conversation which is entirely unnecessary, "idle chatter," as the Sages often refer to it (Meiri).

EVEN WITH ONE'S OWN WIFE: It is a known thing that for the most part conversation with women has to do with sexual matters. That is why Yose ben Johanan says that much talk with them is forbidden, for by such talk a man brings evil upon himself (Maimonides).

Yose ben Johanan is not restricting necessary conversation with one's wife, be it short or long, in such affairs as household needs or expenses or suchlike matters. For so long as a husband speaks with his wife about necessary matters, no evil comes about, because then the mind is concentrating on the advice it is receiving. . . . What the Sage warns against is unnecessary conversation, unnecessary greetings, chitchat of what has been happening, and things of that sort. If it should sometimes happen, says Yose ben Johanan, that the husband has gotten into a conversation over such things, he ought not to talk too much. And this applies even to his own wife, so that he will not bring evil upon himself, for he is a man and should be working or studying, and not be distracted (Meiri).

If a man came to the study house and was not treated with honor, or if he fell out with his fellow, he is not to go and tell his wife "Thus and so did I fall out with my fellow, he said this to me and I said that to him." For [in so doing] he disgraces himself, disgraces his wife, and disgraces his fellow. And his wife, who used to treat him with honor, now stands and scoffs at him. Then his fellow hears of it and cries: "Woe unto me! Words between himself and me he went and told his wife!" And thus such a person disgraces himself, disgraces his wife, disgraces his fellow (ARN).

——

JOSHUA BEN PERAHYAH AND NITTAI THE ARBELITE TOOK OVER FROM THEM.

JOSHUA BEN PERAHYAH SAYS: PROVIDE THYSELF WITH A TEACHER, GET THEE A COMRADE, AND JUDGE EVERYONE WITH THE SCALE WEIGHTED IN HIS FAVOR.

TOOK OVER FROM THEM: From Yose ben Joezer and Yose ben Johanan (Vitry).

PROVIDE THYSELF WITH A TEACHER: Provide thyself with a teacher [from whom] to learn and get thee a comrade [with whom] to review (ARNB).

Rabbi Meir used to say: He that studies Torah with a single teacher, to whom may he be likened? To one who had a single field, part of which he sowed with wheat and part with barley, and planted part with olives and part with oak trees. Now that man is full of good and blessing. But when one studies with two or three teachers he is like him who has many fields: one he sows with wheat and one he sows with barley, and plants one with olives and one with oak trees. Now this man's attention is divided between many pieces of land without good or blessing (ARN).

If you have learned from one teacher everything he has to teach you, do not sit back and say, "It is enough for me." Rather, go to another teacher and learn from him . . . . Shall we say that a person should first study with a teacher who is located far off and then study with one who is nearby? The verse says, *Drink waters out of thine own cistern* (Proverbs 5:15) (ARNB).

Do not depend entirely upon yourself where Halakah is at stake (Vitry).

[There are times] when a person is not really qualified to be your teacher; nevertheless let him teach you, make it possible for him to teach you. If you do this you will acquire wisdom—for there is no comparison between studying by oneself and studying with another person. When one studies with another person, he remembers better what he has learned, the material is more clearly understood by him, even when his companion is no more than his equal in wisdom, or even when his companion is inferior to him (Maimonides).

The philosophers used to say: Even the greatest of kings needs another's counsel (Meiri).

GET THEE A COMRADE: This teaches that a man should get a comrade for himself, to eat with him, drink with him, study Scripture with him, study Mishna with him, sleep with him, and reveal to him all his secrets, the secrets of the Torah and the secrets of worldly things.

When two sit studying Torah and one of them makes a mistake in a matter of halakah or of a chapter heading— or says of the unclean that it is clean, or of the clean that it is unclean; or of the forbidden that it is permitted, or of the permitted that it is forbidden—his comrade will correct him (ARN).

It is sometimes possible for a man to provide himself with a teacher [from whom] to learn, but acquiring a comrade [with whom] to review comes only with great difficulty (ARNB).

Note that the idiom used here is " 'get thee' (buy) a companion," not just "provide thyself with" a companion or "attach thyself" to others or some similar expression. The reason for this is that, if necessary, a man should buy a devoted friend for himself. . . . As the Sages used to say (Taanit 23a): Give me friendship or give me death. And if a person cannot easily find a friend, he must strive with all his heart to do so, even if he has to go so far as compel the person to love him, even if he has to buy his love and friendship (Maimonides).

The Greek philosophers used to say: A friend is somebody outside yourself and yet in truth he is you; that is to say, though the bodies of the two friends are separate and distinct, their souls cling and cleave to each other (Aknin).

There are some who interpret "get thee a comrade" as "buy yourself books," but the true interpretation is the literal one (Duran).

AND JUDGE EVERYONE WITH THE SCALE WEIGHTED IN HIS FAVOR: There was once a young girl who had been taken captive and two saintly folk went after her to ransom her. One of them entered the harlots' apartment. When he came out he asked his companion: "What didst thou suspect me of?" The other replied: "Of finding out perhaps for how much money she is being held." Said the first: "By the Temple service, so it was!" And he added: "Even as thou didst judge me with the scale weighted in my favor, so may the Holy One, blessed be He, judge thee with the scale weighted in thy favor" (ARN).

If there is some person whom you do not know to be either righteous or wicked, and you see him doing something or saying something which might be interpreted either favorably or unfavorably, interpret his action favorably and do not suspect him of evil. But if the person is well known as a righteous man, always doing good, and some action of his seems to be bad—only with extreme difficulty can one justify it—then it is proper to judge it favorably, since there is at least a remote possibility that the action is a good one; and it is not permitted to suspect such a person of evil. It is in this connection that the Sages said (Shabbat 97a): He who suspects the upright should be whipped! However, if there is a person notorious for his wicked ways, and you see him do something which seems to be good, but there is a remote possibility that it is evil, then it is wise to beware of him, not to assume that he is doing good. It is of such a person that the verse says, *He that hateth dissembleth with his lips . . . when he speaketh fair, believe him not* (Proverbs 26:24 ff.) (Maimonides).

———

NITTAI THE ARBELITE SAYS: KEEP FAR AWAY FROM AN EVIL NEIGHBOR, DO NOT ASSOCIATE WITH THE WICKED, AND DO NOT SHRUG OFF ALL THOUGHT OF CALAMITY.

NITTAI THE ARBELITE SAYS: He comes to add to what his colleague had said, namely, that just as one has to draw nigh to good persons and judge them favorably, so must one keep far away from the wicked and judge them unfavorably when the day of their punishment and calamity comes (Duran).

KEEP FAR AWAY FROM AN EVIL NEIGHBOR: Whether it be your neighbor indoors or your neighbor out of doors or your neighbor out in the field. This teaches that plagues come only because of the iniquity of the wicked: the iniquities of the wicked cause the wall of the righteous to be torn down. How so? If there is a wall separating the wicked from the righteous, and a plague appears in the house (see Leviticus 14:33 ff.) of the wicked on the wall separating him from the righteous, the wall of the righteous has to be torn down because of the iniquity of the wicked.

Rabbi Ishmael, son of Rabbi Johanan ben Baroka says: Woe to the wicked and woe to his neighbor! The iniquities of the wicked cause the wall of the righteous to be torn down (ARN).

When a person wishes to rent an apartment . . . he should investigate whether his neighbors are evil—so that he might keep far from them—or good—so that he might get close to them (Rabbi Jonah).

"Keep far away from an evil neighbor" for two reasons: to beware of being harmed along with them and of being influenced by their works; for associating with evil persons leads to a deterioration of character. Again and again the Sages have said (Mishna Negaim 12:6): Woe to the wicked and woe to his neighbor (Meiri).

The evil neighbor mentioned here is one who is evil toward mankind, who is a robber or brigand—who does the kind of things that the evil impulse craves to do; and even the good person might very speedily be influenced to imitate such conduct (Duran).

DO NOT ASSOCIATE WITH THE WICKED: For whoever associates with the wicked must in the end carry away some slight impact by him, as it is said, *Now a word was stealthily brought to me, and mine ear received a whisper thereof* (Job 4:12) (ARNB).

"Do not associate with the wicked" even for the study of Torah (ARN).

"The wicked" refers to the evil impulse which dwells at the opening of the heart. For when a person seeks to commit a transgression, the evil impulse bends all the limbs over which it rules to that end (ARNB).

Lest a person say: "I shall take care not to live in the neighborhood of an evil person because that would involve constant association, but I shall associate with him occasionally for purposes of business," . . . he is therefore warned now: "Do not associate with the wicked," that is to say, in any kind of association (Meiri).

Just as we have been warned to keep far away from a neighbor who is evil toward mankind, so we have been warned against association with a person who is wicked toward Heaven. . . . A parable is told: If one enters a tanner's shop, even if he took nothing from it he will carry away a bad smell with him (Duran).

AND DO NOT SHRUG OFF ALL THOUGHT OF CALAMITY: This teaches that a man's heart should be in a state of fear at all times and he should say, "Woe unto me! Perhaps calamity will come upon me today, perhaps tomorrow." He will thus be in a state of fear at all times; for thus is it said of Job, *The thing which I did fear has come upon me* (Job 3:25). Another interpretation. When a man sees his affairs prosper let him not say, "Because I have merited it, God has given me food and drink in this world and the stock is laid up for me for the world to come." Instead let him say, "Woe unto me! Perhaps no more than one good deed was found before Him in my behalf. And He has given me food and drink in this world so that He might destroy me in the world to come" (ARN).

Nittai puts the statement "do not shrug off" close to "do not associate with the wicked" to teach that if you associate with the wicked man, by all means beware of calamity . . . for it will certainly come (Vitry).

The Sage tells us that if you sin or see somebody sinning, do not think confidently that God will punish the wicked only in the world to come; do not give up hope of speedy retribution for that sin (Maimonides).

Let him who is enjoying good fortune not shrug off all thought of calamity . . . and let him who is in the midst of calamity not despair of good fortune (ARNB).

JUDAH BEN TABBAI AND SIMEON BEN SHETAH TOOK OVER FROM THEM.

JUDAH BEN TABBAI SAYS: DO NOT PLAY THE PART OF CHIEF JUSTICE; AND WHEN THERE ARE LITIGANTS STANDING BEFORE THEE, LOOK UPON THEM AS LIKELY TO BE GUILTY; BUT WHEN THEY DEPART FROM THY PRESENCE LOOK UPON THEM AS LIKELY TO BE INNOCENT, AS SOON AS THEY HAVE ACCEPTED THE SENTENCE.

DO NOT PLAY THE PART OF CHIEF JUSTICE (*Orekhe Ha-Dayyanim*): This teaches that if thou hast come to the study house and heard an interpretation or a statement of halakah, do not be in haste to dispute it. Instead, sit still and ask for what reason it was said, in what connection was the judgment or the halakah which has been discussed (ARN).

Orekhe Ha-Dayyanim means "Chief Justice" . . . and Judah ben Tabbai warns: Do not act like chief justices, that is, do not speak up first in the company of those older than you (Nahmias).

Orekhe Ha-Dayyanim are those who teach the litigants how to arrange their arguments cleverly (Vitry), saying to the litigants, "If the judge should say this, you answer this way; if your opponent should argue such-and-such, let that be your answer" (Maimonides).

Judah ben Tabbai is not warning against teaching a litigant how to argue deceitfully, for that is altogether wicked. . . . What he warns against is saying to a litigant, "Do such-and-such, so that you might win the suit"—even when one knows that this litigant is right (Duran).

WHEN THERE ARE LITIGANTS STANDING BEFORE THEE: When two litigants come before thee for judgment, one poor and one rich, say not: "How shall I acquit the poor and condemn the rich?" or, "How shall I acquit the rich and condemn the poor? For if I condemn the poor one, he will be my enemy; and if I acquit the poor one, the rich one will be my enemy." And say not: "How shall I take the money from the one and give it to the other?" Yea, the Torah hath said, *Ye shall not respect persons in judgment* (Deuteronomy 1:17).

Rabbi Meir used to say: Why does the verse say, *Ye shall hear the small and the great alike* (Deuteronomy 1:17)? So that one of the litigants shall not be kept standing and the other sit, one be allowed to speak his fill while to the other thou sayest "Cut thy words short!" Rabbi Judah said: I have heard that if the judges wished to have both alike sitting, they may be seated. What is forbidden is that one be standing and the other sitting.

Let a minor lawsuit be to thee like a major lawsuit, a lawsuit over a *perutah* like a lawsuit over a hundred *mina* (ARN).

WHEN THEY DEPART FROM THY PRESENCE LOOK UPON THEM AS LIKELY TO BE INNOCENT, AS SOON AS THEY HAVE ACCEPTED THE SENTENCE: Although you know that in the course of the litigation one of them must have been arguing falsely, do not assume that he is a liar. . . . Once he has accepted the sentence, it is not right to continue treating him with suspicion, even though he has been found guilty. One is rather to assume that he repented, that he intends never to behave this way again (Rabbi Jonah).

SIMEON BEN SHETAH SAYS: AGAIN AND AGAIN EXAMINE THE WITNESSES; AND BE GUARDED IN THY SPEECH LEST FROM IT THEY LEARN TO LIE.

AND BE GUARDED IN THY SPEECH: This is a warning to the judge not to say anything in the presence of the litigants or the witnesses which might lead them to perceive how to win the suit (Duran).

SHEMAIAH AND ABTALYON TOOK OVER FROM THEM.
SHEMAIAH SAYS: LOVE WORK, HATE LORDSHIP, AND SEEK NO INTIMACY WITH THE RULING POWERS.

LOVE WORK: This teaches that a man should love work and that no man should hate work. For even as the Torah was given as a covenant, so was work given as a covenant; as it is said, *Six days shalt thou labor and do all thy work* (Exodus 20:9). . . . Rabbi Simeon ben Eleazar says, Even Adam tasted nothing before he worked, as it is said, *And He put him into the Garden of Eden to dress it and to keep it;* [only thereafter] *Of every tree of the garden thou mayest freely eat* (Genesis 2:15-16) (ARN).

Rabbi says: How important is work! For whoever does not engage in work is the subject of everybody's conversation: "How does So-and-so get food, how does he get drink?" A parable is told: to what may this be likened? To a woman who has no husband but struts about in the market place in all her finery, and men talk about her (ARNB).

Let no man neglect to work, for idleness will throw a man into depression (Rabbi Jonah).

Even the rich must love work, that is to say, must engage in some worthwhile occupation, and not remain idle—for idleness is the cause of terrible things (Meiri).

By work the world is sustained and one's learning is sustained. For if a man has no work he will be dependent on others and in the end have to resort to robbing. . . . In many places of the Talmud (see, for example, Berakot 16b) the Sages, of blessed memory, have praised the person who lives on the income from his own labors (Duran).

HATE LORDSHIP: This teaches that no man should put a crown on his head of his own accord; instead let others put it on him, as it is said, *Let another man praise thee and not thine own mouth, a stranger and not thine own lips* (Proverbs 27:22).

Said Rabbi Akiba: Whoever exalts himself above the words of the Torah, to what may he be likened? To a carcass abandoned on the highway—every passerby puts his hand to his nose, turns away from it and walks off (ARN).

Rabbi Yose says: Go down to come up and up to come down —if a man has humbled himself he will be exalted, but if he has exalted himself he will be humbled (ARNB).

Let no man regard himself as so important as not to engage in work. As Rab once said to Rab Kahana (Pesahim 113a): "If necessary make your living by dressing hides in the market place; do not say I am a priest, I am a great man, and such work is beneath me" (Vitry).

Lordship puts its possessors into the grave, the very dust of royalty is fatal (ARNB).

The Sages have warned against lordship; that is to say, let not a rich man be seduced by his wealth to pursue triumph and power over others, for this would only cause everyone to hate him. . . . The Sages, of blessed memory, used to say (see Maimonides on Abot 1:10): "When a man has been appointed the head of a community, on high they regard him as wicked," because the chances are that he demands the kind of authority and awe toward himself which is not for the sake of Heaven (Meiri).

If you hate lordship you will be able to obey the commandment to love work, for he who loves lordship does not engage in work—and the meaning of lordship is love of power. Under no circumstance however should a man be held back from struggling to arrive at the lordship of learning (Duran).

AND SEEK NO INTIMACY WITH THE RULING POWERS: This teaches that one's name should not come to the attention of the ruling powers. For once his name comes to the attention of the ruling powers they cast their eye upon him and slay him and take away all his property from him (ARN).

Even if you exercise lordship, if it has been bestowed upon you by the ruling powers, do not get fond of it—because in the end there will be some accusation against you and everything you have will be taken away from you (Vitry).

If a man is not well known to the ruling powers let him not strive for such intimacy; for close association with the ruling powers will lead a person to neglect everything except serving them, and turn all his days to things of naught (Meiri).

———

ABTALYON SAYS: SAGES, WATCH YOUR WORDS LEST YOU INCUR THE PENALTY OF EXILE AND BE CARRIED OFF TO A PLACE OF EVIL WATERS, AND YOUR DISCIPLES WHO COME AFTER YOU DRINK THEREOF AND DIE—AND THUS THE NAME OF HEAVEN BE PROFANED.

SAGES, WATCH YOUR WORDS: Lest you decide something not in accord with the teaching of the Torah (ARN).

Take care as regards those whom you teach, that is, present your teachings to disciples who fear the Lord, not to simpletons —lest these decide not in accordance with the words of the Torah; and for this you will incur the penalty of exile (Vitry).

Take care to explain clearly the words that come out of your mouth so that it will be impossible for the listener to interpret heretically what you say. Do not say, "Why be concerned with the audience? If they do not understand what we said, let them come up and ask what we meant"—because it may sometimes happen that your words have been uttered in a place where the listeners do not want to ask; indeed they already incline to a false interpretation and are pleased with it (Meiri).

EVIL WATERS: This is a reference to the heathen nations, as it is said, *They mingled themselves with the nations, and learned their works* (Psalm 106:35) (ARNB).

"Evil waters" is a term for heresy. Abtalyon says: When you speak in public watch your words so that they do not lend themselves to a false interpretation. For if there are heretics present they will interpret your words in accordance with their false beliefs. The disciples who have listened to these words will also turn to heresy thinking all the time that this was your belief too. In this way the Name of God is profaned (Maimonides).

AND THUS THE NAME OF HEAVEN BE PROFANED: I think this is what Abtalyon means: "Sages, watch your words," that is, do not be easygoing with the laws of the Torah, even if you now find yourselves in a place of Torah-scholars, about whom you are confident that they will not be turned to heresy by your words. For it is possible that you may have to go into exile—as was the case with many scholars who had to leave the Land of Israel for Babylonia, or Babylonia for the Land of Israel—and you find yourself in a place of ignoramuses whose ways are bad. The disciples who appear subsequently learn these ways and by example become even more easygoing with the words of the Torah. They will die, as it is written, *For she hath cast down many wounded* (Proverbs 7:26). "And thus the Name of Heaven be profaned," for people will say, "Woe to So-and-so! He studied Torah, yet see what happened to him." It is to such a danger the Talmud (Erubin 6a) refers when it reports that "Rab found an open plain, and hedged it in well" (Vitry).

———

HILLEL AND SHAMMAI TOOK OVER FROM THEM.
HILLEL SAYS: BE OF THE DISCIPLES OF AARON, LOVING PEACE AND PURSUING PEACE, LOVING MANKIND AND DRAWING THEM TO THE TORAH.

BE OF THE DISCIPLES OF AARON: This teaches that one should love peace in Israel between man and man the way Aaron loved peace in Israel between man and man. . . . When two men had quarreled with each other, Aaron would go and sit down with one of them and say to him: "My son, mark what thy fellow is saying! He beats his breast and tears his clothing, saying, 'Woe unto me! How shall I lift my eyes and look upon my fellow! I am ashamed before him, for I it is who treated him foully.'"

He would sit with him until he had removed all rancor from his heart, and then Aaron would go and sit with the other one and say to him: "My son, mark what thy fellow is saying. He beats his breast and tears his clothing saying, 'Woe unto me! How shall I lift my eyes and look upon my fellow! I am ashamed before him, for I it is who treated him foully.'"

He would sit with him until he had removed all rancor from his heart. And when the two men met each other they embraced and kissed one another (ARN).

LOVING PEACE AND PURSUING PEACE: This teaches that
whoever establishes peace on earth is accounted by Scripture
as though he had made it on high. . . .

Another interpretation. Even if you pursue peace from
town to town, from city to city, and country to country, do
not refrain from establishing peace anywhere else, for it is
equal to all the commandments of the Torah (ARNB).

The Sages have said (Genesis Rabba 38:6): Even when
Israel worship idols, so long as there is peace in their midst,
no people or nation can have dominion over them. . . .
Controversy is a terrible thing, for even if Israel carry out all
the commandments of the Torah, if there is controversy in
their midst, anybody may do with them what he pleases
(Vitry).

LOVING MANKIND: A man must love his fellow man and
show him proper respect. If the ministering angels, in whom
there is no evil impulse, respect one another, all the more
so men, in whom there is the evil impulse!

In the Scroll of Saints it is said: If you wish to attach
to yourself a devoted friend, do things for his welfare
(ARNB).

One should love mankind and not hate mankind. For thus
we find regarding the men of the Generation of Dispersion—
because they loved one another, the Holy One, blessed be
He, had no desire to wipe them out of the world; instead
He scattered them to the four corners of the earth. As for
the Men of Sodom, because they hated one another, the Holy
One, blessed be He, wiped them out of this world and the
world to come (ARN).

AND DRAWING THEM TO THE TORAH: This teaches that
one should bend men to and lead them under the wings of
the Shekinah, the way Abraham our father used to bend
men to and lead them under the wings of the Shekinah. And
not Abraham alone did this, but Sarah as well; for it is said,
*And Abram took Sarai his wife, and Lot his brother's son,
and all their substance that they had gathered, and the souls
that they had made in Haran* (Genesis 12:5). Now, not all
the inhabitants of the world together can create even a single
gnat! How then does the verse say *and the souls that they
had made in Haran?* This teaches that the Holy One, blessed
be He, accounted it to Abraham and Sarah as though they
had made them (ARN).

Aaron had a habit of associating with evil people until

they grew embarrassed and thought, "Woe unto us! If Aaron knew what we are like, what our life is like, he would resolve never again to set eye upon us. He must think we are worthy people. We ought at least to try to make our conduct correspond to his thinking." In that way they would be drawn to association with him and learning Torah from him (Meiri).

————

HE USED TO SAY: A NAME MADE GREAT IS A NAME DESTROYED; HE THAT DOES NOT INCREASE SHALL CEASE; HE THAT DOES NOT LEARN DESERVES TO DIE; AND HE THAT PUTS THE CROWN TO HIS OWN USE SHALL PERISH.

A NAME MADE GREAT IS A NAME DESTROYED: This teaches that one's name should not come to the attention of the Ruling Power. For once a man's name comes to the attention of the Ruling Power, the end is that it casts its eye upon him, slays him, and confiscates all his wealth (ARN).

If somebody's name becomes well known in the city— "So-and-so is handsome, So-and-so is strong"—you will go looking for him on the morrow and not find out even when he departed from the world (ARNB).

He who appropriates for himself the fame of the Torah, that is, he who studies Torah in order to be able to boast of it, not for the sake of the study, will not acquire a name for himself (Vitry).

If one does whatever he does not for the sake of Heaven, but only to get a reputation, his name will be cut off in the end (Aknin).

HE THAT DOES NOT INCREASE SHALL CEASE: This teaches that if a man studies one or two or three tractates and does not add to them, he will forget the first ones in the end (ARN).

He who is a scholar and does not want to increase his learning, but says to himself, "I have learned the whole Torah, I know its ways and paths; what will it avail me to wear out my days uselessly, why ponder over what I will not understand"— ... why should such a man continue living, seeing he has given up learning? (Rabbi Jonah).

One who is not always striving to improve will come to an end, that is to say, the very memory of him will perish. . . . Hence the Sages have said that one should always be adding to his learning, and if he has learned a number of Talmudic tractates or a number of things, let him yearn to study what remains to be learned (Meiri).

HE THAT DOES NOT LEARN DESERVES TO DIE: And he that does not attend upon the Sages deserves to die. The story is told: There was once a certain man of Bet Ramah who cultivated a saintly manner. Rabban Johanan ben Zakkai sent a disciple to examine him. The disciple went and found him taking oil and putting it on a pot-range, and taking it from the pot-range and pouring it into a porridge of beans.

"What art thou doing?" the disciple asked him.

"I am an important priest," he replied, "And I eat heave-offering in a state of purity."

The disciple asked: "Is this range unclean or clean?"

Said the priest: "Have we then anything in the Torah about a range being unclean? On the contrary, the Torah speaks only of an oven being unclean, as it is said, *Whatsoever is in it shall be unclean*" (Leviticus 11:33).

Said the disciple to him: "Even as the Torah speaks of an oven being unclean, so the Torah speaks of a range being unclean, as it is said, *Whether oven or range for pots, it shall be broken in pieces, they are unclean*" (Leviticus 11:35). The disciple continued: "If this is how thou hast been conducting thyself, thou hast never in thy life eaten clean heave-offerings!" (ARN).

He who has not studied at all is like a beast, for he was created solely for the purpose of learning and studying Torah, whose ways are ways of pleasantness. Now if a person has not studied at all, and if he persists in such wickedness, he does not deserve to live even one day, even one hour (Rabbi Jonah).

AND HE THAT PUTS THE CROWN TO HIS OWN USE SHALL PERISH: Whoever makes use of the Tetragrammaton has no share in the world to come (ARN).

He who makes use of the crown of Torah, is forever puffing himself up and lording it over people, and demands to be honored by virtue of the crown of Torah which he can show he has acquired, will perish and be driven out of the world. He will pass away like a shadow, unable to prolong his days, because he does not fear God—he does not study Torah for its own sake, but for personal advantage . . . Another interpretation. One who makes use of the crown of Torah will vanish, that is, in the Future he will receive no reward for his study of Torah, since he has already taken his reward in the honor people show him for his learning (Vitry).

"He that puts the crown to his own use," that is to say, he makes his living by the Torah. . . . It is forbidden to accept personal services from a scholar save from one's own disciples (Maimonides).

A man is permitted to have his own disciple wait upon him, because in that way he teaches and trains him (Aknin).

———

HE USED TO SAY: IF NOT I FOR MYSELF, WHO THEN? AND BEING FOR MYSELF, WHAT AM I? AND IF NOT NOW, WHEN?

IF NOT I FOR MYSELF, WHO THEN? If I do not acquire merit for myself in this world who will acquire merit for me in the life of the world to come, [where] I have no father, I have no mother, I have no brother, where Father Abraham cannot redeem Ishmael, Father Isaac cannot redeem Esau (ARNB).

If I do not lay up merit in my lifetime, acquire knowledge of the Torah and the doing of good works, who will acquire them for me? For these obligations have been turned over to me, and freedom of action has been granted me, as it is written, *See I have set before thee this day life and good, and death and evil* (Deuteronomy 30:15). That is why one who does good is rewarded and one who transgresses is punished: for if our actions were determined by Heaven and not by ourselves, if man were compelled to do what he does, it would not be just to reward those who do good and to punish those who transgress (Aknin).

Every man should acquire merit for himself and not depend upon the merit of others being laid up in his behalf (Duran).

AND BEING FOR MYSELF, WHAT AM I? If I do not lay up merit in my own behalf, who will lay up merit for me in my behalf? (ARN).

If I do good works only as much as I am able, only as much as I am inclined to do so, it will still not be sufficient for me (Aknin).

If I do not take the trouble to bestir myself to seek out the commandments that have to be carried out, I will be left empty-handed; for even "being for myself," even when I do strive to carry out the commandments, I accomplish only a very little (Rabbi Jonah).

It seems to me that this is how this statement is to be interpreted: Since everything is in my power, "being for myself," that is to say, taking care of my bodily needs only without paying attention at the same time to the obligation of serving the Lord and perfecting my soul, "what am I?" In such conduct I am no more than a beast (Meiri).

Since a man is under obligation to do good himself and make others do good . . . it is therefore not enough that he see to it that he himself walks in upright ways; he must also direct others along the right path. That is why Hillel says, Even when I strive in my own behalf to do the right thing, "what am I?", that is to say, what have I accomplished? Have I fulfilled my obligation? Certainly not—for I must still strive to teach others the right way (Midrash Shemuel).

IF NOT NOW, WHEN: If I do not lay up merit in my lifetime, who will lay up merit for me after I am dead? And so too it says, For a living dog is better than a dead lion (Ecclesiastes 9:4): For a living dog is better refers to the wicked who is alive in this world. If he repents, the Holy One, blessed be He, receives him. But the righteous, once he dies, can no longer lay up additional merit (ARN).

If now, in the days of my youth, I do not acquire good qualities, when shall I acquire them? In my old age? For it is very difficult to abandon habits at that time, because by then behavior patterns have become firmly fixed (Maimonides).

Let no man say, "Today I am busy with my work; tomorrow I will turn to the task of perfecting myself." Perchance the opportunity will not present itself. And even if it does present itself, that particular day has vanished utterly and an opportunity of serving the Lord has been lost; it can never again be recovered (Rabbi Jonah).

———

SHAMMAI SAYS: MAKE OF THY STUDY OF THE TORAH A FIXED PRACTICE; SAY LITTLE AND DO MUCH; AND RECEIVE ALL MEN WITH A CHEERFUL COUNTENANCE.

MAKE OF THY STUDY OF THE TORAH A FIXED PRACTICE: This teaches that if one has heard something from the mouth of a Sage in the study-house, he is not to treat it casually, but to treat it attentively. And what a man learns, let him practice himself and then teach others that they may practice it (ARN).

Do not be lenient with thyself and severe with others, or lenient with others and severe with thyself. Rather, even as thou art lenient with thyself, be thou lenient with others, and as thou art severe with thyself, be severe with others (ARNB).

Set a fixed time to study Torah, and withdraw from other occupations; for if you will not do this because of your involvement in worldly occupations, you will neglect the study of Torah altogether (Vitry).

Make study of the Torah your chief interest in life; let all your other occupations be secondary to it (Aknin).

Even in the midst of your labors, attend to them only insofar as they will provide for your bodily and household needs, so that you may be able to turn your thoughts principally to the study of Torah and wisdom (Meiri).

At the Final Judgment the first thing a person will have to account for, is: why had he not set fixed times for studying Torah. . . . In *Abot de-Rabbi Natan* (28) it is taught: He who makes his study of Torah primary and his worldly occupation secondary will be made primary in the world to come; but he who makes his worldly occupation primary and his study of Torah secondary, will be made secondary in the world to come (Duran), that is to say, even if he were not guilty of transgression, since he did not make Torah study primary, though he is worthy to be in Paradise, he will there be secondary (Rabbi Jonah).

SAY LITTLE AND DO MUCH: The righteous say little and do much, but the wicked say much and do not do even a little. And how do we know that the righteous say little and do much? For thus we find concerning Abraham our father who said to the angels: "You shall eat bread with me today"—as it is said, *And I will fetch a morsel of bread, and stay ye your heart* (Genesis 18:5). But in the end, see what Abraham did for the ministering angels: for he went and prepared for them three oxen and nine measures of fine meal. . . . So too the Holy One, blessed be He, said little and did much, as it is said, *And the Lord said unto Abram: know for a surety that thy seed shall be a stranger in a land that is not theirs, and shall serve him, and they shall afflict them four hundred years; and also that nation whom they shall serve, will I punish; and afterward shall they come out with great substance* (Genesis 15:13 f.): He promised him no more than punishment by means of his D and N Name (*Adonai*); but in the end when the Holy One, blessed be He, requited Israel's enemies, He did so in fact by means of His seventy-two-letter (mystical) Name. . . .

And how do we know that the wicked say much and do not do even a little? For thus we find concerning Ephron, who said to Abraham, *A piece of land worth four hundred shekels of silver, what is that betwixt me and thee?* (Genesis 23:15). But in the end when he weighed the silver to him, *And Abraham hearkened unto Ephron; and Abraham weighed to Ephron,* etc. (*ibid.* : 16) (ARN).

Concerning this Rabbi Saadia Gaon, of blessed memory, said: If when God made a promise to our fathers and referred to Himself by his two-letter Name, He performed for them any number of miracles and wonders; how much the more extraordinary will be His works at the Future Redemption, about which so many pages, so many scrolls, and so many books full of promises and comfort have been written (Rabbi Jonah).

AND RECEIVE ALL MEN WITH A CHEERFUL COUNTENANCE: This teaches that if one gave his fellow all the good gifts in the world with a downcast face, Scripture accounts it to him as though he had given him naught. But if he receives his fellow with a cheerful countenance, even though he give him naught, Scripture accounts it to him as though he had given him all the good gifts in the world (ARN).

Let a man show a happy face to people, so that all men will be pleased with him (Rabbi Jonah).

Even if your heart does not rejoice when your fellow visits you, pretend to be cheerful when he arrives; let him think that your face lights up with joy at his coming (Meiri).

Shammai is here urging three things, corresponding to three human attainments . . . wisdom, strength, riches. As regards wisdom, he says: Make thy study of Torah a fixed practice; as regards riches, he says: Say little and do much; as regards strength, he says: Receive all men with a cheerful countenance, that is, let a person master his anger: "Who is it that is mighty? He that subdues his evil impulse." . . . A cheerful countenance is the opposite of arrogance and anger (Duran).

RABBAN GAMALIEL SAYS: PROVIDE THYSELF WITH A TEACHER, AND ESCHEW DOUBTFUL MATTERS, AND TITHE NOT OVERMUCH BY GUESSWORK.

PROVIDE THYSELF WITH A TEACHER: Here "provide thyself with a teacher" does not refer to study but to rendering a decision: appoint for yourself some master on whom you can depend in matters of the forbidden and permitted, and thus eschew doubtful matters. . . . And so too Rabban Gamaliel instructs us to flee from the practice of tithing by guesswork, because this is an example of "doubtful matters" (Maimonides).

I asked my teacher, of blessed memory: Where there is a controversy between the codifiers, what shall a person do? . . . He answered: If one has a tradition from his teacher, let him follow and practice what he learned from his teacher; otherwise, let him select one of the great codes and follow the one that seems best to him. And this is the meaning of "provide thyself with a teacher and eschew doubtful matters" (Nahmias).

ESCHEW DOUBTFUL MATTERS: In matters of halakah, do not persist in doubt; instead, "provide thyself with a teacher." Another interpretation. Avoid such things as may possibly be forbidden (Vitry).

AND TITHE NOT OVERMUCH BY GUESSWORK: That is, do not get into the habit of tithing by guesswork. For although when one overtithes, his own produce is fit [for personal consumption], nevertheless it is possible that sometimes [by guesswork] he will not set aside the required amount, and then his own produce will be unfit for personal consumption (Vitry).

"Tithing by guesswork" is a figure of speech, for the way certain views are arrived at. A person should not arrive at these views by conjecture, but by thinking the matter through thoroughly.— For this is not always the case. There are occasions when alternative views are possible; a scholar inclines to one view, though he well understands that another scholar might hold a different view but he prefers his own view. [It is in regard to such views that we are urged "Tithe not overmuch by guesswork."] There are however occasions when what a scholar proposes is required by logical reasoning; here no alternative is possible and no disagreement is possible (Rabbi Jonah).

It is also possible to interpret this statement as a reference to rendering decisions: namely, a person should not get into the habit of rendering a decision by guesswork and conjecture when the case is not entirely clear to him. Instead let him examine the laws meticulously until the whole subject has become clear to him, or let him call in others in consultation (Meiri).

SIMEON HIS SON SAYS: ALL MY LIFE I GREW UP AMONG THE
SAGES AND HAVE FOUND NOTHING BETTER FOR ANYBODY
THAN SILENCE; NOT STUDY IS THE CHIEF THING, BUT AC-
TION; AND HE WHO IS VERBOSE BRINGS ON SIN.

NOTHING BETTER FOR ANYBODY THAN SILENCE: If for the
wise silence is becoming, how much more for the foolish!
(ARN).

I learned from the Sages that there is no better behavior
than silence for a man, that there is nothing better than holding his peace when a man is abused. So we have learned
(Gittin 36b): Of those who are abused and do not abuse in
turn, who hear themselves being humiliated and do not retort, the verse says, *But they that love Him are as the sun
when he goeth forth in his might* (Judges 5:31). . . . Moreover, even pertaining to the Torah, better is he who keeps
quiet and carries out the commandments than he who studies
and teaches others but does not practice (Vitry).

Our Sages have said (Megilla 18a): "A word is worth a
sela; silence is worth two." . . . And the philosophers have
said: "Spare your tongue as you would spare your wealth";
or again, "The fewer the words, the fewer the errors" (Meiri).

One of the chief signs of the wise man is silence, one of the
chief signs of the fool is verboseness (Duran).

NOT STUDY IS THE CHIEF THING, BUT ACTION: Wisdom
does not lead to words; nor is it words that lead to wisdom—
only works (ARN).

One should not teach the law to others, and himself not
carry it out; rather, let him first practice and then teach others.
As our Sages, of blessed memory, said (Yebamot 63b):
Speech is becoming only in the mouth of those who practice
what they preach (Rabbi Jonah).

Simeon has not come to tell us that practice without study
is the ideal. For if a person is without knowledge, how will
he know what to do? It is of such a person that we are told,
"The ignorant cannot be a saint, the boor cannot fear sin."
What Simeon comes to tell us is that study which leads to
practice is the best of all—because it is practice which comes
as a consequence of study. And since the person's objective
is practice, it is enough for him to listen to and learn the right
action from his teachers, and hold his peace in their presence
(Duran).

AND HE WHO IS VERBOSE BRINGS ON SIN: As it is said, *In the multitude of words there wanteth not transgression* (Proverbs 10:19), and it says, *Even as a fool, when he holdeth his peace, is counted wise* (Proverbs 17:28) (ARN).

Needless to say in the case of slanderous talk, for foul speech is under all circumstances forbidden and verbosity is here irrelevant; ... but even in regard to words of praise, a person ought not to be excessive in his speech (Vitry).

Let no man say, since it is praiseworthy to hold forth at length about wisdom, I shall carry on orally or write a book with plenty of words though few ideas—let a man beware of doing this! (Aknin).

This statement about verboseness refers to the subject of Torah, that is, a man should not rush into speech in matters of halakah; he ought rather to take his time and think of what he is saying, his words ought to be measured and unhurried, because "in the multitude of words there wanteth not transgression" (Rabbi Jonah).

Notice that man has two ears but only one tongue, suggesting that his speech ought to be little and his hearing much (Duran).

———

RABBAN SIMEON BEN GAMALIEL SAYS: BY THREE THINGS IS THE WORLD SUSTAINED: BY JUSTICE, BY TRUTH, AND BY PEACE, AS IT IS SAID, *Truth and justice and peace judge ye in your gates* (Zechariah 8:16).

This is the meaning of the statement: The world is sustained by obedience to law; but even if law is followed, the world will not be sustained unless the judgment is a judgment of truth ... ; and even if men judge and sentence in accordance with the truth, the world will not be sustained unless there is peace, for O how great is the power of peace! (Vitry).

JUSTICE: By this is meant righteous government (Maimonides).

TRUTH: By truth is meant knowledge of the First Cause, that is, knowing that it is God, may He be exalted on high, Who brings into being all creatures, those in the heavens and those on the earth, ... knowing that all these exist thanks to His will and His mercy (Aknin).

A man is to walk in the ways of repentance, for He is truth and His Torah is truth; and one who walks in the ways of the Holy One, blessed be He, walks in truth (Rabbi Jonah).

By truth is meant, literally, speaking the truth to one's fellow. And because the world has grown accustomed to lying talk, people do not consider it an evil thing, they do not perceive that it *is* evil. It is regarding this that the prophet cries out, *And truth is lacking* (Isaiah 59:15). . . . Just as the world "rests" on worship, so it is sustained by truth—for by falsehood it is impossible to serve the God of truth (Duran).

I asked my teacher, of blessed memory, If there is truth, what need is there for law? And he replied: There are times when both litigants are truly under the impression that each one is right; then the judge comes and renders his decision. Here you have law (justice) and truth together (Nahmias).

PEACE: By peace is meant the right "truths" which a man adopts for his conduct. These are the truths of the *via media,* the avoidance of extremes. And this is the way of the Lord which He commanded us to walk in (Aknin).

Peace embraces all the good in the world, and there is no limit to its benefits (Rabbi Jonah).

By peace is meant that there be peace in the world, that there be no wars either between kingdoms, or between man and his fellow man. For just as acts of lovingkindness are one of the pillars of the universe, so is peace—which is an expression of acts of lovingkindness: it sustains the world (Duran).

Chapter II

RABBI SAYS: WHICH IS THE RIGHT COURSE THAT A MAN OUGHT TO CHOOSE FOR HIMSELF? WHATEVER IS DEEMED PRAISEWORTHY BY THE ONE WHO ADOPTS IT AND [FOR WHICH] HE IS ALSO DEEMED PRAISEWORTHY BY MEN.

BE AS ATTENTIVE TO A MINOR COMMANDMENT AS TO A MAJOR ONE, FOR THOU KNOWEST NOT WHAT IS THE REWARD TO BE GIVEN FOR THE COMMANDMENTS. TAKE INTO ACCOUNT THE LOSS INCURRED BY FULFILLING A COMMANDMENT AGAINST THE REWARD FOR IT, AND THE PROFIT GAINED BY TRANSGRESSION AGAINST THE LOSS IT ENTAILS.

MARK WELL THREE THINGS AND THOU WILT NOT FALL INTO THE CLUTCHES OF SIN: KNOW WHAT IS ABOVE THEE— AN EYE THAT SEES, AN EAR THAT HEARS, AND ALL THINE ACTIONS RECORDED IN THE BOOK.

THE RIGHT COURSE: Whatever course is proper and becoming to the man who adopts it and follows it, and is at the same time deemed becoming by other men—when all agree this course is praiseworthy and desirable—that is the right course: for example, the ways of truth, of justice, of peace, and others like these which are approved by everybody (Vitry).

By the right course is meant good actions, that is, actions in accord with the "golden-mean" ideal, for by means of these a man acquires for himself an important pattern of conduct and then his relationship with other human beings is a good one. And this is the meaning of "deemed praiseworthy by him who adopts it and for which he is also deemed praiseworthy by men" (Maimonides).

The Holy One, blessed be He, is glorified when the commandments are carried out; and this is also to the glory of those who carry them out. For such is the true glory one enjoys among men. This is the course a man should choose for himself; and he will enjoy the praises of men when he carries out the commandments at the proper time, as it is said, *How good is a thing in its proper season* (Proverbs 15:23)—for it is possible to carry out the commandments at a time when it would be displeasing to other human beings; a person would then not be praised for his actions, and that would not be carrying out a commandment to perfection (Rabbi Jonah).

Two conditions are here laid down. The first is that the course should be deemed praiseworthy by him who adopts it, . . . that he himself regard it as praiseworthy, so that if some other person had adopted it, he would have praised him for it; and if that person had taken the opposite course he would have reproved him for it. But for such a course a man might still not be honored by other men. Moreover, it sometimes happens that others honor a man for the course he adopts, but he himself feels that it is not praiseworthy. That is why the conditions laid down are that the course must be deemed as praiseworthy by him who adopts it as by other people. . . . Some read this statement of our Mishna as follows: "The right course . . . whatever is deemed praiseworthy by his Creator will bring him praises from men" . . . that is to say, a man should choose a course which will bring glory and honor to the Holy One, blessed be He; in that way the man will win the praises of men (Duran).

BE AS ATTENTIVE TO A MINOR COMMANDMENT AS TO A MAJOR ONE: Rabbi Hiyya taught (Pesikta Rabbati 121b) by way of parable: A king brought laborers into one of his orchards, but did not inform them in advance what would be the compensation for the respective plants they would cultivate. For had he given this information, each of them would have looked for that plant for which the compensation was liberal and taken care of *it*. As a result only some of the work in the orchard would have been taken care of; some would have been neglected. Said Rabbi Aha in the name of Rabbi Abba bar Kahana: The Holy One did not reveal what would be the reward for the different commandments of the Torah, lest only some of these be carried out, while some would be neglected (Vitry).

One must be as attentive to a commandment which he regards as minor—for example, rejoicing during the festivals, learning the Holy Tongue (Hebrew)—as to a commandment of whose major importance we have been informed—for example, the law of circumcision, Fringes (Numbers 15:37-41), the paschal offering. . . . For as regards "positive commandments," we have never been informed what is the reward set aside by the Lord, blessed be He, for each of them . . . ; and that is why we must be attentive to all of them (Maimonides).

There may be a commandment which seems minor to you, but from it may be derived one of the basic principles of the Torah: for example, in your eyes the "benediction of the day" in the Kiddush prayer of the Sabbath may seem a minor matter; yet it is something which fixes in men's hearts the belief in *creatio ex nihilo* (Meiri).

TAKE INTO ACCOUNT THE LOSS INCURRED BY FULFILLING A COMMANDMENT AGAINST THE REWARD FOR IT: If it seems to you that by fulfilling a commandment you will be incurring a loss—for example, when you have to dispose at a loss of meats that have become ritually disqualified, or when because of the Sabbath you cannot save produce from being damaged in your field—don't even think of saying, "How shall I stand by and suffer a loss?"; compare rather your present loss with the reward, a thousand times as much!, in store for you in the world to come. Restrain yourself and compare your loss with that gain! . . . And do not covet your fellow's wealth in your heart. Think not of robbing or stealing, or keeping what he has lost and you found. Take stock of what you may profit now as against what your loss will be; take to heart that you will lose a thousand times as much in the world to come (Vitry).

Although we have not been informed how precious each particular commandment is, a distinction between them may be made, thus: In the case of a positive commandment, if you find that the penalty for transgressing it is a heavy one, be sure that the reward for fulfilling it will be a goodly one. . . . If the penalty for a sin which a person commits is a heavy one, then if he refrains from that particular sin, his reward is correspondingly great. This is the meaning of the statement in the Talmud (Makkot, end): Whoever refrains from sinning is rewarded like one who has carried out a commandment (Maimonides).

KNOW WHAT IS ABOVE THEE: In the heavens. The Holy One looks down and takes note of you, like a scout who stands at his watchtower on an elevation. His eye sees what you do and he hears what you say, and it is impossible for you to hide yourself from him, as it is said, *Can any hide himself in secret places that I shall not see him?* (Jeremiah 23:24). AND ALL THINE ACTIONS RECORDED IN THE BOOK: And it is impossible for them to be forgotten, for the individual himself testifies to them and records them, as it is said, *He sealeth up by the hand of every man* (Job 37:7) (Vitry).

When a man stands in the presence of kings or princes or sages or famous people he is ashamed to do in their presence things which should not be done, or to say things that are improper. So let a person always keep in mind that he is, as it were, standing in the presence of the Holy One, blessed be He, as a man stands in the presence of his neighbor. Thus he will keep his ways and his speech from sinning, and his soul from trouble (Rabbi Jonah).

First, KNOW WHAT IS ABOVE THEE, that is to say, believe in the existence of God, blessed be He. Second, AN EYE THAT SEES, AN EAR THAT HEARS, that is to say, that one must believe in His providence and His righteous judgments. . . . Third, AND ALL THINE ACTIONS RECORDED IN THE BOOK, that is to say, if you have committed a transgression, it is impossible for you to escape punishment unless you repent. . . . But there are sins for which repentance cannot altogether undo the punishment. . . . This therefore is the meaning of "And all thine actions recorded in the book," that is, just as a debt is not canceled without some payment, so, figuratively speaking, a sin is not altogether blotted out without some punishment (Meiri).

The eye, the ear, and the book are figures of speech. And the same is true whenever you find such expressions in Scripture. Scripture is simply using human language (Nahmias).

Do not say . . . God, blessed be He, has no organs, and because He has no organs—since on high there is no such thing as body or matter—He therefore cannot have the faculties exercised by those organs, namely, seeing and hearing. So too, do not say that there is forgetfulness before Him because He has no organ with the power of remembrance, as humans have (Duran).

———

RABBAN GAMALIEL, THE SON OF RABBI JUDAH THE PRINCE, SAYS: SPLENDID IS THE STUDY OF TORAH WHEN COMBINED WITH A WORLDLY OCCUPATION, FOR TOIL IN THEM BOTH

PUTS SIN OUT OF MIND; BUT STUDY [TORAH] WHICH IS NOT COMBINED WITH WORK, FALLS INTO NEGLECT IN THE END, AND BECOMES THE CAUSE OF SIN.

LET ALL THOSE WHO LABOR IN BEHALF OF THE COMMUNITY, LABOR IN THEIR BEHALF FOR THE SAKE OF HEAVEN—FOR THE MERIT OF THEIR FATHERS UPHOLDS THEM AND THEIR GRACE ENDURES FOREVER. AND AS FOR YOU, I LAY UP TO YOUR CREDIT A RICH REWARD AS THOUGH YOURSELVES HAD ACCOMPLISHED IT.

STUDY OF TORAH WHEN COMBINED WITH A WORLDLY OCCUPATION . . . PUTS SIN OUT OF MIND: That is to say, removes the evil impulse. . . . For while a man toils away at the study of Torah and at some work task, the evil impulse can have no dominion over him; for so long as he does not wax fat and self-indulgent he will find no pleasure in transgressing. Therefore let a man engage in the study of Torah, which exhausts human strength; let him also engage in some occupation, as much as he needs for his livelihood. Let no man ever stay idle lest he begin to indulge himself, and his heart be lifted up so that he forget the Lord his God, as it is said, *But Jeshurun waxed fat, and kicked* (Deuteronomy 32:15) (Rabbi Jonah).

WORLDLY OCCUPATION (*Derek Erez*): By this is meant trading or other means of making a living. . . . Since on the one hand a man learns from the Torah that you may not oppress, you may not rob, and on the other hand he is engaged in making a living, it will not even occur to him to steal, to rob, or to act with violence (Vitry).

It is also possible to interpret the expression *derek erez* in our passage literally, that is, as good relations with human beings. Let a person receive all men with a cheerful countenance; then many out of love for him will be happy to do his work for him; he will thus have the leisure to study Torah (Aknin).

It is possible to interpret *derek erez* as moral conduct. And when Rabban Gamaliel says "toil in them both puts sin out of mind," he means this: When a sage upbraids people angrily, those who are base resent him and begin searching for his faults, to wit, that he upbraids with anger and hostility. But if the sage is a person of moral character, he upbraids people lovingly and affectionately; then people are careful to honor him. This is what is meant by "puts sin [shortcomings] out of mind" (Meiri).

STUDY WHICH IS NOT COMBINED WITH WORK ... BECOMES THE CAUSE OF SIN: When a man is not engaged in trade or some other occupation like everybody else, his study "falls into neglect in the end"—because he has no way of making a living, he has to wander from place to place seeking a livelihood, and as a result his study is neglected. It "becomes the cause of sin," because all along he has not even learned one skill; now if it should happen that he fails to find a livelihood, he will end up resorting to brigandage and robbery and violence (Vitry).

Many are the sins a man is dragged into when he has no food! (Duran).

LET ALL THOSE WHO LABOR IN BEHALF OF THE COMMUNITY: This is a reference to community leaders; that is, let them engage in communal work for the sake of Heaven, guiding people along an upright course, restraining them from evil ways, reproving them when necessary. And in all this their objective must not be self-aggrandizement, acquiring honor or wealth or power or pride: for a public figure who lords it over the community is despised by God (Aknin).

FOR THE MERIT OF THEIR FATHERS UPHOLDS THEM: Let all those who toil and trouble in behalf of the community, who devote themselves to its needs—for example, representing it before the crown or the military authorities—do so for the sake of Heaven, that is, in order to help the people ... not to capture power for themselves. Then even if the community does not see eye to eye with them and is not pleased by some particular thing, no matter, because "the merit of their fathers upholds them," that is, upholds those who have the responsibility of leadership—they will yet enjoy good favor and success because their intent is Heavenward—and the grace of the Fathers will stand by them, the leaders, forever (Vitry).

That is, the merit of the Fathers of the community, namely, Abraham, Isaac, and Jacob: it upholds them in a good and righteous course; "and their grace endures forever," that is, the grace of the Fathers endures forever. And we do not make arithmetical calculations of the ages already gone by, saying or thinking that the merit of the Fathers will not uphold us, because that merit has already sustained previous generations and therefore that stock of reward is exhausted and cannot support us. The Holy One, blessed be He, has informed us that He promised the Fathers that their merit would endure for their sons and their sons' sons, to the end of all generations (Aknin).

Even though you leaders work in behalf of the community and take care of its needs, it is not you who accomplish this. On the contrary, it is the merit of the community's Fathers which upholds them, it is their grace which endures forever, to the thousandth generation (Rabbi Jonah).

AS FOR YOU, I LAY UP TO YOUR CREDIT A RICH REWARD AS THOUGH YOURSELVES HAD ACCOMPLISHED IT: This is Rabban Gamaliel speaking to those who bear the burden of communal work, to wit: "You who bear this burden, if in your labors you have tried once and despite your efforts have accomplished nothing, do not throw up your hands in despair, saying, 'We shall have no reward, for see, we do not prosper and we labor in vain!' The Holy One will certainly not cut off your reward. On the contrary, He will account it unto you as though you had accomplished your task and you had succeeded at it." Lo, the Sages have said (Kiddushin 40a): Good intentions, the Holy One brings to fruition in action (Vitry).

This is God speaking to those who bear the burden of communal work. For there are times when they are prevented from carrying out a commandment, because they are then engaged in some public task. And so the Lord, blessed be He, says to them that He will lay up reward to their credit as though they had carried out that particular commandment, though they had in fact not done so: because they were busy in behalf of communal matters for the sake of Heaven (Maimonides).

Although the merit of the Fathers upholds the community and its needs are provided for by virtue of this merit and not because of what you do, nevertheless I lay it up to your credit, you who bear the work, as though all the community's needs were taken care of by you and by virtue of your merit. So the earliest commentators, of blessed memory, interpreted this statement. But it is possible to offer another interpretation: "Let all who labor in behalf of the community, labor in their behalf for the sake of Heaven." Do not say: "Why do I need this burden to take on communal responsibilities? Even if the people practice charity, they alone will be rewarded, for it is of their wealth they give." Do not let your thoughts take this turn: for doubly will you be benefiting yourself—since the merit of their Fathers upholds them, in what they do, you will achieve more than you would if you had been acting alone. And I will lay up reward to your credit as though you had done it all of your own, as though out of your own purse you have given all they gave because of you. Thus by the burden you have taken on to get them to give charity, you profit more than you would have if you had met only your own responsibilities—for their works outnumber yours. And everything you undertake the Lord will cause to prosper because "the merit of their Fathers upholds them." That is why he who devotes himself to communal needs brings great benefit to himself—so long as he directs his heart to Heaven (Rabbi Jonah).

———

BEWARE OF THE RULING POWERS! FOR THEY DO NOT BEFRIEND A PERSON EXCEPT FOR THEIR OWN NEEDS: THEY SEEM LIKE FRIENDS WHEN IT IS TO THEIR ADVANTAGE, BUT THEY DO NOT STAND BY A MAN WHEN HE IS HARD-PRESSED.

If government officials come to you for information, flattering and making all kinds of promises to you, beware, don't depend upon their words (Vitry).

This Mishna describes the ruling powers [of ancient times] (Maimonides).

The story is told of a certain king who promoted one of his officers. The king would rise up before him and kiss him on his neck. In the end the king slew him, and said that he used to kiss the spot where his sword would have to land. Folks say: do not think that the lion is smiling when he bares his teeth; it is only to devour. Human monarchs are like lions in the animal kingdom (Nahmias).

Rabban Gamaliel has this in mind: Even when you have to have dealings with the ruling powers, for communal purposes . . . beware of their smiling faces and honeyed words! Let them not seduce you into revealing to them the secrets in your heart (Duran).

———

HE USED TO SAY: DO HIS WILL AS THOUGH IT WERE THY WILL SO THAT HE MAY DO THY WILL AS THOUGH IT WERE HIS WILL; UNDO THY WILL FOR THE SAKE OF HIS WILL SO THAT HE MAY UNDO THE WILL OF OTHERS FOR THE SAKE OF THY WILL.

DO HIS WILL: Rabbi Judah the Prince used to say: If thou hast done His will as though it were thy will, thou hast not yet done His will as He wills it. But if thou hast done His will as though it were not thy will, then thou hast done His will as He wills it. Is it thy wish not to die? Die, so that thou wilt not need to die. Is it thy wish to live? Do not live, so that thou mayest live. Better for thee is it to die in this world, where against thy will thou wilt die, than to die in the age to come, where, if thou wishest, thou needst not die (ARNB).

Strive at all times to do the will of God "as though it were thy will," with a perfect heart and with a ready spirit. And "undo thy will" even if God's will is a burden to you—undo it so that He may undo the will of others who seek to do what is against your wishes: even if God's will seemed to incline toward theirs, it will incline toward yours (Vitry).

If you have carried out the commandments of the Torah and acquired wisdom—know in truth that God exists, walk in His ways so that you may be like Him—and if you have delighted in and yearned for these just as you yearn for the fulfillment of your bodily needs and pleasures; then the Holy One, blessed be He, will grant you your wishes and desires, He will carry them out as you have carried out His will. And if you have bestirred yourself and canceled your will for the sake of His will—engaged in divine occupation and abandoned the pleasures of this world which you naturally desire, and yearned instead to cleave to the ways of the Lord— then the Holy One, blessed be He, will reward you in accordance with what you have done, and He will undo the will of others who wish to harm you, He will destroy their counsels against you. Measure for measure! (Aknin).

There should be no distinction between the will of the Holy One, blessed be He, and one's own will. Both should be the same. That is to say, a man should have no wish except that which is in accordance with what is pleasing to God. . . . And this is the counsel given to men: to rise above their own nature and do eagerly with their wealth and their possessions what God wishes: for it is He who has given us everything, and what men possess is only in trust (Rabbi Jonah).

It seems to me that this is how the statement is to be interpreted: "Do His will as though it were thy will," as though you had no will of your own at all, only His will. Then He will also do your will, your particular will: your wishes will not be merely part of what He does in order to sustain the universe as a whole, righteous and sinners alike; what you wish to carry out will become part of His will, to satisfy your individual wish. So that, even if because of the sins of the generation or because of fate, it may have been necessary to visit you with misfortune, He will carry out your individual wish and protect you from that evil which should have befallen you (Duran).

SO THAT HE MAY UNDO THE WILL OF OTHERS FOR THE SAKE OF THY WILL: This is simply a respectful way of speaking of Heaven. It is as though the statement read, "So that God might undo His will for the sake of Thy will" (Duran).

HILLEL SAYS:

DO NOT WITHDRAW FROM THE COMMUNITY.

PUT NO TRUST IN THYSELF UNTIL THE DAY OF THY DEATH.

DO NOT JUDGE THY COMRADE UNTIL THOU HAST STOOD IN HIS PLACE.

SAY NOT OF A THING WHICH CANNOT BE UNDERSTOOD THAT IN THE END IT WILL BE UNDERSTOOD.

AND SAY NOT "WHEN I HAVE LEISURE I WILL STUDY"— PERCHANCE THOU SHALT HAVE NO LEISURE.

HILLEL SAYS: This is the same Hillel who was mentioned above. But his sayings were interrupted so that the order of the *Nesiim*, who were his descendants, might be completed. Now the other sayings of Hillel are introduced, in order to place them next to those of Rabban Johanan ben Zakkai, who was his disciple (Duran).

DO NOT WITHDRAW FROM THE COMMUNITY: Instead share in their burdens imposed by the government, in their fasts, in their prayers. Thus indeed Mordecai sent to Esther: *Think not with thyself that thou shalt escape in the king's house, more than all the Jews. For if thou altogether holdest thy peace at this time, then will relief and deliverance arise to the Jews from another place, but thou and thy father's house will perish* (Esther 4:13-14). And we have learned in the Talmud (Taanit 11a): If one withdraws from the community, the two ministering angels who accompany a person . . . lay their hands on his head and say: May So-and-so who withdrew from the community not be witness to the comfort of the community (Vitry).

A man should not entertain views far different from those of his community. But if he sees that the opinions the people of his city hold are corrupt, and he is worried lest if he concur with them he might adopt their course, walk in their evil ways, and thus be driven from the way of life, then he must leave their midst immediately, and go to another city the conduct of whose inhabitants is proper, whose views are those right views in accordance with the principle of the *via media.* If he has found no such city close by, let him go to one far off. If he has found no such city at all, let him go off to the wilderness where there are no human beings, as Jeremiah, may he rest in peace, said: *Oh that I were in the wilderness, in a lodging-place of wayfaring men* (Jeremiah 9:1) (Aknin).

Praying together with the congregation is more praise-worthy than praying by oneself. For when a man prays by himself, he might include in his prayers some petition which could be detrimental either to another individual or to the public. Whereas, when the congregation is at prayer, it asks only for those things which are of benefit to everybody. . . . Moreover, by way of parable: in a bundle of reeds, each single reed is weak and easily breakable; but as part of the bundle, a person is unable to break it (Duran).

PUT NO TRUST IN THYSELF UNTIL THE DAY OF THY DEATH: Let no man say, "I may allow myself to ignore what has been forbidden by special decree as an added precaution, because I am careful not to fall into transgression" . . . for lo, John Hyrcanus served eighty years as High Priest and in the end became a Sadducee. An even better example: There are three commandments recorded in the Torah for which Scripture supplies reasons: *Let not the king multiply horses to himself . . . neither shall he multiply wives to himself, that his heart turn not away; neither shall he greatly multiply to himself silver and gold* (Deuteronomy 17:16-17). Solomon however had confidence in his own wisdom and depended on his own prudence [and determined to ignore the commandments because he was certain that he would not be guilty of defection despite such indulgence; and in the end he was!]. This is why reasons for the commandments of the Torah have not been disclosed (Vitry).

Even when some virtue has become second nature to a man, let him not neglect the opportunity for doing good again and again in order to fix the virtue more firmly in his soul. Let him not be overconfident and say: "This virtue I have already mastered successfully, it can never leave me." There is always the possibility that it may! (Maimonides).

Beware in your old age as in your youth not to expose yourself to the possibility of sinning, by being self-confident, regarding yourself so secure in your purity as to be beyond the reach of temptation (Meiri).

It seems to me that this saying has been put next to the one about not withdrawing from the congregation to teach you that it is much better for you to be part of the congregation than to go off by yourself even for one day, even if you are well on in years. For when a person lives solitary, his evil impulse overpowers him through sinful thoughts, from which no man is ever safe . . . and as a result he may come to an evil end. In the company of others he escapes such evil (Duran).

DO NOT JUDGE THY COMRADE UNTIL THOU HAST STOOD IN HIS PLACE: Even if your comrade has been guilty of a transgression, do not condemn him, saying: "He deserves to be burned! He deserves to be stoned! He deserves to be strangled!—because he was guilty of this sin" (Vitry).

If it happened with your comrade that he did not withstand temptation, do not disgrace him. Say instead: "What he did is nothing!" For it is possible that had the same circumstance befallen you, you too would not have been able to withstand the temptation (Aknin).

This is of a piece with the statement that a man is not to trust in himself and be too sure of his own judgment. If a person sees that a companion of his in high office does not behave justly, let him not say: "If I occupied his position I would not do any of the evil things he does." You don't know. Human beings, one's no better than the next! Perhaps that office would have perverted you too. When you have reached his position and his station and revealed a better nature, then you may question his ways (Rabbi Jonah).

Some of my teachers interpreted this saying to me as follows: If you have met some stranger in your city and you find him fastidious in conduct and full of extraordinary virtues, do not conclude on your own that these constitute his real nature until you get to the place where he dwells: note his behavior there, is it like his behavior here? Then you will be in a position to judge him. Many are the cheap and mediocre individuals who show their true colors in one place, and elsewhere put on a show of a saintliness which is not native to them (Meiri).

SAY NOT OF A THING WHICH CANNOT BE UNDERSTOOD THAT IN THE END IT WILL BE UNDERSTOOD: [And do not say: "There is something it will still be possible to hear and in the end it will be heard."] If you are not engaged in some task and it is possible for you to listen to words of Torah now, even if there will be an opportunity to listen to them at some other time, do not say: "Lo, there will be other opportunities for such sessions, and then I shall go and attend"—for you do not know what the day may bring, whether you will be able to attend again or not. Indeed, even if you are engaged in a task, take the time from it to study Torah (Vitry).

Let not the meaning of your words be far removed from their literal sense; say not, "If a person probe deeply, he will see that what I said is right." The Mishna warns against expression of this sort, by exhorting: Let not your words require farfetched interpretation and extraordinary perception before they can be understood (Maimonides).

Do not speak evil of your neighbor and say, "Who can overhear me?" For in the end what you said will be heard of, and you will get into a quarrel (Aknin).

And speak not of anything assuming that it cannot possibly be overheard, for in the end it will be heard. A man ought to be cautious and on his guard against all possibilities. That is why if you have a secret, do not tell it even to him whose soul is bound to yours; do not say, "It is impossible for this thing to become known, seeing there is no other person with us to broadcast it." For the end of the matter is that everything is heard. Even what you tell yourself, do not utter aloud—as the Sages, of blessed memory, used to say (see Leviticus Rabba 32:2) figuratively: Do not mutter even indoors, "for the walls have ears." It is of this Solomon, may he rest in peace, said, *For a bird of the air shall carry the voice, and that which hath wings shall tell the matter* (Ecclesiastes 10:20) (Rabbi Jonah).

AND SAY NOT "WHEN I HAVE LEISURE I WILL STUDY"— PERCHANCE THOU SHALT HAVE NO LEISURE: And thus all your life you will have neglected the study of Torah (Vitry).

This is like what Shammai, his colleague, had enjoined: "Make thy study of Torah a fixed practice" (Maimonides).

As a sage once put it: Time past is gone and vanished, time present is like a fleeting shadow, time future, who knows if you will ever get to it? The fact is, not only should a person not neglect study because of the pursuit of pleasures, he should not neglect it even for his occupation. If you neglect study because of your occupation, you will find yourself adding one task to another, and you will be the loser on every score (Meiri).

————

HE USED TO SAY: THE BOOR IS NO FEARER OF SIN, THE AM HA-AREZ CANNOT BE A SAINT, THE TIMID CANNOT LEARN, THE SHORT TEMPERED CANNOT TEACH; HE WHO IS MOSTLY IN TRADE WILL NOT GROW WISE; AND WHERE THERE ARE NO MEN, STRIVE TO BE A MAN.

THE BOOR . . . THE *Am Ha-Arez:* A boor is one in whom is neither learning nor moral virtue; the *am ha-arez* is one who has no intellectual capacities but does have some moral qualities (Maimonides).

A boor is someone in whom there is neither Torah nor good works, but there are no ingrained evil qualities in him either. . . . And because neither virtues nor vices are fixed in his soul, there can be no fear of sin in him—for he does not know what are the virtues to cleave to and what are the evils to avoid. The *am ha-arez* is a person in whom there is knowledge of right conduct but no Torah. He is called *am ha-arez* ("worldly person") because he is fit for civilized society: he has a knowledge of what is good, folks can get along with him, he is useful to them and they are useful to him. But because there is no learning in him, he does not know how to act in a manner that transcends strict justice, he does not know how to rise above average behavior. . . . It is possible for him to be a fearer of sin because he has a sense of right conduct which teaches him how to get along with other people, so that he learns from such association what is right and what is wrong (Aknin).

Saintliness is attained only by him who is engaged in the study of Torah and who all his days strives for purity of mind—each day striving to add to the purity of his soul. . . . The *am ha-arez* has only one concern: to get along with people correctly so that he may find favor with them. And Hillel's saying comes to teach us that it is the study of Torah which saves a man from sin and leads him to saintliness (Duran).

THE TIMID CANNOT LEARN, THE SHORT TEMPERED CANNOT TEACH: It is written: *If thou hast done foolishly in lifting up thyself, or if thou hast planned devices, lay thy hand upon thy mouth* (Proverbs 30:32). The verse is interpreted as follows: He who is ready to play the fool for the sake of learning Torah, will in the end be lifted up; but he who puts a bit to his mouth, that is, refuses to ask questions, will in the end be asked about some matter of halakah, and he will have to lay his hand on his mouth because he will not know the answer (Vitry).

There are times when a teacher teaches and the student does not understand what has been explained to him, but is ashamed to say to his teacher: "I do not understand, Master, what you said; explain it once again." It is also possible that after the teacher has explained the law to him and asked him, "Do you understand what I said to you?", though the student did not understand he is ashamed to say, "No, I do not understand." Instead he says, "I do understand." The net result is that the student has gained nothing, *And shall take nothing for his labor, which he may carry away in his hand* (Ecclesiastes 5:14) (Aknin).

Bashfulness is a virtue in every respect except in the course of study; as it is said, *When I speak of Thy testimonies in the presence of kings, I am not ashamed* (Psalm 119:46). When David, may he rest in peace, fled from Saul and appeared before the heathen kings, he was never ashamed to speak of the Torah and the commandments, even if they were to mock and ridicule him when he spoke. For bashfulness is not a good thing in study. Moreover, no student ought to say, "How shall a fool like me ask questions of a very great scholar, of a brilliant sage? I have neither knowledge nor understanding." For if this is how he feels all the time, how will wisdom ever come to him? And this is the meaning of the maxim, "Ask like a fool and save like the generous." That is to say, just as the generous do not scatter their wealth, but also do not keep it to themselves—instead they give it gladly and graciously where it will do most good— . . . so in the case of wisdom: one should engage in it with the proper people and at the proper time. . . . But a person should ask every manner of question and not be ashamed to do so, in order that he may learn (Rabbi Jonah).

HE WHO IS MOSTLY IN TRADE WILL NOT GROW WISE: That is to say, not by means of trade alone will a man grow wise. For he who wishes to be wise must engage in all kinds of social enterprises, both in trade and all other instructive affairs, for the ways of the world require an understanding of all manner of things (Vitry).

The Sages have said (Erubin 55a): Learning is to be found neither in the proud nor the arrogant nor those who travel from country to country. And they prove their point by a figurative interpretation of the verse, *It is not in heaven. . . . Neither is it beyond the sea* (Deuteronomy 30:12-13) (Maimonides).

When a man is taken up with business all the time, he has to travel from country to country; then his mind and heart are preoccupied, and he loses that peace of mind necessary for the study of Torah. And even when he does engage in study he cannot concentrate. Thus he learns only what is on the surface of things and cannot attain to any profundity. . . . That is why Hillel says, "He who is mostly in trade will not *grow wise*"; he does not say that such a person cannot learn (Aknin).

If a man spends all his time in trade and makes *it* his constant occupation, and of his study of Torah he makes an incidental pursuit, he will never grow wise (Rabbi Jonah).

WHERE THERE ARE NO MEN, STRIVE TO BE A MAN: Where there is no one to take the initiative and assume responsibility, "strive to be a man," to take on leadership. There is no trace of lordship in this, and we do not charge such a person with arrogance (Vitry).

The early Commentators, of blessed memory, interpreted this as follows: Where there is no one to help you carry out the commandments and to reprove you when necessary, "strive to be a man" and correct yourself to do only that which is good and right in the sight of the Lord. There is another interpretation. "Where there are no men," if you see a generation neglecting the Torah, rise up and strive in its behalf . . . . Still another interpretation is possible: Where there is no one wiser than you, "strive to be a man," that is, do not give up trying to increase in wisdom: even though you do not find in your city someone wiser than you, even if there is no one in that generation as wise as you, consider: what if you were a contemporary of the Talmudic Sages and were in their company! And even if you have attained to their rank, think: what if you were present with the prophets, yea, with Moses our master, may he rest in peace—when will you attain to their rank and wisdom? Thus you will never neglect to study, and every single day you will improve your conduct, for you will be increasing in wisdom and will be like an ever-flowing stream (Rabbi Jonah).

Where there is no one standing in the breach, ready to concern himself with the needs of the community, "strive to be a man" even if it means having to neglect some study of Torah . . . (Duran).

———

MOREOVER HE SAW A SKULL FLOATING ON THE FACE OF THE WATER. HE SAID TO IT: "FOR DROWNING OTHERS THOU WAST DROWNED; AND IN THE END THEY THAT DROWNED THEE SHALL BE DROWNED."

This is something borne out by experience at all times and in all places: whoever does evil and introduces violence and corruption, is himself the victim of the harms caused by those very evils he introduced; for he himself has taught an occupation which can only bring harm to him and to others. So too, he who teaches virtue and introduces some good activity will be rewarded by the results of that very activity; for he teaches something which will do good to him and to others. And the words of the verse are very apt in this connection, namely, *For the work of a man will He requite unto him, and cause every man to find according to his ways* (Job 34:11) (Maimonides).

The purpose of this saying is to teach us to believe that misfortunes are a punishment, they are not accidental events. Evil deeds boomerang (Meiri).

Hillel, may he rest in peace, saw Pharaoh's skull floating on the water. It was Pharaoh who used to take one hundred and fifty young children of Israel every morning, and another one hundred and fifty every evening, and (after extreme torture) . . . cast them into the sea. That is why the Lord slew him and drowned him. And the ancients tell us that the Hillel referred to in this Mishna is really Moses our master, may he rest in peace. . . . And he said to the skull, "Because you slew human beings and threw them into the water, the Lord has slain you and cast you into the water." . . . This is the hidden (mystic) meaning of this statement (Rabbi David the Prince).

———

HE USED TO SAY:

  THE MORE FLESH, THE MORE WORMS.

  THE MORE POSSESSIONS, THE MORE WORRY.

  THE MORE WIVES, THE MORE WITCHCRAFT.

  THE MORE MAIDSERVANTS, THE MORE UNCHASTITY.

  THE MORE SLAVES, THE MORE ROBBERY.

  THE MORE TORAH, THE MORE LIFE.

  THE MORE THE COMPANY OF SCHOLARS, THE MORE WIS-
DOM.

  THE MORE COUNSEL, THE MORE UNDERSTANDING.

  THE MORE CHARITY, THE MORE PEACE.

  IF ONE ACQUIRES A GOOD NAME HE ACQUIRES SOMETHING
FOR HIMSELF.

  IF ONE ACQUIRES FOR HIMSELF KNOWLEDGE OF THE
TORAH HE ACQUIRES FOR HIMSELF LIFE IN THE WORLD TO
COME.

This statement is here to tell us that all increase is profitless
save only increase of learning (Vitry).

THE MORE TORAH, THE MORE LIFE: This is the counterpart
of "the more flesh, the more worms." For by indulgence in
luxury a man's days are cut short; by toil in the Torah they
are prolonged. So too this statement is the counterpart of "the
more possessions, the more worry." For worry over possessions
shortens a man's life; worry over the Torah—even though a
student does worry a great deal in his attempt to understand
the law, to express a thing properly—that worry cannot bring
him evil. Even though the scientists say, "Grief makes the
heart sick, and worry consumes it," for him who worries over
the Torah there is only length of days and a life of peace
(Rabbi Jonah).

THE MORE THE COMPANY OF SCHOLARS, THE MORE WIS-
DOM: As the Sage put it (Taanit 7a): "Much have I learned
from my masters, more from my colleagues, and from my disciples most of all" (Vitry).

IF ONE ACQUIRES A GOOD NAME HE ACQUIRES SOMETHING
FOR HIMSELF: The more good works, [the more] one brings
peace to himself (ARN).

For a good name remains with one; he does not leave it
behind. This is the opposite of possessions, which a man must

leave behind when he dies, and he must depart without the delights they can provide (Rabbi Jonah).

By a "good name" is meant ethical virtues. "He acquires something for himself," that is to say, something profitable to him, which may serve as an introduction and path to the learning of Torah and wisdom (Meiri).

When Monobaz distributed his wealth to the poor, he said (Baba Batra 11a): "My fathers stored up treasures for others to enjoy; I have stored up treasures for myself!" (Duran).

RABBAN JOHANAN BEN ZAKKAI TOOK OVER FROM HILLEL AND SHAMMAI. HE USED TO SAY: IF THOU HAST WROUGHT MUCH IN THE STUDY OF TORAH TAKE NO CREDIT TO THYSELF, FOR TO THIS END WAST THOU CREATED.

Men were created only on condition that they study Torah (ARN).

"If thou hast wrought much in the Torah," that is, if you have studied much, "do not take credit to thyself," saying, "what a great favor I have done to my Creator, I have studied His Torah!" Neither say, "How great I am!", "for to this end wast thou created": You were brought into being to study Torah. ... The Holy One laid it down as a condition with the works of Creation: If Israel will receive the Torah, well and good; otherwise I shall reduce you to chaos again (Vitry).

TAKE NO CREDIT TO THYSELF: Do not say, "I have studied so very much, it is only right that men should honor me." And because Rabban Johanan ben Zakkai had neglected nothing which had to be studied, neither Mishna nor Scripture, he could in all propriety tell others ("Take no credit to thyself") (Maimonides).

If a man has acquired a lot of knowledge in the sciences and philosophy, let him not flatter himself and praise his accomplishments; for it was on this condition that he entered the world, and intelligence was given him so that he might acquire knowledge and do good works to the best of his ability (Aknin).

Even if you have wrought much in the Torah, you are still at the very beginning; when will you get to the middle and the end of it? For the Torah is *longer than the earth, and broader than the sea* (Job 11:9) and it is within no man's ability to reach to its uttermost end. Everyone is far from attaining it. How then shall a person take credit to himself when he has done no more than a thousandth part of what there is to be done? "For to this end wast thou created": the Holy One, blessed be He, brought you into being ex-nihilo only in order to engage in His Torah. Even if you have wrought much in the Torah, take no credit to yourself for this reason: this is the purpose of your creation! Compare this to a borrower who repaid his debt. Does one give him credit for that? The same injunction applies in regard to the commandments. If you have wrought much in carrying out the commandments, "take no credit to thyself, for to this end wast thou created" (Rabbi Jonah).

RABBAN JOHANAN BEN ZAKKAI HAD FIVE DISCIPLES, TO WIT: RABBI ELIEZER BEN HYRCANUS, RABBI JOSHUA BEN HANANIAH, RABBI YOSE THE PRIEST, RABBI SIMEON BEN NATHANEL, AND RABBI ELEAZAR BEN ARAK.

HE USED TO LIST THEIR OUTSTANDING VIRTUES:

RABBI ELIEZER BEN HYRCANUS—A PLASTERED CISTERN WHICH LOSES NOT A DROP.

RABBI JOSHUA—HAPPY IS SHE WHO BORE HIM!

RABBI YOSE—A SAINT.

RABBI SIMEON BEN NATHANEL—FEARS SIN.

RABBI ELEAZAR ARAK—EVER-FLOWING STREAM.

HE USED TO SAY: IF ALL THE SAGES OF ISRAEL WERE IN ONE SCALE OF THE BALANCE AND ELIEZER BEN HYRCANUS WERE IN THE OTHER SCALE, HE WOULD OUTWEIGH THEM ALL.

ABBA SAUL SAYS IN HIS NAME: IF ALL THE SAGES OF ISRAEL WERE IN ONE SCALE OF THE BALANCE, AND EVEN IF RABBI ELIEZER BEN HYRCANUS WERE WITH THEM, AND RABBI ELEAZAR WERE IN THE OTHER SCALE, HE WOULD OUTWEIGH THEM ALL.

PLASTERED CISTERN: He never forgot a thing he learned (Vitry).

HAPPY IS SHE WHO BORE HIM: Happy the mother who bore him, because he was a master of all kinds of knowledge and he also enjoyed entree to the royal palace. I have also heard an additional reason for the tribute: When his mother was pregnant with him, she would keep walking by the study-house, so that the disciples might bless the child she was bearing (Vitry).

A SAINT: For he was engaged in the study of Torah and in acts of lovingkindness (Vitry).

FEARS SIN: He used to keep his distance even from the very shadow of sin (Vitry).

EVER-FLOWING STREAM: In his learning he could even add to the traditions he received and knew how to deduce one thing from another (Vitry).

ELEAZAR BEN ARAK: When Rabban Johanan ben Zakkai's son died, his disciples came in to comfort him. Rabbi Eliezer entered, sat down before him, and said to him: "Master, by thy leave, may I say something to thee?"

"Speak," he replied.

Rabbi Eliezer said: "Adam had a son who died, yet he allowed himself to be comforted for him. And how do we know that he allowed himself to be comforted for him? For it is said, *And Adam knew his wife again* (Genesis 4:25). Thou too, be thou comforted."

Said Rabban Johanan to him: "Is it not enough that I grieve over my own, that thou remindest me of the grief of Adam?"

Rabbi Joshua entered and said to him: "By thy leave, may I say something to thee?"

"Speak," he replied.

Rabbi Joshua said: "Job had sons and daughters, all of whom died in one day, and he allowed himself to be comforted for them. Thou too, be thou comforted. And how do we know that Job was comforted? For it is said, *The Lord gave, and the Lord hath taken away; blessed be the name of the Lord"* (Job 1:21).

Said Rabban Johanan to him: "Is it not enough that I grieve over my own, that thou remindest me of the grief of Job?"

Rabbi Yose entered and sat down before him; he said to him: "Master, by thy leave, may I say something to thee?"

"Speak," he replied.

Rabbi Yose said: "Aaron had two grown sons, both of whom died in one day, yet he allowed himself to be comforted for them, as it is said, *And Aaron held his peace* (Leviticus 10:3)—silence is no other than consolation. Thou too, therefore, be thou comforted."

Said Rabban Johanan to him: "Is it not enough that I grieve

over my own, that thou remindest me of the grief of Aaron?"

Rabbi Simeon entered and said to him: "Master, by thy leave, may I say something to thee?"

"Speak," he replied.

Rabbi Simeon said: "King David had a son who died, yet he allowed himself to be comforted. Thou too, therefore, be thou comforted. And how do we know that David was comforted? For it is said, *And David comforted Bath-Sheba his wife, and went in unto her, and lay with her; and she bore a son, and called his name Solomon* (II Samuel 12:24). Thou too, master, be thou comforted."

Said Rabban Johanan to him: "Is it not enough that I grieve over my own, that thou remindest me of the grief of King David?"

Rabbi Eleazar ben Arak entered. As soon as Rabban Johanan saw him, he said to his servant: "Take my clothing and follow me to the bathhouse, for he is a great man and I shall be unable to resist him."

Rabbi Eleazar entered, sat down before him, and said to him: "I shall tell thee a parable: to what may this be likened? To a man with whom the king deposited some object. Every single day the man would weep and cry out, saying: 'Woe unto me! when shall I be quit of this trust in peace?' Thou too, master, thou hadst a son: he studied the Torah, the Prophets, the Holy Writings, he studied Mishna, Halakah, Agada, and he departed from the world without sin. And thou shouldst be comforted when thou hast returned thy trust unimpaired."

Said Rabban Jonanan to him: "Rabbi Eleazar, my son, thou hast comforted me the way men should give comfort!"

When they left his presence, Rabbi Eleazar said: "I shall go to Emmaus, a beautiful place with beautiful and delightful waters."

But they said: "We shall go to Jamnia where there are scholars in abundance who love the Torah."

Because he went to Emmaus—a beautiful place with beautiful and delightful waters—his name was made least in the Torah. Because they went to Jamnia—where there are scholars in abundance who love the Torah—their names were magnified in the Torah (ARN).

Rabban Johanan ben Zakkai praises Rabbi Eleazar ben Arak for his acute understanding and wonderful mind, that is, for him even profound matters are easy to understand (Maimonides).

RABBAN JOHANAN SAID TO THEM: GO OUT AND SEE WHICH
IS THE RIGHT WAY TO WHICH A MAN SHOULD CLEAVE.

    RABBI ELIEZER REPLIED: A LIBERAL EYE.

    RABBI JOSHUA REPLIED: A GOOD COMPANION.

    RABBI YOSE REPLIED: A GOOD NEIGHBOR.

    RABBI SIMEON REPLIED: FORESIGHT.

    RABBI ELEAZAR REPLIED: GOODHEARTEDNESS.

SAID RABBAN JOHANAN BEN ZAKKAI TO THEM: I PREFER
THE ANSWER OF ELEAZAR BEN ARAK, FOR IN HIS WORDS
YOUR WORDS ARE INCLUDED.

    RABBAN JOHANAN SAID TO THEM: GO OUT AND SEE
WHICH IS THE EVIL WAY WHICH A MAN SHOULD SHUN.

    RABBI ELIEZER REPLIED: A GRUDGING EYE.

    RABBI JOSHUA REPLIED: AN EVIL COMPANION.

    RABBI YOSE REPLIED: AN EVIL NEIGHBOR.

    RABBI SIMEON REPLIED: BORROWING AND NOT REPAY-
ING; FOR HE THAT BORROWS FROM MAN IS AS ONE
WHO BORROWS FROM GOD, BLESSED BE HE, AS IT IS
SAID, *The wicked borroweth, and payeth not; but the
righteous dealeth graciously, and giveth* (Psalm 37:21).

    RABBI ELEAZAR REPLIED: MEANHEARTEDNESS.

    RABBAN JOHANAN SAID TO THEM: I PREFER THE ANSWER
OF ELEAZAR BEN ARAK, FOR IN HIS WORDS YOUR WORDS ARE
INCLUDED.

THE RIGHT WAY TO WHICH A MAN SHOULD CLEAVE: So
that he might inherit the life of the world to come (ARN).

A person should adopt one ideal which he will follow
through to perfection. For it is better for him to adhere perfectly to one ideal—it is indeed then easier to reach out from
this one to all the worthy ideals—than to be a man of parts,
not perfect in any one of them (Rabbi Jonah).

A LIBERAL EYE: One should not begrudge his companion his
good fortune. . . . Moreover, even if one were a scholar, if he
begrudged his comrade in this world, his eyes will be filled
with smoke in the world to come (Vitry).

    To have a liberal eye is to be content with one's portion
and delight in what the Holy One, blessed be He, has given
him; if what he has is little, let him regard it as though it were
plentiful. . . . The opposite of this is "a grudging eye." If one
acquires possessions and riches and honor, but regards it all

as though it were only a little, and pursues the vanities of the world in order to satisfy his appetite for more and more, all his days are filled with pain, deep anguish, sickness, and wrath (Aknin).

By "a liberal eye" is meant generosity (Rabbi Jonah).

A GOOD NEIGHBOR: A man must seek out a good neighbor even more than a good companion. For the behavior of a good companion one sees only in the daytime; but a neighbor one sees day and night. One therefore can learn from his good behavior more than from a companion (Vitry).

One must himself make a good neighbor for all his neighbors. For by himself being a good and loyal friend to five or eight people, it will be easier for him to love all the inhabitants of the world (Rabbi Jonah).

FORESIGHT: One who takes it to heart to think, "If I do the following thing I shall finally be brought to such and such an end," will weigh the possibilities before him, will "take into account the loss incurred by fulfilling a commandment against the reward for it, and the profit gained by transgression against the loss it entails" (Vitry).

With foresight it is as with medicine: at first it tastes bad, but it makes the body recover from sickness in the end. But a person who follows only his heart's desires turns things upside down. If at the moment things seem pleasant, he does them and does not examine if in the end they will be good or bad. And perhaps, had he acted intelligently and with perception he might have discovered that these things are bitter as wormwood, fatal as a two-edged sword (Aknin).

GOODHEARTEDNESS: Toward Heaven and toward mankind (ARN). For the Holy One, blessed be He, seeks out the heart principally (Vitry).

By "goodheartedness" is meant that good conduct which comes from following the *via media*. This is the ideal and it includes contentment with one's portion, the love of good men, and other virtues. That is why Rabban Johanan ben Zakkai said that in Rabbi Eleazar's answer all the other words were included. Contrariwise, "meanheartedness" is the lowest of qualities and includes all the vices which the Sages warned against (Maimonides).

It seems to me that by "goodheartedness" is meant the capacity for long-suffering, one's not being short-tempered. Such a person shuns anger, always makes reply softly; even when something evil is done to him, he puts up with it, and no bitterness comes from his mouth (Rabbi Jonah).

IN HIS WORDS YOUR WORDS ARE INCLUDED: For he in whom is goodheartedness will be generous, will get him good companions, set up a residence next to good neighbors; and because of his goodheartedness he will also practice foresight and beware lest he be the cause of anything untoward. He will be at peace with God and with men (Duran).

THE EVIL WAY WHICH A MAN SHOULD SHUN: So that he may enter the world to come (ARN).

A GRUDGING EYE: There are a number of virtues whose absence does not necessarily suggest that one is evil. For example, saintliness: it is a very great virtue. But if a person does not cultivate saintliness, he is not to be described as evil. This is the reason Rabbi Eliezer wants to emphasize the evil of "a grudging eye" (the opposite of "a liberal eye"). That is: Let no man say that miserliness is not a bad thing, that because he has neither oppressed nor robbed his neighbor, [his life is free of sin]—for great is the evil of miserliness. It is the basis of every kind of evil! (Rabbi Jonah).

BORROWING AND NOT REPAYING: This is a tradition I received: When a person borrows from another and does not repay, it is as though from the beginning he had borrowed from God. For that creditor was not putting his trust in the borrower but in the third party who was with them, namely, He who issued the commandments. This is similar to a story told in the Palestinian Talmud (J. Berakot 2:3, 4c): There was a certain man who used to wear tefillin, and people entrusted him with valuables. Then he denied that he had them. Said the victim to him: "It was not in you that I put my trust, but in Him who commanded you to put the tefillin on your head!" (Vitry).

One who does not exercise foresight will not shun evil ways. An example of this is the one who borrows and does not repay. For at the time of the loan he should have reflected and considered if he would be able to return the loan when it was due (Rabbi Jonah).

———

EACH OF THEM SAID THREE THINGS.

RABBI ELIEZER SAYS: LET THE HONOR OF THY FELLOW BE AS DEAR TO THEE AS THINE OWN. BE NOT EASILY ANGERED. REPENT ONE DAY BEFORE THY DEATH.

AND KEEP WARM AT THE FIRE OF THE SAGES, BUT BEWARE OF THEIR GLOWING COAL LEST THOU BE SCORCHED: FOR THEIR BITE IS THE BITE OF A JACKAL, AND THEIR STING THE STING OF A SCORPION, AND THEIR HISS THE HISS OF A SERPENT—MOREOVER ALL THEIR WORDS ARE LIKE COALS OF FIRE.

LET THE HONOR OF THY FELLOW BE AS DEAR TO THEE AS THINE OWN: This teaches that even as one looks out for his own honor, so should he look out for his fellow's honor. And even as no man wishes that his own honor be held in ill repute, so should he wish that the honor of his fellow shall not be held in ill repute (ARN).

If you wish that no man should help himself to what is yours, do not help yourself to what belongs to your fellow; if you wish that no one should gossip about you, do not gossip about anyone else (ARNB).

And thou shalt love thy neighbor as thyself (Leviticus 19:18), and the Sages have laid it down (Shabbat 31a) as a principle: "What is hateful to thee, do not do to thy fellow" (Aknin).

BE NOT EASILY ANGERED: This teaches that one should be patient like Hillel the Elder and not short tempered like Shammai the Elder.

What was this patience of Hillel the Elder? The story is told:

Once two men decided to make a wager of four hundred *zuz* with each other. They said: "Whoever can put Hillel into a rage gets the four hundred *zuz*."

One of them went [to attempt it]. Now that day was a Sabbath eve, toward dusk, and Hillel was washing his head. The man came and knocked on his door. "Where's Hillel? Where's Hillel?" he cried.

Hillel got into a cloak and came out to meet him. "My son," he said, "what is it?"

The man replied: "I need to ask about a certain matter."

"Ask," Hillel said.

The man asked: "Why are the eyes of the Tadmorites bleary?"

"Because," said Hillel, "they make their homes on the desert sands which the winds come and blow into their eyes. That is why their eyes are bleary."

The man went off, waited a while, and returned and

knocked on his door. "Where's Hillel?" he cried. "Where's Hillel?"

Hillel got into a cloak and came out. "My son," he said, "what is it?"

The man replied: "I need to ask about a certain matter."

"Ask," Hillel said.

The man asked: "Why are the Africans' feet flat?"

"Because they dwell by watery marshes," said Hillel, "and all the time they walk in water. That is why their feet are flat."

The man went off, waited a while, and returned and knocked on the door. "Where's Hillel?" he cried. "Where's Hillel?"

Hillel got into a cloak and came out. "What is it thou wishest to ask?" he inquired.

"I need to ask about some matter," the man said.

"Ask," Hillel said to him. . . .

Said the man: "Is this how princes reply! May there be no more like thee in Israel!"

"God forbid!" Hillel said, "tame thy spirit! What dost thou wish?"

The man asked: "Why are the heads of Babylonians long?"

"My son," Hillel answered, "thou hast raised an important question. Since there are no skillful midwives there, when the infant is born, slaves and maidservants tend it on their laps. That is why the heads of Babylonians are long. Here, however, there are skillful midwives and when the infant is born it is taken care of in a cradle and its head is rubbed. That is why the heads of Palestinians are round."

"Thou hast put me out of four hundred *zuz!*" the man exclaimed.

Said Hillel to him: "Better that thou lose four hundred *zuz* because of Hillel than that Hillel lose his temper."

What was this impatience of Shammai the Elder? The story is told:

A certain man once stood before Shammai and said to him: "Master, how many Torahs have you?"

"Two," Shammai replied, "one written and one oral."

Said the man: "The written one I am prepared to accept, the oral one I am not prepared to accept."

Shammai rebuked him and dismissed him in a huff.

He came before Hillel and said to him: "Master, how many Torahs were given?"

"Two," Hillel replied, "one written and one oral."

Said the man: "The written one I am prepared to accept, the oral one I am not prepared to accept."

"My son," Hillel said to him, "sit down."

He wrote out the alphabet for him [and pointing to one of the letters] asked him: "What is this?"

"It is *aleph*," the man replied.

Said Hillel: "This is not *aleph* but *bet*. What is that?" he continued.

The man answered: "It is *bet*."

"This is not *bet*," said Hillel, "but *gimmel*."

[In the end] Hillel said to him: "How dost thou know that this is *aleph* and this *bet* and this *gimmel*? Only because so our ancestors of old handed it down to us, that this is *aleph* and this *bet* and this *gimmel*. Even as thou hast taken this in good faith, so take the other in good faith."

A certain heathen once passed behind a synagogue and heard a child reciting: *And these are the garments which they shall make: a breastplate, and an ephod, and a robe* (Exodus 28:4). He came before Shammai and asked him: "Master, all this honor, whom is it for?"

Shammai said to him: "For the High Priest who stands and serves at the altar."

Said the heathen: "Convert me on condition that thou appoint me High Priest, so I may serve at the altar."

"Is there no priest in Israel," Shammai exclaimed, "and have we no high priests to stand and serve in high priesthood at the altar, that a paltry proselyte who has come with naught but his staff and bag should go and serve in high priesthood!" He rebuked him and dismissed him in a huff.

The heathen then came to Hillel and said to him: "Master, convert me on condition that thou appoint me High Priest, so that I may stand and serve at the altar."

"Sit down," Hillel said to him, "and I will tell thee something. If one wishes to greet a king of flesh and blood, is it not right that he learn how to make his entrances and exits?"

"Indeed," the heathen replied.

"Thou wishest to greet the King of kings of kings, the Holy One, blessed be He: is it not all the more right that thou learn how to enter into the Holy of Holies, how to fix the lights, how to approach the altar, how to set the table, how to prepare the row of wood?"

Said the heathen: "Do what seems best in thine eyes."

First Hillel wrote out the alphabet for him and taught it to him. Then he taught him the Book of Leviticus. And the heathen went on studying until he got to the verse, *And the common man that draweth nigh shall be put to death* (Numbers 1:51). Forthwith, of his own accord, he reasoned by inference as follows: "If Israel, who were called children of God and of whom the Shekinah said, *And ye shall be unto Me a kingdom of priests, and a holy nation* (Exodus 19:6), were nevertheless warned by Scripture, *And the common man that draweth nigh shall be put to death,* all the more I, a paltry proselyte, come with naught but my bag!" Thereupon that proselyte was reconciled of his own accord.

He came to Hillel the Elder and said to him: "May all the blessings of the Torah rest upon thy head! For hadst thou been like Shammai the Elder I might never have entered the community of Israel. The impatience of Shammai the Elder well-nigh caused me to perish in this world and the world to come. Thy patience has brought me to the life of this world and the one to come" (ARN).

Do not lend yourself to quick anger and rage. The Sages have said some very sharp things in disgrace of anger and rage, and their strongest comment (Shabbat 105b) is, "He who is angry is like an idol-worshipper" (Maimonides).

It is well known that anger is a very bad thing, but by nature men are drawn to it. That is why Rabbi Eliezer says: Since against your wish you will sometimes get angry, beware not to be angered easily. . . . Weigh the matter wisely: is it worth getting angry over? And if you find any excuse to dismiss anger, dismiss it. Then when there is reason to be genuinely angry, your anger will not fail you. . . . And this is what the Sages meant by their saying (Erubin 65b): "By three things a man gives himself away: by his tumbler, his tipping, and his temper" (Rabbi Jonah).

REPENT ONE DAY BEFORE THY DEATH: Rabbi Eliezer was asked by his disciples: "Does, then, a man know on what day he will die, that he should know when to repent?"

"All the more," he replied; "let him repent today lest he die on the morrow; let him repent on the morrow lest he die the day after: and thus all his days will be spent in repentance" (ARN).

This is the meaning of the verse, *Let thy garments be always white* (Ecclesiastes 9:8) (ARNB).

In the Midrash Kohelet (Ecclesiastes Rabba 9:8) there is the following parable: A sailor's wife was in the habit of putting on her finery every day. Said her neighbors to her:

"Your husband is overseas; for whom are you getting yourself
up so fine?" She said to them: "My husband is a sailor. If by
chance he hits upon a wind he may be at my doorstep before I
know it. Better that he find me attractive than messy!"
(Duran).

The reason the day of death has been concealed from men
is this: If a man knew he was about to die, he would not
engage in anything useful to the world; if he knew his day
of death was far off, he would not engage in good works, for
he would say, "There is still time" (Nahmias).

KEEP WARM AT THE FIRE . . . : The statements which
follow are those Rabbi Eliezer transmitted in the name of
other authorities from whom he heard them. They are not
original with him. That is why there are more than three
sayings here; the closing statements are not to be included in
the number three the Mishna cites (Maimonides).

BEWARE . . . LEST THOU BE SCORCHED: Do not transgress
the words of the Sages, as it is written, *Thou shalt not turn
aside* (Deuteronomy 17:11), "lest thou be scorched," for the
words of the Torah are compared to fire. . . . And just as
in the case of fire, if a man is found worthy he may enjoy it
and its warmth, otherwise he is scorched; so with the words
of the Torah: if a man is worthy he acquires the life of the
world through them; otherwise he is driven out of the world
(Vitry).

In your association with Sages and men of rank . . . approach
only to the extent that they invite you. Do not approach them
more than they allow, lest you lose even that relationship
they were planning to share with you and you turn their love
into hatred—and the benefits you hoped for, now be lost
entirely to you. Rabbi Eliezer compared this to warming
oneself at a fire. If a person keeps his distance from the flame,
he will enjoy the warmth and get the benefit of the fire. But
if he foolishly gets too close he will be burned (Maimonides).

A person should not behave frivolously in the presence of
scholars (Rabbi Jonah).

ALL THEIR WORDS: This includes even their ordinary conversation. As the Talmud (Sukkah 21b) puts it: Even the
small talk of scholars deserves study (Aknin).

———

RABBI JOSHUA SAYS: A GRUDGING EYE, EVIL IMPULSE, AND
HATRED OF MANKIND PUT A MAN OUT OF THE WORLD.

A GRUDGING EYE: This teaches that even as a man looks out for his own home, so should he look out for the home of his fellow. And even as no man wishes that his own wife and children shall be held in ill repute, so should no man wish that his fellow's wife and his fellow's children be held in ill repute. Another interpretation. . . . One should not begrudge another his learning. There was once a certain man who begrudged his companion his learning. His life was cut short and he passed away (ARN).

A grudging eye is a passion for wealth (Maimonides).

He who is not content with his lot and is constantly envying his fellow who is richer than he, wondering when he will become as wealthy—brings evil upon himself and his fellow. So the philosophers teach us: From grudging thoughts, the things a person craves for are themselves consumed; then he destroys himself, for he craves for impossible things—from excessive impatience his body is ruined, and thus one who craves for what is evil is put out of the world (Rabbi Jonah).

Nothing satisfies a grudging eye. It always yearns for what others have—and in the end puts a man out of the world (Rabbi David the Prince).

EVIL IMPULSE: By thirteen years is the evil impulse older than the good impulse. In the mother's womb the evil impulse begins to develop and is born with a person. If he begins to profane the Sabbath, it does not prevent him; if he commits murder, it does not prevent him; if he goes off to another heinous transgression, it does not prevent him.

Thirteen years later the good impulse is born. When he profanes the Sabbath, it reprimands him: "Wretch! lo it says, *Every one that profaneth it shall surely be put to death*" (Exodus 31:14). If he goes to commit murder, it reprimands him: "Wretch! lo it says, *Whoso sheddeth man's blood, by man shall his blood be shed*" (Genesis 9:6). If he goes off to another heinous transgression, it reprimands him: "Wretch! lo it says, *Both the adulterer and the adulteress shall surely be put to death*" (Leviticus 20:10).

When a man bestirs himself and goes off to some unchastity, all his limbs obey him, for the evil impulse is king over his two hundred and forty-eight limbs. When he goes off to some good deed, all his limbs begin to drag. For the evil impulse within man is monarch over his two hundred and forty-eight limbs, while the good impulse is like a captive in prison, as it is said, *For out of prison he came forth to be king* (Ecclesiastes 4:14), that is to say, the good impulse. . . .

Rabbi Reuben ben Astroboli says: How can a man escape from the evil impulse within him? For the first seminal drop a man puts into a woman is the evil impulse! And the evil impulse lies verily at the opening of the heart, as it is said, *Sin coucheth at the door* (Genesis 4:7). . . .

Rabbi Simeon ben Eleazar says: Let me tell thee by way of parable to what this may be compared. The evil impulse is like iron which one holds in a flame. So long as it is in the flame one can make of it any implement he pleases. So too the evil impulse: its only remedy is in the words of the Torah, for they are like fire, as it is said, *If thine enemy be hungry, give him bread to eat, and if he be thirsty, give him water to drink: for thou wilt heap coals of fire upon his head, and the Lord will reward thee* (Proverbs 25:21 f.)—read not *will reward thee* (*yeshallem lak*) but *will put him at peace with thee* (*yashlimennu lak*).

Rabbi Judah the Prince says: I shall tell thee a parable; to what may this be likened? With the evil impulse it is as when two men enter an inn and one of them is seized as a brigand. When asked "Who is with thee?" he could say "No one is with me." Instead he decides: "Since I am to be slain, let my companion be slain along with me." So too the evil impulse says: "Since all hope for me is lost in the world to come, I shall destroy the whole body" (ARN).

The dominion of the evil impulse is overwhelming and only very few in each generation escape from its evil effects. These few are the only ones who are truly free, who are not slaves of their passions; on the contrary, they rule over their impulse and appetites, and such people are very few in number (Aknin).

Evil impulse refers to unchastity (Meiri).

Evil impulse refers to excessive appetite in food and sexual relations; whoever yields to his appetite when the evil impulse drives him on, will die early. For many serious sicknesses come upon a person from excessive eating and drinking; his body is worn out from excessive sexual indulgence; and as a result he departs from the world (Duran).

HATRED OF MANKIND: For God will uproot from the world everyone who hates his fellow man (ARNB).

Rabbi Simeon ben Eleazar says: Under solemn oath was this statement pronounced, *But thou shalt love thy neighbor as thyself* (Leviticus 19:18): [for] I the Lord have created him —if thou lovest him, I am faithful to reward thee in goodly measure; but if not, I am the judge to punish (ARN).

This is evil spirit. It is the sickness of melancholy which leads a man to despise the sight of his own kind and to hate everything; then he prefers the society of animals, going off alone into deserts and wilderness; he prefers places far from all habitation. Without a doubt this will put a person to death (Maimonides).

When a man withdraws from human beings, hates them, and does not want to associate with them, men begin to hate him, seek to do him evil, and plot to kill him. They will not help him in his need, and so he is left completely on his own to do things he has to do—then he can do these only with the greatest difficulty and pain. Now, this is something we know from psychology, that the association of men with each other and support of each other is an absolute good, for everybody helps his fellow. Withdrawal from human society is an absolute evil, unless of course the people of one's time are utterly depraved and turn completely from the good way to the evil way and abandon the Lord. In such times a man must of course separate from his contemporaries so that he will not learn their ways and perish with them (Aknin).

There are some who interpret hatred of mankind as follows: a person who is hard to get along with, thereby causes men to hate him; then they curse him and their curse takes effect and he perishes (Duran).

———

RABBI YOSE SAYS: LET THY FELLOW'S PROPERTY BE AS DEAR TO THEE AS THINE OWN. MAKE THYSELF FIT FOR THE STUDY OF TORAH, FOR IT WILL NOT BE THINE BY IN-HERITANCE. LET ALL THINE ACTIONS BE FOR THE SAKE OF HEAVEN.

THY FELLOW'S PROPERTY: This teaches that even as one has regard for his own property, so should he have regard for his fellow's property; and even as no man wishes that his own property be held in ill repute, so should he wish that his fellow's property shall not be held in ill repute.

Another interpretation: When a scholar comes to thee saying, "Teach me," if it is in thy power to teach, teach him. Otherwise, send him away at once and do not take his money from him (ARN).

If your fellow has lost something, search for it as though it were your own (Vitry).

If a buyer asks someone about the merchandise or possessions of his fellow and they are good, let him praise them. If they are not good, let him not say that they are bad; instead let him say, "I do not know" (Aknin).

MAKE THYSELF FIT FOR THE STUDY OF TORAH: If knowledge of the Torah could be acquired by inheritance, a man would pass it on to his son and his grandson and his sister's son, to the end of all generations. Thus we find in the case of Moses; when he thought that his sons would succeed him, what did he say? *And Moses spoke unto the Lord, saying: Let the Lord, the God of the spirits of all flesh, set a man over the congregation, who may go out before them* (Numbers 27:15 ff.). Come now, note what God answered him: *Take thee Joshua* (Numbers 27:18) (ARNB).

Make yourself fit and bestir yourself to study Torah. Do not say: "My father was a scholar, I shall therefore be like him without effort and labor." Certain it is that if you do not bestir yourself and labor over it, you will not know Torah (Vitry).

The early Sages used to say that at the time of his birth a person is not created to be by nature either the author of good works or bad works—just as there is no one by nature a craftsman. . . . Without training no one is by nature a craftsman or builder or weaver or dyer or farmer. . . . He has to learn these arts. It is possible that by nature a man may be born potentially capable of doing good rather than evil, or vice versa; then such action will be easier for him to do than its opposite; and when he does something which is contrary to his nature, he will have to do it with pain and difficulty. . . .

Pay no attention to the foolish and stupid things the astrologers tell you, to wit, the star in the ascendancy when a man is born, and the position of the planets at that time, determine whether he shall be wise or foolish, righteous or wicked, upright or crooked, strong or weak, rich or poor. . . . All these things are vanity and nonsense. . . .

And because study in this world leads a man to inherit the world to come, Rabbi Yose says, "Make thyself fit for the study of Torah": abandon bodily appetites, excessive food and drink, lavish raiment, many wives. . . . These things will seduce you, they will leave you no time or leisure to study and do good (Aknin).

Even if your ancestors were scholars, do not say, "This is second nature to me! For me a little study will suffice." "It is not thine by inheritance": O the seas that have run dry! O the stones that brought forth water! (Meiri).

LET ALL THINE ACTIONS BE FOR THE SAKE OF HEAVEN: Like Hillel's. When Hillel used to go out to a certain place, folks would say to him: "Where are you going to?" [He would reply,] "I am going to carry out some commandment."
  "Which commandment, Hillel?"
  "I am going to the privy."
  "Is this, then, a commandment?"
  "Indeed," he would say, "so that the body do not deteriorate."
[Or again:] "Where are you going to, Hillel?"
  "I am going to carry out some commandment."
  "Which commandment, Hillel?"
  "I am going to the bathhouse."
  "Is this, then, a commandment?"

He would say to them: "Indeed, to make the body clean. Know that this is so: if for the statues put up in royal palaces, he who is appointed to keep them clean receives an annual salary from the government, and what is more, is exalted . . . , all the more he who has been created in the image and likeness of God, as it is said, *For in the image of God made He man*" (Genesis 9:6) (ARNB).

"Let all thine actions be for the sake of Heaven," that is, for the sake of Torah, as it is said, *In all thy ways acknowledge Him and He will direct thy paths* (Proverbs 3:6) (ARN).

We have been taught (Nazir 23b): Greater is sin for the sake of the good, than the good not for its own sake (Vitry).

Even things permitted to you, like eating, drinking, sitting down, rising up, walking, lying down, sexual intercourse, conversation and all bodily needs, let them all be in the service of your Creator or contribute to whatever leads you to serve Him. . . . This is the end of the matter: a man must set his eyes and heart to his ways and weigh all his actions in the scale of intelligence. When he sees that there is something which leads to the service of the Creator, blessed be He, let him do that; if not, let him shun it (Rabbi Jonah).

A man certainly has to be engaged in worldly and social affairs for the benefit of his body. But he has been warned that even when he engages in these he should have only one purpose, perfection of his soul. Thus he will be found meritorious even when engaged in such activities, since the intention was not the activities themselves, but the perfection of his soul (Meiri).

Sin is a shameful thing under all circumstances. But if a man has to transgress the will of his Creator because of an emergency, let him even then have in mind to carry out the will of his Father in Heaven. . . . When a man gathers wealth, let him have in mind to be able to buy books and carry out the commandments, and give these books over as an inheritance to his children so that they may be found worthy to study Torah. . . . And when a man finds that his body has grown weak from [too much] study and for a while he has to walk about out-of-doors and in the streets, let him have in mind bringing relief to himself, so that he may return to his study (Duran).

———

RABBI SIMEON SAYS: BE ALERT IN RECITING THE SHEMA AND THE PRAYER. WHEN THOU PRAYEST, DO NOT MAKE OF THY PRAYER SOMETHING AUTOMATIC, BUT A PLEA FOR COMPASSION, A SUPPLICATION BEFORE GOD, BLESSED BE HE, FOR IT IS SAID, *For He is a God gracious and compassionate, long-suffering and abundant in mercy, and repenteth Him of the evil* (Joel 2:13). AND BE NOT WICKED IN THINE OWN SIGHT.

BE ALERT IN RECITING THE SHEMA AND THE PRAYER: Be prompt to recite the Shema at the prescribed time, so that you may receive that reward reserved for those who carry out the commandments at their prescribed time (Vitry).

Direct your heart properly and accept the yoke of the kingdom of Heaven with love and fear and awe, and do not let words come out of your mouth while your heart turns to worldly preoccupations and your thoughts wander. . . . Let rather your mouth and heart be at one in the love of God. And know before whom you are standing, before the King of kings of kings, the Holy One, blessed be He. He tests the heart and searches out one's thoughts and knows the hidden things. So plead before Him for your soul which sins, and for your heart which strays (Aknin).

WHEN THOU PRAYEST, DO NOT MAKE OF THY PRAYER SOMETHING AUTOMATIC: When you pray, make not of your prayer a chattering (ARN).

Things automatic become a burden to a man and he hastens to get rid of them. This is not the proper form of respect, the way of supplication even in the presence of a king of flesh and blood! (Vitry).

A man should recite his prayers like a poor person pleading and beseeching for something which he needs (Rabbi Jonah).

AND BE NOT WICKED IN THINE OWN SIGHT: Do not do something which you yourself know to be evil, though others do not recognize it as such. This is an interpretation I have received. . . . In the name of Rabbenu Tam I heard the following: "Do not be wicked in thine own sight" means, do not regard yourself as wicked. So too we are taught in the Talmud (Kiddushin 40b): Let a man look upon himself as though he were half-righteous, half-wicked. Then when he does one good deed, how fortunate for him! For he has placed himself and the whole world on the balance side of merit. But when a man regards himself as wicked, he despairs of doing any more good, for he feels that it would be of no avail. Thus he grows more and more wicked (Vitry).

When a man has a mean opinion of himself, then any meanness he is guilty of does not seem outrageous to him (Maimonides).

Rabbi Solomon, of blessed memory, explained this saying as follows: Do not do something which later, today or to-morrow, you will condemn yourself for. Somebody once said to his son: "If you are more ashamed because of what others may think, than because of what you yourself think, then your own self is worthless to you" (Duran).

———

RABBI ELEAZAR SAYS: BE DILIGENT IN THE STUDY OF TORAH, AND KNOW HOW TO ANSWER AN EPICUROS. KNOW IN WHOSE PRESENCE THOU ART TOILING; AND FAITHFUL IS THY TASK-MASTER TO PAY THEE THE REWARD OF THY LABOR.

BE DILIGENT IN THE STUDY OF TORAH: "Diligence" may be interpreted either in the sense of the word in the verse (Jeremiah 1:12), *For I am diligent in regard to my word*, that is to say, quick and energetic; or it may mean regularity and faithful attendance, as in the verse (Proverbs 8:34),

Watching daily at my gates (Maimonides—in the Hebrew translation, but wanting in the Arabic original).

KNOW HOW TO ANSWER AN EPICUROS: In the Talmud (Sanhedrin 99b) several explanations of the term Epicuros are offered. Some say the term refers to one who despises scholars; some say it refers to him who interprets the Torah slanderously—like Manasseh, the son of Hezekiah, who used to sit and expound false teachings (Vitry).

You have to learn the arguments with which to refute Gentile non-believers. . . . Now, it is said in the Talmud (Sanhedrin 38b): Such debate is permitted only with a Gentile non-believer, but not with a Jewish one, for him argument only leads to deny even more, that is, he gets to despise and ridicule the Torah even more. That is why one should not enter into debate with him at all, for there is no remedy for him, no cure at all. . . . Now then, even though you study the teachings of the Gentiles in order to know how to answer them, beware lest any of these teachings enter into your heart. Know that He before whom you serve knows the secret of your heart. That is why our statement is followed by "Know in whose presence thou art toiling" (Maimonides).

In addition to what you have to know for understanding the commandments and for study, you need to learn those speculative teachings of the Torah which will make you able to answer an unbeliever who contradicts it, either with false or inconclusive arguments—so that, if he attacks a basic principle of the Torah, you will be able to destroy his proofs, and if he raises philosophical questions, you will be able to establish your views by conclusive reasoning (Meiri).

Fill your belly with Torah and then argue with the Epicuros. For if you do not first fill yourself with Torah, he may knock you over with a straw and you will be bested by him (Nahmias).

Epicuros was the name of one of the Greeks who denied the reality of God, blessed be He, and said, "There is no God." Our Sages, of blessed memory, applied this term to all those who deny the teachings of our faith, either denying the existence of God or, in their denial, saying that there is more than one God. . . .

This statement is the source of the permission which we have taken to study philosophy, so that we may know how to refute the philosophers in their own words, for they have no arguments by which to undermine the words of the Torah and the Prophets (Duran).

FAITHFUL IS THY TASKMASTER TO PAY THEE THE REWARD OF THY LABOR: I do not think that this statement refers back to the statement about answering an Epicuros. Rather, it applies to every true believer, namely, that he ought not despair in his service of God, but grow stronger and stronger in it (Duran).

———

RABBI TARFON SAYS: THE DAY IS SHORT, THE WORK IS PLENTIFUL, THE LABORERS ARE SLUGGISH, AND THE REWARD IS ABUNDANT, AND THE MASTER OF THE HOUSE PRESSES.

THE DAY IS SHORT, THE WORK IS PLENTIFUL, THE LABORERS ARE SLUGGISH, AND THE REWARD IS ABUNDANT: Do not remove thyself from the measure which hath no limit and the work which hath no end. A parable: to what may this be likened? To one who keeps drawing up sea water and pouring it on dry land: the sea is not diminished and the dry land is not flooded. If he should grow impatient, he is told: "Wretch! Why dost thou grow impatient? Every day take thy reward, a golden denar!" (ARN).

"The day is short," that is, the days of your life in this world, as it is written, *The days of our years are threescore years and ten* (Psalm 90:10), and it says, *We bring our years to an end as a tale that is told* (Psalm 90:9). And the work of the Torah is plentiful, it is impossible to learn it all within one's lifetime without pressing hard upon time. That is why a man should strive to study as much Torah as he can, so that he may receive an abundant reward. For the more one studies, the more abundant will be the reward for it. "The laborers are sluggish" and are not always studying. "And the master of the house," that is, the Holy One from whom you receive your reward, "presses" . . . proclaiming, *But thou shalt meditate therein day and night* (Joshua 1:8). And you are obliged to be quick in carrying out His command (Vitry).

The measure of man's life is short and his days are too few to acquire all the wisdom and knowledge that there is, because these are endless. For every science, *The measure thereof is longer than the earth, and broader than the sea* (Job 11:9), and if this is true of Medicine, as Prince Hippocrates the Saint has it, how much the more so of the Torah, the Mysteries of Creation and the Mysteries of the Chariot (Aknin).

The forty days that Moses our master, may he rest in peace, spent on Mount Sinai, he did not sleep at all. Compare this to a king who said to his servant: "Count gold pieces from now until tomorrow, and whatever you count off will be yours." How can such a person sleep? Why, the time he spent in sleep he would be losing a fortune! So said Moses: "If I go to sleep, how many precious words of the Torah I would lose!" All the more so in our case: let us give no sleep to our eyes nor slumber to our eyelids (Rabbi Jonah).

———

HE USED TO SAY: IT IS NOT THY DUTY TO FINISH THE WORK, BUT THOU ART NOT AT LIBERTY TO NEGLECT IT. IF THOU HAST STUDIED MUCH TORAH, THOU SHALT BE GIVEN MUCH REWARD: FAITHFUL IS THY TASKMASTER TO PAY THEE THE REWARD OF THY LABOR. AND KNOW THAT THE REWARDING OF THE RIGHTEOUS IS IN THE AGE TO COME.

IT IS NOT THY DUTY TO FINISH THE WORK: Not the whole Torah must thou take upon thyself to finish (ARN).

Though the work is plentiful, as I have told you, and I have said that your days are swifter than flight, do not say: "I shall drive myself excessively in my study, the way workers do who have to finish a fixed task." For if you act this way you will in the end grow weak and sluggish and cease from the work altogether. He who tries to do more than he is able, will in the end do less, because he wears out his body, dulls the sharpness of his mind, slackens his enthusiasm, and his soul grows too limp for study. And having been worn out, you will withdraw altogether (Aknin).

BUT THOU ART NOT AT LIBERTY TO NEGLECT IT: For it was on this condition that the Holy One, blessed be He, redeemed us from Egypt, to receive the Torah and His commandments (Vitry).

Do not say: "Since I am not obliged to finish the work, I shall not go to great pains; instead I will study an hour a day." No, no. You are the Torah's bondsman, to meditate therein day and night (Rabbi Jonah).

IF THOU HAST STUDIED MUCH TORAH: He that more and more studies, more and more increases his reward (ARN).

THE REWARDING OF THE RIGHTEOUS IS IN THE AGE TO COME: Let not your heart mislead you not to study Torah, so that you say: "I see people who do not study, but are nevertheless filled with all manner of good"; why therefore should you toil in vain? Say rather that "faithful is thy taskmaster." . . . He will not be niggardly in rewarding you, for the rewarding of the righteous is only in the age to come (Vitry).

By "age to come" is meant the world to come, and there the righteous receive their reward. . . . Maimonides, of blessed memory, explains this as the time after death, he applies it to the world where there are only souls. But Nahmanides, of blessed memory, explains it as the era after the world of souls, he applies it to the Age of the Resurrection of the dead, which world will come after this world (Duran).

Chapter III

AKABYA BEN MAHALALEL SAYS: MARK WELL THREE THINGS, AND THOU WILT NOT FALL INTO THE CLUTCHES OF SIN. KNOW WHENCE THOU ART COME, WHITHER THOU ART GOING, AND BEFORE WHOM THOU ART DESTINED TO GIVE AN ACCOUNT AND RECKONING.

"WHENCE THOU ART COME?" FROM A PUTRID DROP.

"WHITHER THOU ART GOING?" TO A PLACE OF DUST, WORM, AND MAGGOT.

"AND BEFORE WHOM THOU ART DESTINED TO GIVE AN ACCOUNT AND RECKONING?" BEFORE THE KING OF KINGS OF KINGS, THE HOLY ONE, BLESSED BE HE.

AKABYA: Up to this chapter the Mishna cited authorities according to some sequence. From here on no particular sequence is followed. The Sages are now quoted neither according to chronological order nor according to their excellence, and not even according to some sequence of subject matter (Duran).

MARK WELL: Give your mind to these things, and never again will it even occur to you to join the company of transgressors (Vitry).

WHENCE THOU ART COME: Rabbi Simeon ben Eleazar says: I shall tell thee a parable: to what may this be likened? To a king who built a large palace and decorated it, but a tannery pipe led through it and emptied at its doorway. Says every passerby: "How handsome and magnificent this palace would be if it were not for the tannery pipe coming through it!"

So too is man. If then, with a foul stream issuing from his bowels, he exalts himself over other creatures, how much the more would he exalt himself over other creatures if a stream of precious oil, balsam, or ointment issued from him! (ARN).

118

To a Place of Dust, Worm, and Maggot: With such thoughts in mind it will never enter your heart to seek a crown for yourself, to regard yourself as exempt from the commandments—for you are not worthy of such sovereign independence. Nevertheless, if your evil impulse continues to be overpowering, consider in your heart before whom you are destined to give an account and reckoning for your deeds. It is He by whom everything is seen, and it is impossible for you to escape His notice (Vitry).

Reflection on his origin will lead a man to humility. When he contemplates his ultimate end, he will get to despise mundane matters. And when he contemplates the majesty of the Commander, he will come to obey His commandments speedily. And when a person succeeds in keeping his mind on these three things, he will sin no more (Maimonides).

Before the King of Kings of Kings, the Holy One, Blessed Be He: All these titles are listed in order to intensify man's fear of God. For when one stands in the presence of some minor king he is in terror; the more so in the presence of the King of kings of kings! . . . So too we read in the Talmud (Berakot 28b): When Rabban Johanan ben Zakkai fell sick, his disciples came to call on him and found him weeping. "Why are you weeping?" they asked him. He said to them: "If I were being led before a king of flesh and blood—who is here today and in the grave tomorrow; whose anger, if he were angry at me, is not an everlasting anger; whose punishment, if he punished me, is not an eternal punishment; whose slaying, if he slew me, is not an eternal death; whom I can bribe with wealth or appease with words—I would still be in terror. All the more now that I am being led before the King of kings of kings, the Holy One, blessed be He, who lives and endures forever and to all eternity; whose anger, if He gets angry at me, is an eternal anger; whose punishment, if He should punish me, is an eternal punishment; whose slaying, if He should slay me, is an eternal death; whom I cannot bribe with wealth or appease with words! Moreover, there are before me two roads, one to Paradise and one to Gehenna, and I know not on which I am to be led! And shall I not weep?" (Duran).

———

RABBI HANANIAH, PREFECT OF THE PRIESTS, SAYS: DO THOU PRAY FOR THE WELFARE OF THE EMPIRE, BECAUSE WERE

IT NOT FOR THE FEAR IT INSPIRES, EVERY MAN WOULD
SWALLOW HIS NEIGHBOR ALIVE.

So too it says, *And seek the peace of the city whither I
have caused you to be carried away captive, and pray unto
the Lord for it; for in the peace thereof shall ye have peace*
(Jeremiah 29:7) (Vitry).

Were it not for the fear that the masses have of the king,
men would try to get power over one another, would kill
each other, oppress each other, rob each other—they would
be like the fish where the bigger one is always swallowing the
smaller one, and there is none to prevent it. . . . That is
why when the Lord of the universe, blessed be He, has brought
it to pass that there be someone through whom men enjoy their
existence, it is proper to pray for his welfare, and to beseech
and supplicate in his behalf that his days be lengthened and
that those who rise against him be cut off; as it is written,
And pray for the life of the king, and of his sons (Ezra 6:10)
(Aknin).

A man should pray for the welfare of the whole world
and share in the grief of others. This is indeed the way of
the righteous, as David, may he rest in peace, said, *But as
for me, when they were sick, my clothing was sackcloth,
I afflicted my soul with fasting* (Psalm 35:13). For no man
ought to offer up supplications and prayers for his own
needs only. He ought to pray in behalf of all men, that they
enjoy well-being. And in the peace of the government there
is peace for the world (Rabbi Jonah).

The conduct of human life may be divided into two parts:
there is the intellectual part, and it is the domain of the
philosophers; and there is the political part, and it is the
domain of the ruling powers and judges. Now, when philosophical conduct is lacking, political life does not necessarily
fail; but when political conduct is lacking, then everything
fails. For where there is no fear of the government, every
man is in fear of his fellow. . . . That is why Rabbi Hananiah
emphasizes that we must pray in its behalf; and this is
intended not merely in behalf of a Jewish government, but
in behalf of Gentile ones too (Meiri).

———

RABBI HANANIAH BEN TERADYON SAYS: IF TWO SIT TO-
GETHER AND THE WORDS BETWEEN THEM ARE NOT OF
TORAH, THEN THAT IS A SESSION OF SCORNERS, AS IT IS

SAID, *Nor hath sat in the seat of the scornful* (Psalm 1:1). BUT IF TWO SIT TOGETHER AND THE WORDS BETWEEN THEM ARE OF TORAH, THEN THE SHEKINAH IS IN THEIR MIDST, AS IT IS SAID, *Then they that feared the Lord spoke one with another; and the Lord hearkened, and heard, and a book of remembrance was written before Him, for them that feared the Lord and that thought upon His name* (Malachi 3:16). NOW I KNOW IT IS SO OF TWO; HOW DO WE KNOW THAT EVEN WHEN ONE SITS STUDYING THE TORAH, THE HOLY ONE, BLESSED BE HE, FIXES A REWARD FOR HIM? FOR IT IS SAID, *Though he sit alone and quietly he has surely received his* [*reward*] (Lamentations 3:28).

SEAT OF THE SCORNFUL: The verse in Psalms continues, *But his delight is in the Law of the Lord.* That is to say, he whose delight is in the Law of the Lord is not one to sit in the seat of the scornful; but one who has no delight in the Law of the Lord does sit in the seat of the scornful (Vitry).

In our passage, "seat of the scornful" refers to those who set aside regular sessions to engage in idle conversations and neglect the study of Torah (Rabbi Jonah).

BUT IF TWO SIT TOGETHER AND THE WORDS BETWEEN THEM ARE OF TORAH: When two sit studying Torah and one of them makes a mistake in a matter of halakah or of a chapter-heading—or says of the unclean that it is clean or of the clean that it is unclean, or of the forbidden that it is permitted or of the permitted that it is forbidden—his comrade will correct him. And where do we hear that when his comrade corrects him and studies with him they are well rewarded for their labor? For it is said, *Two are better than one; because they have a good reward for their labor* (Ecclesiastes 4:9). . . .

When two sit studying Torah, their reward is stored up on high, as it is said, *Then they that feared the Lord spoke one with another; and the Lord hearkened . . . and a book of remembrance was written before Him, for them that feared the Lord, and that thought upon His name* (Malachi 3:16) (ARN).

WHEN ONE SITS STUDYING THE TORAH: When one sits by himself studying Torah, his reward is stored up on high. . . . A parable is told: to what may this be likened? To one who had a young son whom he left at home when he went out to the market place. The child then proceeded to take down a scroll, laid it in his lap, and sat studying it. When his father returned from the market place, he exclaimed: "See what my little son, whom I left alone when I went out to the market place, has done! By himself he proceeded to take down the scroll, laid it in his lap and sat studying it." Thus thou dost learn that even when one sits by himself studying Torah, his reward is stored up on high (ARN).

FIXES A REWARD FOR HIM: As though the Torah had been brought down altogether for his sake only (Maimonides).

———

RABBI SIMEON SAYS: WHEN THREE EAT AT ONE TABLE AND DO NOT SPEAK WORDS OF TORAH THERE, IT IS AS THOUGH THEY HAD EATEN OF THE SACRIFICES OF THE DEAD, AS IT IS SAID, *For all tables are full of filthy vomit, when God is absent* (Isaiah 28:8). BUT WHEN THREE EAT AT ONE TABLE AND DO SPEAK WORDS OF TORAH THERE, IT IS AS THOUGH THEY HAVE EATEN FROM THE TABLE OF GOD, BLESSED BE HE, AS IT IS SAID, *And He said unto me, this is the table that is before the Lord* (Ezekiel 41:22).

———

SACRIFICES OF THE DEAD: That is, an idolatrous offering. . . . The table is called an altar, and the food on it is regarded as an offering. . . . Now therefore, when words of the Torah are spoken at a table, it is regarded as the atonement altar and the food as a meat offering; but when words of the Torah are not spoken at table, since you cannot regard the offering as an offering to God, you must regard it as an idolatrous offering. . . . So long as there was the Temple, atonement was possible for man by means of the altar. Now that there is no Temple, a man achieves atonement by means of his table, by his giving food and drink to the poor (Vitry).

A session of three people sitting together is called an assembly for then they recite the Grace as a group. . . . And when the words between them are not of the Torah, what takes place is a casting off of the yoke of the Torah: for they eat and drink and indulge themselves, and the very mention of the Torah does not enter their minds. Woe to them and woe to their pleasures! (Rabbi Jonah).

———

RABBI HANANIAH BEN HAKINAI SAYS: IF ONE WAKES IN THE NIGHT, OR WALKS BY HIMSELF ON THE HIGHWAY, AND TURNS HIS HEART TO IDLE MATTERS, HE IS MORTALLY GUILTY.

A man is to be engaged only in the study of the Torah. ... If one wakes in the night and turns his heart from idle matters to words of the Torah, it is a good sign for him; as it is said, *When thou walkest, it shall lead thee* (Proverbs 6:22) in this world; *when thou liest down, it shall watch over thee* (*ibid.*) at the hour of death; *and when thou awakest, it shall talk with thee* (*ibid.*) in the world to come (ARNB).

Rabbi Hananiah ben Jacob says: If one is kept awake in the night by words of the Torah, it is a good sign for him; if by [idle] conversation, it is a bad sign for him.

Rabbi Jacob ben Hananiah says: If one wakes in the night and the first words out of his mouth are not words of the Torah—it might have been better for him if . . . he had never been born and beheld the world (ARN).

The night hours are very valuable, and therefore one should contemplate in them only things that please God, blessed be He, such as words of the Torah. How important are those hours, how excellent for thinking about the Torah! For at that time a man has no work to do and he is not distracted by the noise of other people. Now, if he turns his heart to idle matters he is mortally guilty, because he wastes the time when he might have had clear thoughts, and removed his mind from thoughts of the Torah (Rabbi Jonah).

The meaning of Rabbi Hananiah's statement is that a man should engage in no thing which can induce the heart's falling into slumber and the mind's growing numb (Meiri).

———

RABBI NEHUNYA BEN HA-KANA SAYS: HE WHO TAKES UPON HIMSELF THE YOKE OF TORAH WILL BE RELIEVED OF THE YOKE OF THE GOVERNMENT AND THE YOKE OF MUNDANE MATTERS; BUT HE WHO REMOVES FROM HIMSELF THE YOKE OF TORAH WILL HAVE IMPOSED UPON HIM THE YOKE OF THE GOVERNMENT AND THE YOKE OF MUNDANE MATTERS.

He who gives over his heart to words of the Torah is relieved of words of folly; but he who gives over his heart to words of folly will be deprived of words of the Torah (ARNB).

Rabbi Hananiah, prefect of the priests, says: He who takes to heart the words of the Torah is relieved of many preoccupations—preoccupations with hunger, foolish preoccupations, unchaste preoccupations, preoccupations with the evil impulse, preoccupations with an evil wife, idle preoccupations, and preoccupations with the yoke of flesh and blood. For thus is it written in the Book of Psalms by David king of Israel: *The precepts of the Lord are right, rejoicing the heart; the commandment of the Lord is pure, enlightening the eyes* (Psalm 19:9). But he who does not take to heart the words of the Torah is given over to many preoccupations—preoccupations with hunger, foolish preoccupations, unchaste preoccupations, preoccupations with the evil impulse, preoccupations with an evil wife, idle preoccupations, preoccupations with the yoke of flesh and blood. For thus is it written in Deuteronomy by Moses our master: *And they shall be upon thee for a sign and for a wonder, and upon thy seed for ever; because thou didst not serve the Lord thy God with joyfulness, and with gladness of heart, by reason of the abundance of all things: therefore shalt thou serve thine enemy whom the Lord shall send against thee, in hunger, and in thirst, and in nakedness, and in want of all things* (Deuteronomy 28:46 ff.) (ARN).

YOKE OF TORAH: That is, diligent study (Maimonides).

By "yoke of Torah" is meant the discipline of study, attending upon scholars, being quick to carry out the commandments and self restraint from transgression (Aknin).

YOKE OF THE GOVERNMENT: I have not found an interpretation of this; but it seems to me to refer to what is spoken of in the Talmud (Baba Batra 8a) . . . that taxes and tribute are not to be imposed on scholars (Vitry).

By "yoke of the government" is meant the imposts of and extortions by the ruler (Maimonides).

"Yoke of the government" refers to *corvées* (Nahmias).

YOKE OF MUNDANE MATTERS: That is, livelihood worries. Heaven will provide for [the scholar] (Vitry).

"Mundane matters" refers to the necessity of providing for temporal needs (Maimonides).

By the "yoke of mundane matters" is meant a person's preoccupation with the details of living, bodily needs like food and drink and clothing and a place to live and marrying and raising children and other such things (Aknin).

HE WHO REMOVES FROM HIMSELF THE YOKE OF TORAH: For example, the *am ha-arez* (Vitry).

One "who removes from himself the yoke of Torah," is he who says the Torah is from Heaven but I will not submit to it (Maimonides).

One who takes upon himself the yoke of the Torah makes his study of Torah primary and his own needs secondary. Such a person the Holy One, blessed be He, protects from every evil, so that he does not need to neglect his study of Torah, and God sees to it that those tyrants who commandeer people to do work for them, shall not take this man. . . . [Moreover,] the work of the righteous man prospers, and he is content with his portion. But he who removes from himself the yoke of the Torah . . . thinks that he will be able to do more of his own work if he neglects the work of the Torah. But the Lord, blessed be He, will make void his plans; and He puts it into the heart of the king to seize this man for the king's service. . . . Such a person will have to wander after and toil for his livelihood, but will not find it. Even when he finds it he will not be content with his portion (Rabbi Jonah).

The Gentile philosophers write: There was once a certain ascetic who kept wandering from place to place for food. He arrived in a certain city and there found an idol-worshipper. He said to the idol-worshipper, "Why do you worship this idol?" The idol-worshipper replied, "So that it provide me with a livelihood." Said the ascetic to him, "How can you be so blind? Has this idol any power to provide you with livelihood? It cannot even stir from its place!" Said the idol-worshipper to him, "And whom do you serve?" Replied the ascetic, "The God of the heavens, whose might prevails in the whole universe and who can feed His creatures everywhere." Said the idol-worshipper to him, "Look here, your own actions contradict your words. If this God whom you serve is everywhere, why did you leave your home and wander from one place to another to seek a livelihood?" The ascetic had to admit that the idol-worshipper was right, and returned to his place (Duran).

RABBI HALAFTA OF KEFAR HANANIÁH SAYS: WHEN TEN
SIT STUDYING THE TORAH, THE SHEKINA RESIDES IN THEIR
MIDST, AS IT IS SAID, *God standeth in the congregation of
God* (Psalm 82:1). HOW DO WE KNOW THAT THE SAME IS
TRUE OF FIVE? FOR IT IS SAID, *This band of His He hath
established on the earth* (Amos 9:6). HOW DO WE KNOW
THAT THE SAME IS TRUE OF THREE? FOR IT IS SAID, *In
the midst of the judges He judgeth* (Psalm 82:1). HOW DO
WE KNOW THAT THE SAME IS TRUE OF TWO? FOR IT IS
SAID, *Then they that feared the Lord spoke one with another;
and the Lord hearkened, and heard* (Malachi 3:16). HOW DO
WE KNOW THAT THE SAME IS TRUE OF ONE? FOR IT IS
SAID, *In every place where I cause My name to be mentioned
I will come unto thee and bless thee* (Exodus 20:21).

TEN . . . CONGREGATION: The word "congregation" is
applied to a group of ten (Vitry).

FIVE . . . BAND: The word "band" (*agudah*) is related to
the verb *agad,* as in the expression "what a man gathers
into one of his hands." Now the hand has five fingers . . .
and the sum of these five fingers may be called "band"
(Maimonides).

THREE . . . JUDGES: The minimum number for a court of
judges is three (Rabbi Jonah).

———

RABBI ELEAZAR OF BARTOTA SAYS: GIVE TO HIM OF HIS
OWN, FOR THOU AND THINE ARE HIS. AND SO TOO OF
DAVID IT SAYS, *For everything is from Thee and of Thine
own we have given to Thee* (I Chronicles 29:14).

This statement refers both to a man's body and to his
wealth. And it says that a man should withhold neither himself
nor his wealth from the wishes of Heaven. This is what is
meant by "For thou and thine are his." For you give nothing
of your own, of your own body or of your own wealth, but
of what belongs to God, blessed be He. For the wealth a
man enjoys is given to him only in trust (Rabbi Jonah).

No man ought to be grudging in the giving of charity or
in the expenditure of funds to the glory of God (Meiri).

The Sages have said (Derek Erez Zuta 2): If you have
done much good, let it be little in your eyes; and do not

say, "I have done good out of what is mine"—say rather, "Out of what was mercifully given to me" (Nahmias).

———

RABBI SIMEON SAYS: IF ONE IS STUDYING AS HE WALKS ALONG THE HIGHWAY, AND HE INTERRUPTS HIS STUDY AND EXCLAIMS, "HOW HANDSOME IS THIS TREE, HOW HANDSOME THIS FIELD!", SCRIPTURE (Deuteronomy 4:9) ACCOUNTS IT TO HIM AS THOUGH HE WERE MORTALLY GUILTY.

This statement may be interpreted as follows: It is said, *And thou shalt talk of them when thou sittest in thy house, and when thou walkest by the way* (Deuteronomy 6:7); and it is written, *When thou walkest, it shall lead thee, when thou liest down, it shall watch over thee* (Proverbs 6:22). That is to say, so long as a man does not distract his mind from the words of the Torah, his knowledge of the Torah will keep. And since this man did allow his attention to wander from the Torah, he has come close to jeopardizing his soul, for it is written, *Wilt thou let thine eyes wander from it? behold it is gone* (Proverbs 23:5) (Vitry).

I have already explained that a man is permitted to speak only of the Torah, its praiseworthy qualities, the good fortune of those who seek it as their portion, the disgrace of sinning, and the abomination of those guilty of transgression. In such things a man ought to engage all his days, if possible; only the smaller part of his life should he devote to bodily needs; but his heart and soul should be given over to the Torah. Now this man's exclamation expresses neither words of the Torah nor practical matters, but idle things. Because he neglected a subject which gives life to his soul, namely, words of the Torah, and neglected what could provide for his bodily needs, and engaged in idle matters, it is accounted to him as though he were mortally guilty. Now note our statement says *"as though* he were mortally guilty"; but in the statement of the man who wakes in the night and turns his heart away from the Torah it says "he *is* mortally guilty." That is because here at least a man combined words of the Torah with idle matters, for the major part of his thinking was with the words of the Torah. In the other statement we are told that he turned his heart to idleness and that he did not speak words of the Torah at all. That is why he is actually sinning against his soul and deserves punishment for it. In our statement too the man is regarded as having sinned against his soul, because he had been engaged in words of the Torah . . . and therefore it was not proper for him to break off and begin to engage in matters of vanity and emptiness which are of no avail. . . . But the sin of such a person is not like the sin of one who turns his heart to idleness and does not engage in matters of the Torah at all. That is why our statement reads, *"as though* he were mortally guilty" (Aknin).

The reason for such strong condemnation is this: by nature man is drawn to vanity and idle matters; [if he does not resist his nature] he will be drawn on from such habits to throwing off the yoke of the Torah completely (Meiri).

The Torah is a source of life to those who study it, and he who breaks off his study withdraws from life. And so too we read in the Talmud (Abodah Zara 3b): Said Rab Judah in the name of Samuel: What is the meaning of the verse, *And Thou makest men as the fishes of the sea* (Habakkuk 1:14)? Even as the fish of the sea die the moment they come on dry land, so human beings die the moment they withdraw from words of the Torah. And although in our passage the Sage speaks specifically of the exclamation, "How handsome is this tree, how handsome this field!"— the same is true of any other chatter. But the Sage is referring to something commonplace, for it is customary for those who walk on the highway to talk of what they see along the way (Duran).

———

RABBI DOSTAI BAR YANNAI SAYS IN THE NAME OF RABBI MEIR: IF ONE FORGETS ANY THING OF HIS STUDIES, SCRIPTURE ACCOUNTS IT TO HIM AS THOUGH HE WERE MORTALLY GUILTY, FOR IT IS SAID, *Only take heed to thyself, and keep thy soul diligently, lest thou forget the things which thine eyes saw* (Deuteronomy 4:9). IS THIS TRUE EVEN OF ONE WHOSE STUDIES PROVED TOO DIFFICULT FOR HIM? THE VERSE SAYS, *And lest they depart from thy heart all the days of thy life (ibid.):* LO, ONE IS NOT MORTALLY GUILTY UNTIL HE DELIBERATELY REMOVES THEM FROM HIS HEART.

IF ONE FORGETS ANY THING OF HIS STUDIES: That is, he puts out of mind all thought of reviewing his studies, so that he finally forgets them (Vitry).

MORTALLY GUILTY: Because he does not take to heart the fact that forgetfulness is quite common among human beings. That person should have reviewed his study many times, he should have been thinking on it day and night, so that it would not vanish out of mind—and this he did not do. And he is mortally guilty because he then renders decisions on the basis of his memory and says, "So my teacher told me"; and he forbids what is permitted and permits what is forbidden (Rabbi Jonah).

UNTIL HE DELIBERATELY REMOVES THEM FROM HIS HEART: One may learn Torah for ten years and forget it all in two years. How so? For example: If for six months one neglects to review, he then says of the unclean "It is clean" and of the clean "It is unclean." If for twelve months he does not review, he then confuses the Sages with one another. If for eighteen months he does not review, he forgets the chapter-headings. If for twenty-four months he does not review, he forgets the treatise-headings. And after saying of the unclean "It is clean" and of the clean "It is unclean," after confusing the Sages with one another, after forgetting the chapter-headings and treatise-headings, he sits and keeps quiet in the end. And of him said Solomon, *I went by the field of the slothful, and by the vineyard of the man void of understanding; and lo, it was all grown over with thistles; the face thereof was covered with nettles, and the stone wall thereof was broken down* (Proverbs 24:30 f.): for once the wall of the vineyard falls, the whole vineyard is destroyed (ARN).

How does a man remove the words of the Torah from his heart? He neglects to review, he gives up studying the Torah. In that way he certainly forgets the whole Talmud, today a little, tomorrow a little, the day after even more; and so each day more is forgotten than on the previous one: as it is written, "Forsake Me a day, I will forsake you two" (J. Berakot, 9, 14d) (Aknin).

The heart of study is reviewing, and this is what is meant by study for its own sake. For when a man studies something once, he studies in order to understand. But when he studies it a second time, he studies it for its own sake (Nahmias, quoting his teacher, Rabbi Asher).

———

RABBI HANINA BEN DOSA SAYS: HE WHOSE FEAR OF SIN TAKES PRECEDENCE OVER HIS WISDOM, HIS WISDOM WILL

ENDURE; BUT HE WHOSE WISDOM TAKES PRECEDENCE OVER
HIS FEAR OF SIN, HIS WISDOM WILL NOT ENDURE.

HE USED TO SAY: HE WHOSE WORKS EXCEED HIS WISDOM,
HIS WISDOM WILL ENDURE; BUT HE WHOSE WISDOM EXCEEDS
HIS WORKS, HIS WISDOM WILL NOT ENDURE.

HE WHOSE FEAR OF SIN TAKES PRECEDENCE OVER HIS
WISDOM: As it is said, *The fear of the Lord is the beginning
of wisdom* (Psalm 111:10) (ARN).

Rabban Johanan ben Zakkai was asked: "If one is wise and
fears sin, what is he like?"

He replied, "Lo, that's a craftsman with the tools of his
craft in his hand."

"If one is wise but does not fear sin, what is he like?"

"Lo, that's a craftsman without the tools of his craft in his
hand," he replied.

"If one fears sin but is not wise, what is he like?"

He replied: "He is no craftsman, but the tools of the craft
are in his hand" (ARN).

This is something the philosophers also agree with: if cul-
tivation of good habits takes precedence over the pursuit of
knowledge, and the habits are firmly fixed, when an individual engages in study, the study will reinforce these habits,
he will get greater joy out of his learning, and will strive
to perfect himself in it. But if the pursuit of evil is put before
everything else, and the individual hopes that study will teach
him self-restraint, then the learning becomes too much of a
burden for him, and he will abandon it too (Maimonides).

Practice takes a long time before it is firmly fixed in a man.
That is why a person should first observe the ways most Jews
follow—carry out the commandments they carry out and flee
from those things they regard as transgressions—even if at
first he does not understand the reasons why. Then let him go
on to investigate and study the Torah to learn the reasons. If
one acts this way his study will be solidly established, for what
he learns will command him to continue in those ways he
followed even before he began to study. . . . But one who
studies and pays no attention to conduct, simply follows what
seems proper in his own sight, carries out only what seems
good or bad to him . . . then wicked conduct and sin become
firmly fixed in him (Aknin).

The "precedence" spoken of in our passage is not a precedence in time, for how is it possible for fear of sin to come

before wisdom? If a man has no wisdom, how can he fear sin? Have we not already learned that "the boor does not fear sin"? The precedence spoken of is a precedence in thinking, that is, if first in his thoughts a man determine to fear sin, then he will acquire wisdom, and it will be firmly established in him. . . . This may be compared to the person who says: "Planning for this house came before building." For if there had been no thought of a residence, the house would not have been built. And what begins in thought, ends in action (Duran).

HE WHOSE WORKS EXCEED HIS WISDOM: As it is said, *We will do, and study thereafter* (Exodus 24:7) (ARN).

This is what the Holy One, blessed be He, says to the wicked: "You have in your possession no good works, and do you seek to study Torah?" As it is said, *But unto the wicked God saith: What hast thou to do to declare My statutes* (Psalm 50:16): My statutes you do not keep, how dare you speak of them? *seeing thou hatest instruction* (*ibid.*) (ARNB).

Rabbi Simeon ben Eleazar says: He whose works exceed his wisdom, to what may he be likened? To one who rides a horse with a bit in its mouth. He can direct the horse wherever he wishes to. But one whose wisdom exceeds his works is like a person who rides a horse without a bit in its mouth. When he rides upon the animal, he falls off and breaks his neck (ARNB).

"He whose wisdom exceeds his works" is one who does not carry out what he learns; therefore his knowledge of the Torah will not keep, for through lack of practice he gradually forgets. And as we say in the Talmud (Sanhedrin 99a, ARN 23): He who studies but does not practice is like a man who sows but does not reap, like a woman who gives birth to children and buries them. "He whose works exceed his wisdom" is one who sets up many fences and hedges and precautions about the Torah and strives to act even beyond the demands of law—"his wisdom will endure," for he will never fall into transgression (Virty).

When a man's works exceed his wisdom he loves to know even more than he knows; thus every single day he adds to what he already knows. But if one's wisdom exceeds his works, his wisdom will not endure: because he knows more than he wishes to know, and thus what he has learned constantly diminishes (Quoted by Rabbi Jonah).

Works exceeding wisdom, that is to say, the person is meticulous in carrying out the commandments, and engages in their practice even more than seems to him necessary in the light of his learning (Meiri).

———

HE USED TO SAY: ONE WITH WHOM MEN ARE PLEASED, GOD IS PLEASED; AND ONE WITH WHOM MEN ARE DISPLEASED, GOD IS DISPLEASED.

It is said, *Find grace and good favour in the sight of God and man* (Proverbs 3:4) (Vitry).

The Sages have taught (Yoma 86a): When a man studies Scripture and Mishna and speaks decently with people, and his give and take in the market place are upright, and he is trustworthy in his dealings, what do men say of him? "What a blessed man, for he studied Torah! How blessed his father, how blessed his teacher who taught him Torah! Woe to those who have not studied Torah! So-and-so studied Torah, how comely is his conduct! how fine are his works!" Of such a person the verse says, *And He said unto me: Thou art My servant, Israel, in whom I will be glorified* (Isaiah 49:3). But when a man studies Scripture and Mishna and does not speak decently to people, and is not trustworthy in his dealings, and his give and take in the market place are unbecoming, what do men say of him? "Woe to So-and-so who studied Torah! How hideous is his conduct! how degenerate his ways!" And of such a person the verse says, *And they profaned My holy name; in that men said of them: These are the people of the Lord, and are gone forth out of His land* (Ezekiel 36:20) (Aknin).

Our statement speaks of "him with whom men are pleased," not of "him with whom *all* men are pleased"; for there is no man pleasing and acceptable to all human beings. And so of Mordecai it says, *And acceptable to most of his brethren* (Esther 10:3), not, to *all* his brethren (Nahmias).

Man must be beloved on earth not because this love is very important as such. But when a man is beloved on earth, he will be beloved on high, because thus the Name of the Lord is sanctified. . . . And how is the Holy One, blessed be He, glorified through human beings? By their right actions, carried out in accordance with the Torah. For then men honor the Torah, and at all times bless Him who gave it. This is what God desires from His creatures (Duran).

———

RABBI DOSA BEN HARKINAS SAYS: MORNING SLEEP, MIDDAY
WINE, CHILDREN'S PRATTLE AND SITTING IN THE GATHERING
PLACES OF THE AM HA-AREZ PUT A MAN OUT OF THE WORLD.

He who withdraws from these four things is second only
to the ministering angels (ARNB).

These things prevent a man from developing good character,
and the end is that he perishes (Maimonides).

MORNING SLEEP: What is that? This teaches that a man
should not plan to sleep until the time for reciting the Shema
has passed. For when a man sleeps until the time for reciting
the Shema has passed, he thereby neglects the study of Torah,
as it is said, *The sluggard saith: There is a lion in the way;
yea, a lion is in the streets. The door is turning upon its
hinges, and the sluggard is still upon his bed* (Proverbs
26:13 f.) (ARN).

MIDDAY WINE: What is that? This teaches that a man should
not plan to drink wine at midday. For when a man drinks wine
at midday, he thereby neglects the study of Torah, as it is said,
*Woe to thee, O land, when thy king is a boy, and thy princes
feast in the morning* (Ecclesiastes 10:16)! It says also,
*Happy are thou, O land, when thy king is a free man, and thy
princes eat in due season, in strength and not in drunkenness*
(*ibid.* :17) (ARN).

CHILDREN'S PRATTLE: What is that? This teaches that a man
should not plan to stay at home and study. For when a man
stays home to study, he chatters away with his children and
with the folk in his household, and thus neglects the study of
Torah. And it is said, *This book of the Torah shall not depart
out of thy mouth, but thou shalt meditate therein day and
night* (Joshua 1:16) (ARN).

By "children's prattle" is meant prolonged talk with young-
sters, youths who while away their time at idle gatherings
(Vitry).

THE GATHERING PLACES OF THE *Am Ha-Arez*: What is that?
This teaches that a man should not plan to sit down with those
that loiter at street corners in the market place. For when a
man sits down with those that loiter at street corners in the
market place, he neglects the study of Torah. And it is said,
*Happy is the man that hath not walked in the counsel of the
wicked, nor stood in the way of sinners. . . . But his delight
is in the Torah of the Lord* (Psalm 1:1 f.).

Rabbi Meir says: What does the verse mean by, *Nor sat in the seat of the scornful* (*ibid.*)? It is a reference to the theaters and circuses of the heathen, for in these, lives are condemned to death; and it is said, *I hate the gathering of evildoers, and will not sit with the wicked* (Psalm 26:5).

Now, *evildoers* are none but the wicked, as it is said, *For the evildoers shall be cut off. . . . And yet a little while, and the wicked is no more* (Psalm 37:9 f.). Now what will be their punishment in the age to come? As it is said: *For behold the day cometh, it burneth as a furnace, and all the proud and all that work wickedness shall be stubble* (Malachi 3:19). And the *proud* are none but the scornful, as it is said, *A proud and haughty man, scorner is his name* (Proverbs 21:24).

Once as Rabbi Akiba sat teaching his disciples and remembered what he had done in his youth, he exclaimed:

> "I give thanks unto Thee,
> O Lord my God,
> that Thou hast set my portion
>   amongst those that sit in the study-house,
> and didst not set my portion
>   amongst those that loiter at street corners
>   in the market place."   (ARN)

Why was man created? Only for the purpose of studying Torah. It will give him length of days and add years to his life. And if a man prefers the four things mentioned in our Mishna, what does he need life for? (Rabbi Jonah).

The conversation of the *am ha-arez* is seductive, for they speak only about daily happenings. And neglecting Torah for one hour brings on neglect for another hour, and finally a person departs from the world without any knowledge of Torah. Moreover a person is attracted to the *am ha-arez* by their eating and drinking habits and their frivolity (Duran).

RABBI ELEAZAR OF MODAIM SAYS: HE WHO PROFANES THE SACRED THINGS, AND DESPISES THE FESTIVALS, AND PUBLICLY DISGRACES HIS FELLOW, AND ANNULS THE COVENANT OF ABRAHAM OUR FATHER, MAY HE REST IN PEACE, AND IS CONTEMPTUOUS TOWARDS THE TORAH—EVEN THOUGH HE HAVE TORAH AND GOOD WORKS TO HIS CREDIT, HAS NO SHARE IN THE WORLD TO COME.

PROFANES THE SACRED THINGS: That is, he does not take the necessary precautions with them and is careless when

The Wisdom of the Fathers 135

consuming them. Another interpretation is possible: He acts
as did the sons of Eli ... of whom it is written, *Yea, before
the fat was made to smoke, the priest's servant came, and
said to the man that sacrificed: Give flesh to roast for the
priests* (I Samuel 2:15). Of them it is also written, *And the
sin of the young men was very great before the Lord* (*ibid.*
:17) (Aknin).

DESPISES THE FESTIVALS: That is, the "intermediate days" of
the festivals: he is lax about the law, and on these days engages
in work even though he would have incurred no loss [had he
waited for the holiday to pass] (Vitry).

To despise the festivals is not to prepare festive meals for
them, not to go to special expense in their honor, not to buy
delicacies and nice clothing for his wife and children as he
can well afford (Aknin).

PUBLICLY DISGRACES HIS FELLOW: A man should sooner
fling himself into a fiery furnace than disgrace his fellow in
public (Vitry).

The Tanna taught (Baba Mezia 58b) in the presence of
Rab Nahman bar Isaac: If one disgraces his fellow in public,
it is as though he sheds blood (Aknin).

ANNULS THE COVENANT OF ABRAHAM OUR FATHER: Annuls
the covenant in the flesh (ARN), that is, refuses to fulfill the
commandment of circumcision (Vitry).

"Annuls the covenant" is a reference to him who tries to
remove all signs of his circumcision [so that he may appear
like the uncircumcised] (Maimonides).

CONTEMPTUOUS TOWARDS THE TORAH: That is, seeks to
ascribe disgraceful or improper meanings to the contents of
the Torah (Vitry).

One who "is contemptuous towards the Torah" is a person
who transgresses the commandments of the Torah in public,
and "contemptuous towards the Torah" is the idiom of the
Sages to describe such behavior (Maimonides).

A person who despises the Torah or despises those who
devote themselves to it, that is to say, the scholars—if he is
guilty of either of these—is called "contemptuous towards the
Torah" (Aknin).

The transgressions spoken of in our Mishna are not such
as a man is led to by an overpowering evil impulse—for
example, like eating forbidden foods or committing some un-

chaste act. . . . The transgressions spoken of arise from a tendency towards heresy. Being contemptuous towards the Torah is of this character too. That is to say, the individual pretends to know the secret meanings of the Torah; he then puts them forth although they are not in accordance with the halakah. For example, he rejects completely the manifest meaning of a commandment, and insists that this was not the Lord's intention but that the words are only a metaphor for something else, and the plain meaning is not to be taken seriously at all. Now, this is rooted in heresy; for although there is in some of the commandments a hidden intent, it is beyond any doubt that the essence of every commandment is in its manifest terms. This requires some explanation. A person of false belief will say, "It was not the intention of the Torah that a man should not eat swine's flesh. When the Torah forbids swine's flesh that is only a figure of speech for the injunction that our behavior should not be shameful and foul." Now, if anyone in our nation does say something like this, he is called a heretic and he has no share in the world to come. If he wishes, he may say, "Swine's flesh has unquestionably been forbidden and the reason for the prohibition is that everything that is like a swine is hateful in His eyes." Or he may offer some other reason—even though it is not proper to put forth reasons, especially since the reasons are not known, except as views of different sages, one suggesting one reason and another suggesting another. It is even possible that an individual may fall into error, thinking he knows the true reason. A scholar may think he knows the reason and may even feel he can depend on his own thinking . . . but even in a case like this, it is not proper to broadcast his views. One might be misled by "leaning on his own understanding," and say, "I will fulfill the intent without carrying out the commandments" . . . (Meiri).

HAS NO SHARE IN THE WORLD TO COME: That is, if he has not repented (Maimonides).

———

RABBI ISHMAEL SAYS: BE SUPPLIANT TO A SUPERIOR, SUBMISSIVE UNDER COMPULSORY SERVICE (*Tishhoret*), AND RECEIVE EVERY MAN HAPPILY.

BE SUPPLIANT TO A SUPERIOR: Be supple as the reed which bends this way and that, and alert—the way a commoner is when about to greet the chief of a city and its officers (Vitry).

When you stand in the presence of a person of superior station, consider yourself his inferior—serve him, be at his beck and call, and consider yourself of no great value before him (Maimonides).

SUBMISSIVE UNDER *Tishhoret*: Be submissive in the presence of a chief of a city, follow his orders and his counsel—do not quarrel with him, nor resist him. . . . And so the saying goes: "There's something about the royal servant too," "Cleave to an officer and you too will be saluted." The word *tishhoret* refers to the royal official who imposes the corvée on people (Vitry).

When you are with a person the color of whose hair is still black, that is to say, with a young person, . . . do think of your own importance, do not act frivolously or overfamiliarly with him (Maimonides, who understands the second clause of Rabbi Ishmael's statement as, Be staid in the presence of the young, *tishhoret,* the black-haired).

In all matters, when in the presence of the powerful, one should be submissive and not vaunt himself in give and take with them. The ethical philosophers also declare: "It's risky lording it over lords" (Meiri).

AND RECEIVE EVERY MAN HAPPILY: Do not think that when I warned you against familiarity with the young, you must therefore receive them with sullen and scowling countenance. On the contrary, you must receive every man—small and great, free man and slave, every sort of person—happily and in good cheer. And this is even stronger than Shammai's statement, "Receive every man with a cheerful countenance" (Maimonides).

Receive happily all who come to you, as Shammai said, "Receive every man with a cheerful countenance" (Meiri).

RABBI AKIBA SAYS:

    MERRIMENT AND FRIVOLITY ACCUSTOM ONE TO UNCHASTITY.

    TRADITION IS A HEDGE ABOUT THE TORAH.

    TITHES ARE A HEDGE ABOUT RICHES.

    VOWS ARE A HEDGE ABOUT ABSTINENCE.

    A HEDGE ABOUT WISDOM—SILENCE.

MERRIMENT AND FRIVOLITY: When a man is after frivolity

and merriment in the company of a woman, he will in the end seduce her to harlotry (Vitry).

Merriment and idle conversation along with frivolity accustom one to unchastity; but seriousness and fear of God are a hedge to unchastity (Rabbi Jonah).

One who keeps in mind that the Shekinah hovers over him, will conduct himself with seriousness (Duran).

TRADITION IS A HEDGE ABOUT THE TORAH: This is a reference to those masoretic comments which are added to the margins of Biblical books, and these are known as the Great Masorah. He who knows these notes well will know the correct interpretation of most of Scripture and will avoid error and confusion (Vitry).

Rabbi Isaac ben Reuben, of blessed memory, explained "tradition" as a reference to the mnemonic signs which a person devises for his study. These preserve his learning, so that it is not forgotten. But we think the word "tradition" may be derived from the verb meaning "to bind together" . . . that is, gathering and assembling. And the meaning is to organize subject matter properly, logically arrange it, and then classify all of one's learning under general principles so that the subject may be easy to learn and then not be forgotten (Aknin).

This refers to the traditions of textual readings and punctuation of the Scripture which the Sages have handed on to their disciples, and these traditions are a hedge about the written Torah. For you will not find variant readings in copies of Biblical books except in very few places. This is utterly unlike the situation with regard to copies of the Talmud, for in many passages there are variant readings (Rabbi Jonah).

Some interpret the word "tradition" as a reference to the Oral Torah . . . that is, it serves as a hedge to the Written Torah (Nahmias).

TITHES ARE A HEDGE ABOUT RICHES: If one wishes to grow rich, let him give tithes liberally. . . . And charity is like tithes, so that if one increases his charitable gifts, he will increase his wealth (Rabbi Jonah).

There was once a certain man who made his living from a field that produced a thousand measures. Of these he used to give one hundred measures as tithe. Before his death he instructed his son to continue such practice. But the son ignored these instructions. As a result, every single year that field kept producing less and less, until it produced no more than one tenth of what it had been accustomed to yield. Said the man's relations to him, "Until now you were the owner and the Holy One, blessed be He, was the priest. Now the Holy One, blessed be He, is the owner and you are the priest. You receive only one tenth" (Duran).

VOWS ARE A HEDGE ABOUT ABSTINENCE: When a man makes vows and keeps them, he succeeds in developing the ability of self-restraint; this habit grows stronger and stronger in him so that it becomes ever easier for him to abstain, that is to say, to keep from things that defile (Maimonides).

One should hedge himself about only when his evil impulse is too strong for him. Then he might make vows as a kind of healing measure. But he who is in control of himself and is capable of abstinence without vowing, ought not to make vows (Rabbi Jonah).

A HEDGE ABOUT WISDOM—SILENCE: The Sages have said (Pesahim 99a): If silence becomes the wise, how much more so the foolish (Vitry).

A person should not speak in the presence of someone greater than himself in wisdom. For example, when a person studies in the presence of his master, and a certain interpretation strikes him as the correct one, let him not immediately think that this must be the true interpretation. He should not blurt it out before his teacher has finished speaking. For if he acts [impatiently] he will miss what his teacher is saying, and not learn the views of the ancient Sages—for his attention will be distracted and he will not learn what these ancient views are. Moreover, even one's own views cannot be clear until he has first heard what the ancients have said and then weighed in his own mind which view is the more correct. That is why silence on the part of a student in the presence of his teacher, or of anybody greater than he in wisdom, is a hedge (Rabbi Jonah).

"The beginning of wisdom is silence" for there is nothing as useful as silence for a person who has to study; thus he will listen and give ear to the words of the Sage and carve them on the tables of his heart. Such conduct will bring a person to wisdom (Meiri).

In one of the fables it is told of someone who saw a person talking more than listening. So he said to that person, "Note the difference between your ears and your mouth. For the

Holy One, blessed be He, created for you two ears and one mouth, so that you might listen twice as much as speak" (Nahmias).

———

HE USED TO SAY: BELOVED IS MAN FOR HE WAS CREATED IN THE IMAGE. EXTRAORDINARY IS THE LOVE MADE KNOWN TO HIM THAT HE WAS CREATED IN THE IMAGE, AS IT IS SAID, *For in the image of God made He man* (Genesis 9:6).

BELOVED ARE ISRAEL FOR THEY WERE CALLED CHILDREN OF GOD. EXTRAORDINARY IS THE LOVE MADE KNOWN TO THEM THAT THEY WERE CALLED CHILDREN OF GOD, AS IT IS SAID, *Ye are the children of the Lord, your God* (Deuteronomy 14:1).

BELOVED ARE ISRAEL FOR TO THEM WAS GIVEN A PRECIOUS IMPLEMENT. EXTRAORDINARY IS THE LOVE MADE KNOWN TO THEM THAT THEY WERE GIVEN THE PRECIOUS IMPLEMENT WITH WHICH THE WORLD WAS CREATED, AS IT IS SAID, *For I give you good doctrine, forsake ye not My Torah* (Proverbs 4:2).

THE IMAGE: God made men in His very own image (Vitry).

Rabbi Isaac ben Reuben said that this statement comes to teach that one dare not treat the human face disrespectfully (Aknin).

By "image," no physical likeness is intended. The term image refers to the intelligence and understanding. . . . And it is by this image that man is distinguished from the beasts and the fowl (Nahmias).

EXTRAORDINARY IS THE LOVE: The fact that God created man in His own image is a sign of the extraordinary love He bore him (Vitry).

By making known to man that He loves him, God exhibits His additional love to man. There are times when a person does someone a favor merely out of pity, and does not even bother to let him know what favor he did him because he regards the beneficiary as beneath him. [But God so loves man as to tell him of His love.] (Maimonides, who takes the statement of the Mishna as, "Extraordinary is the love in that it was made known to him that he was created in the image.")

I found in a French prayer book a nice version of our Mishna, to wit: "Beloved is man for he was created in the image. Extraordinary love is made known to him in that he was created in the image of God. . . . Beloved are Israel for they were called children. Extraordinary love is made known to them in that they were called children of God. . . . Beloved are Israel for to them was given a precious implement. Extraordinary love is made known to them in that they were given a precious implement with which the world was created. . . ." Now according to this version the extraordinary love is illustrated by the phrases "image of God," "children of God," and precious implement "with which the world was created" (Duran).

PRECIOUS IMPLEMENT WITH WHICH THE WORLD WAS CREATED: It is written, *With the beginning God created the heaven and the earth* (Genesis 1:1), and the word "beginning" refers only to the Torah, as it is said, *The Lord acquired me as the beginning of His way* (Proverbs 8:22). It says also, *Then I was by Him as the instrument of His craft* (Proverbs 8:30): Says the Torah, "I was the instrument made use of by the Holy One at the very beginning"—for God studied it and created the universe accordingly (Vitry).

Everything that was created, was created only for the purpose of fulfilling the Torah. All the things under the heavens, all of them, are only the means of satisfying the needs of those who devote themselves to the Torah (Rabbi Jonah).

The Torah is not like all other possessions. With these, when a person makes an exchange with his fellow, he no longer owns what he had, and what he did not have he now owns. With the Torah it is not so. If one knows one treatise and his fellow knows another treatise, and each teaches the other what he knows, then each becomes the possessor of two treatises (Duran).

———

EVERYTHING IS FORESEEN, YET FREEDOM OF CHOICE IS GRANTED; IN MERCY IS THE WORLD JUDGED; AND EVERYTHING IS ACCORDING TO THE PREPONDERANCE OF WORKS.

EVERYTHING IS FORESEEN: Everything is foreseen and everything is revealed, yet everything happens according to man's will (ARN).

The Holy One sees in advance all the works of men, as it is said, *The eyes of the Lord . . . run to and fro through the whole earth* (Zechariah 4:10). And when a man sets out to do something improper, He sees and knows of it but does not prevent it, for freedom of choice is granted to each man. If he wishes he may sin; if he wishes he may refrain from sinning; as it is written, *See, I have set before thee this day life and good, and death and evil* (Deuteronomy 30:15), and it is written, *Therefore choose life* (Deuteronomy 30:19). It would have been impossible to tell a person, "Choose," if he had no freedom of choice.

There are some who read [instead of "Everything is foreseen"] "Everything is stored away," all human actions are stored with the Holy One, as it is said, *Is this not laid up in store with Me, sealed up in My treasuries* (Deuteronomy 32:34) (Vitry).

Do not think that because God knows what will happen things are predetermined and therefore a man is predestined to act as he does. It is not so. Man has the freedom to choose what he wants to do (Maimonides).

Whatever is in the heavens or on the earth God knows, and nothing is hidden from His sight, and He knows the secrets of the heart, as it is written, *The secret things belong unto the Lord our God* (Deuteronomy 29:28) (Aknin).

IN MERCY IS THE WORLD JUDGED: The Lord's judgment of men is indeed a merciful one, it is not what strict justice requires. And so we are told of God's ways, *Long-suffering, and abundant in goodness and truth* (Exodus 34:6); and our Sages, of blessed memory, said (Erubin 22a), He is long-suffering toward the righteous and the wicked (Maimonides).

Even the wicked are judged by Him mercifully, as it is said, *The Lord is good to all* (Psalms 145:9), and the wicked are part of the "handiwork" of the Holy One, blessed be He (Rabbi Jonah).

The Lord created the evil impulse, but He created Torah and repentance as its remedy. And the world is judged in mercy in that the sinner's repentance is found acceptable; and this is a merciful act of the Lord toward His creatures (Meiri).

The Holy One, blessed be He, judges the world with His attribute of mercy; and when a person is neither thoroughly righteous nor thoroughly wicked, the Holy One, blessed be He, judges him with His attribute of mercy as a righteous man. And this is what is meant by the verse *abundant in goodness* (Exodus 34:6) (Duran).

AND EVERYTHING IS ACCORDING TO THE PREPONDERANCE OF WORKS: The good qualities a man acquires are not the product of a single great act, but of the recurrence of many good works—only this way is virtue firmly acquired. For example, a charitable nature is not acquired when a person gives one needy individual a thousand gold pieces on one occasion . . . whereas a person who gives away a thousand gold pieces on a thousand occasions does acquire a charitable nature. . . . Being charitable once represents no more than that the individual has been suddenly stirred to carry out one good act; thereafter it may leave him (Maimonides).

Even though the world is judged in accordance with God's mercy, not everyone enjoys the same measure of it. For him who does much good there is great mercy, for him who does little good there is little mercy (Rabbi Jonah).

Man is judged according to the preponderance of his works: if most of these are righteous, he is meritorious; if they are sinful, he is wicked ("Rashi").

We may interpret our Mishna as follows: Even though "everything is foreseen, freedom of choice is granted." And although we cannot understand this great mystery, for "everything is foreseen" and "freedom of choice is granted" seems like a contradiction in terms, nevertheless do not question this matter—for "in mercy is the world judged," the judgment of the Holy One, blessed be He, is a merciful judgment, whether he punishes or rewards. "And everything is according to the magnitude of the work," that is to say, according to the greatness of the Creator's work—we are unable to grasp this mystery, as it is written, *For My thoughts are not your thoughts, neither are your ways My ways* (Isaiah 55:8) (Nahmias).

The Holy One sustains the world in accordance with the dictates of His mercy, and not in accordance with the human actions which predominate; that is, although there are both sinners and righteous in the world, the world is judged in accordance with God's mercy: He does not follow a course dictated by the preponderance of wicked works in the world to destroy it (Vitry, who reads the last two clauses of the Mishna as "In mercy is the world judged, not according to the preponderance of works").

HE USED TO SAY: EVERYTHING IS GIVEN AGAINST A PLEDGE
AND A NET IS CAST OVER ALL THE LIVING: THE SHOP IS
OPEN, THE SHOPKEEPER EXTENDS CREDIT, THE LEDGER LIES
OPEN, THE HAND WRITES, AND WHOEVER WISHES TO BORROW
MAY COME AND BORROW; AND THE COLLECTORS MAKE THE
ROUNDS CONTINUALLY, EVERY DAY, AND EXACT PAYMENT
OF MAN WITH HIS CONSENT OR WITHOUT IT. THEY HAVE
WHAT TO BASE THEIR CLAIMS ON. AND THE JUDGMENT
IS A JUDGMENT OF TRUTH. AND EVERYTHING IS PREPARED
FOR THE FEAST.

EVERYTHING IS GIVEN AGAINST A PLEDGE: Whatever credit
the Holy One extends to man is given against a pledge; from
the moment of man's birth God begins to extend credit to
him. And the soul of man serves as surety for all the limbs
of his body. When they behave righteously, his soul is regarded
as righteous too; when they are unrighteous, it is punished
along with them (Vitry).

A man is held responsible for everything he receives in
this world, and his children are responsible too. Let not a
person who inherits from his father and mother think, "This
wealth is my inheritance, I can do with it what I please." The
fact is, nothing belongs to him, everything is the Lord's and
whatever he received, he received only on credit, and the Lord
will exact payment for it. This may be compared to a person
who entered a city and found no one there. He walked into a
house and there found a table set with all kinds of food and
drink. So he began to eat and drink, thinking, "I deserve
all this, all of it is mine, I shall do with it what I please."
He didn't even notice that the owners were watching him
from the side! He will yet have to pay for everything he ate
and drank, for he is in a spot from which he will not be able
to escape (Rabbi Jonah).

The Lord will collect from every man what he owes Him,
that is to say, He will punish everyone for his sins (Meiri).

All man's actions are carried out against a pledge. And
who acts as surety? His body and his soul, his wife and the
members of his family (Nahmias).

A NET IS CAST OVER ALL THE LIVING: That is to say, the net
of the angel of death, for no man can escape the day of death
and Day of Judgment (Vitry).

Some men are caught by the net, that is to say, they are
trapped by the bait that is put in the net. These are the fools

who have been trapped by the vanities of the world. . . . But the wise, the men of intelligence, know that the bait inside the net was not put in purposelessly, but to deceive human beings; so they circumvent the net and never fall in it (Aknin).

THE SHOP IS OPEN: That is to say, the ways of good and evil are opened up to a man . . . , for a man's legs will lead him to the course he wishes to walk in. And he is allowed to sin. But subsequently he is taken to account—the way it is when a shopkeeper allows folk to take things on credit, and extends it, but finally demands what is coming to him. That is why the Mishna says: "The shopkeeper extends credit," that is, the evil impulse gives one leeway, a little now, and then a little more, until the individual has satisfied his desires. But when a man has satisfied his desires, the evil impulse begins to tax him and then all kinds of tribulation overtake him (Vitry).

The world has been compared to a shop because, as in a shop, many things are found in it of different nature—some are bitter, some are sweet; some are hot, some are cold; some are moist, some are dry; some are hard, some are soft; and the choice is left to the purchaser to buy what he wishes, either the bitter or the sweet. Such a shop is the world and man is the purchaser, and it is in his power to do either evil or good, either little or much. In saying that "The shopkeeper extends credit" the Mishna is figuratively expressing that the Lord, blessed be He, does not punish the sinner immediately, but is long-suffering (Meiri).

THE LEDGER LIES OPEN: It is said, *And behold the angels of God ascending and descending on it* (Genesis 28:12). This teaches that two angels accompany a man by day and two angels accompany him by night. Those who accompany him by day write down what he did during the day; those who accompany him by night write down what he did at night. Then they all come and testify before the Holy One (Vitry).

There is no forgetfulness before the Lord, blessed be He, and all the actions of men are written down and sealed in the ledger, the way it is when a shopkeeper writes down whatever the purchasers have taken from his shop (Aknin).

The expression "the ledger lies open," is used for two reasons: first, as a figure of speech, to suggest that there is no forgetfulness before the throne of His glory. . . . That is to say, big things and little ones, all of them, are, as it were, written down before Him and He does not forget even the earliest iniquities. The second reason is this: to teach us that there is no interval between the committing of a sin and the opening of the ledger. Rather when the sinful act has been committed it is already written down, so that not a moment is lost during which a person's sin is not charged against him. For although sins are forgiven to those who repent, the sins are first taken into account as soon as they have been committed; only afterwards, if a person repents, is he forgiven (Rabbi Jonah).

THE COLLECTORS MAKE THE ROUNDS: The collectors are the angels of death who are sent in God's wrath to exact payment for the transgressions which man in his freedom committed, and from which he did not repent, although they waited for his repentance (Vitry).

"The collectors" is a figure of speech for death and other sufferings that are visited upon man (Maimonides).

EVERYTHING IS READY FOR THE FEAST: What amounts a shopkeeper cannot collect from those who are in debt to him, he leaves in their possession for a while. These funds he earmarks for some feast which on some future day he will hold. . . . So the Holy One sends His messengers to search out the ways of men and to collect what they owe Him, whether they consent to it or not. . . . Those sins for which He has not punished them as yet are set aside for an accounting on some future day to which they have to come, namely, the Day of Judgment. Rabbi Meshullam bar Kalonymos of Rome interpreted the word "feast" as "the day of death," as we read later in our treatise, "The end of man is death." And why is death called a feast? To teach that when men are invited to a feast they all enter through one doorway, but when they sit down they do not sit down pell-mell but each one according to his station and dignity. So too departing from the world is the fate of every man, of the righteous and the wicked, but only in accordance with his worth does each one receive what is coming to him for his works (Vitry).

The end purpose of everything our Mishna has described is the life of the world to come (Maimonides).

All men are destined for reward in the world to come and for the enjoyment at a feast of the fruits of their good works. Now there are some who are not admitted to that feast, because of the corruption of their works and the perversion of their ways—such are driven away from that feast. . . . It is also possible to interpret "Everything is prepared for the feast" as follows: Both the righteous and the wicked receive a reward commensurate with their works; some receive what they deserve in accordance with their evil works, and in regard to such punishment it is said, *Woe unto the wicked! It shall be ill with him; for the work of his hands shall be done to him* (Isaiah 3:11). The expression "feast" is used principally because of the reference to the righteous, as the verse puts it, *Say ye of the righteous, that it shall be well with them; for they shall eat the fruit of their doings* (Isaiah 3:10) (Aknin).

Just as a man finds prepared for his feast only such things as he took the trouble to buy and bring home—meat and cheese or any kind of food—so shall souls find a feast prepared for them in the world to come, made up of what they have "purchased" in this world. For some it will be bitter, for some, sweet (Meiri).

———

RABBI ELEAZAR BEN AZARIAH SAYS: WHERE THERE IS NO TORAH, THERE'S NO RIGHT CONDUCT, WHERE THERE IS NO RIGHT CONDUCT, THERE'S NO TORAH; WHERE THERE IS NO WISDOM, THERE'S NO PIETY, WHERE THERE IS NO PIETY, THERE'S NO WISDOM; WHERE THERE IS NO PERCEPTION, THERE'S NO KNOWLEDGE, WHERE THERE IS NO KNOWLEDGE, THERE'S NO PERCEPTION; WHERE THERE IS NO BREAD, THERE'S NO TORAH, WHERE THERE IS NO TORAH, THERE'S NO BREAD.

WHERE THERE IS NO TORAH: No man can have real knowledge of *savoir-faire* unless he has studied Torah, for it is in the Torah that one finds all kinds of wisdom and counsel, and a knowledge of how to behave. . . . If a man has not cultivated right behavior, his knowledge of Torah will be useless to him and will not survive. . . . When a man does not fear sin he does not refrain from transgressing, and since he does not refrain from transgressing he is not wise. . . . When a man is not profound in his learning he cannot properly understand or discover the meaning of fear of Heaven (Vitry).

A person who does not know any Torah—does not know how to cleave to the commandments and to avoid transgression—will fail in social intercourse. And without social intercourse the Torah he did study will be useless, he will be like one who has not studied, because he has not acted in accordance with the teachings of study, to enter into relationships with human beings uprightly and properly. For learning and proper conduct are interdependent, the one on the other. . . . If a person has not studied philosophy and thereby acquired, to the best of his capacity, an understanding of the Creator, there can be no adequate piety in him—because he does not understand the nature of God, to which testify the might of His creative powers and the greatness of His deeds and the perfect wisdom with which everything was created; as it is written, *How manifold are Thy works, O Lord! In wisdom hast Thou made them all* (Psalm 104:24). Job says too, *Out of my flesh shall I see God* (Job 19:26): that is, I have come to understand the nature of God from the wisdom that went into the forming of the limbs of my body and the power of my soul. Now then, if one can perceive the nature of God from a microcosm, how much the more from a knowledge of all things created, the heavens and the earth and what is between them. . . . And when one perceives the genuine greatness of these things, he begins to understand the nature of Him who created them and then fears to sin before Him. So too a person without a sense of fear in the presence of his Creator can have no wisdom. . . . When a slave rebels against a mighty master, is he not a fool and senseless? . . . How much the more the rebel against the King of kings of kings, the Holy One, blessed be He (Aknin).

One who does not know the Torah cannot be perfect in his ethical conduct because most of the highest ethical principles are to be found in the Torah—such as, *If there be among you a needy man . . . thou shalt surely open thy hand unto him, and shalt surely lend him sufficient for his need in that which he wanteth* (Deuteronomy 15:7 f.), or, *If thy brother . . . be sold unto thee . . . when thou lettest him go free from thee, thou shalt not let him go empty; thou shalt furnish him liberally out of thy flock, etc.* (Deuteronomy 15:12 ff.), or, *Just balances, just weights . . . shall ye have* (Leviticus 19:36), and many similar commandments. . . . But first a man must perfect his conduct; then the Torah will stay with him. For the Torah does not stay with a person whose conduct is not good. It is impossible first to study Torah and then to adopt the commandments. . . . Now, without learning there can be no perfect piety, for learning strengthens piety and illuminates the way for it. But the piety must come before the learning, otherwise in the end the learning will not endure. For when a man's conduct is not proper and he does not fear the Holy One, he will come to despise his studies and abandon them (Rabbi Jonah).

Were it not for the commandments of the Torah . . . no man could achieve perfect ethical behavior in his worldly conduct, even if by nature he was ideally suited for it; for no man can achieve ideal ethical conduct as effectively as the one who holds on to the ways of the Torah. And so too, if a person has no natural inclination toward ethical conduct, the commandments of the Torah will not be sufficient to bring him to such perfection. For the commandments put a man in the right path only in a general way, they are unable to provide for subtle and new problems which constantly require the guidance of morality and ethics (Meiri).

WHERE THERE IS NO PERCEPTION: What a person learns from his master is called knowledge; what he perceives with his own mind is called perception. . . . [Now then] if one is ignorant of the tradition, he can have no perception, he can have no insight into the words of the Torah—for without a tradition, how is he to have insight. . . . And if he has no capacity for insight and for reasoning on his own, and for adding to what he has received from the tradition, he can have no knowledge. That is to say, of what use to him is everything he learned? He will not be able to sustain it if he does not add to what he has received (Vitry).

The knowledge spoken of here refers to the capacity implanted in man at birth to acquire knowledge. . . . Perception is what comes to a man as a result of his strivings at study and research (Meiri).

WHERE THERE IS NO BREAD: If a man does not have what to eat he cannot study Torah, since he is haunted by insecurity. . . . That is why a man ought to engage in some occupation or trade along with his study. And "where there is no Torah, there's no bread": It is written, *Length of days is in her right hand; in her left hand are riches and honor* (Proverbs 3:16). From this positive statement [about the rewards of Torah] you can deduce the negative too [to wit, where there is no Torah, there will be no riches and honor] (Vitry).

When a man is Torah-less his food is useless too—for the only purpose of riches is to provide for a man's needs so that he may have the leisure to study Torah (Rabbi Jonah).

There are some who interpret this statement as follows: If there were no one paying attention to worldly chores—to plow and to sow, to harvest, to thresh, to winnow, to sift, to grind, to knead and to bake—and everyone was engaged in the study of Torah, the world would perish and the Torah would perish along with it. . . . And if all men were taken up with the chores of the world and no one engaged in the study of Torah, the world would not be able to survive (Nahmias).

HE USED TO SAY: HE WHOSE WISDOM EXCEEDS HIS WORKS, TO WHAT MAY HE BE LIKENED? TO A TREE WHOSE BRANCHES ARE NUMEROUS BUT WHOSE ROOTS ARE FEW. THE WIND COMES ALONG AND UPROOTS IT AND SWEEPS IT DOWN, AS IT IS SAID, *For he shall be like a tamarisk in the desert, and shall not see when good cometh; but shall inhabit the parched places in the wilderness, a salt land and not inhabited* (Jeremiah 17:6). BUT HE WHOSE WORKS EXCEED HIS WISDOM, TO WHAT MAY HE BE LIKENED? TO A TREE WHOSE BRANCHES ARE FEW BUT WHOSE ROOTS ARE NUMEROUS. THEN EVEN IF ALL THE WINDS OF THE WORLD COME ALONG AND BLOW AGAINST IT THEY CANNOT STIR IT FROM ITS PLACE, AS IT IS SAID, *For he shall be as a tree planted by the waters, and that spreadeth out its roots by the river, and shall not see when heat cometh, but its foliage shall be luxuriant; and shall not be anxious in the year of drought, neither shall cease from yielding fruit* (Jeremiah 17:8).

HE WHOSE WISDOM EXCEEDS HIS WORKS: That is, he does not carry out what he learned. . . . Works are compared to roots because they are the principal thing. . . . Wisdom is like the branches of a tree (Vitry).

HE WHOSE WORKS EXCEED HIS WISDOM: Elisha ben Abuyah says: One in whom there are good works, who has studied much Torah, to what may he be likened? To a person who builds first with stones and afterwards with bricks: even when much water comes and collects by their side, it does not dislodge them. But one in whom there are no good works, though he studied Torah, to what may he be likened? To a person who builds first with bricks and afterwards with stones: even when a little water gathers, it overthrows them immediately.

He used to say: One in whom there are good works who has studied much Torah, to what may he be likened? To lime poured over stones: even when any number of rains fall on it, they cannot push it out of place. One in whom there are no good works, though he studied much Torah, is like lime poured over bricks: even when a little rain falls on it, it softens immediately and is washed away.

He used to say: One in whom there are good works who has studied much Torah, to what may he be likened? To a cup that has a base. But one in whom there are no good works, though he studied much Torah, to what may he be likened? To a cup that has no base: as soon as the cup is filled it overturns, and whatever was in it spills.

He used to say: One in whom there are good works who has studied much Torah, to what may he be likened? To a horse that has a bridle. But one in whom there are no good works, though he has studied much Torah, to what may he be likened? To a horse that has no bridle: when one mounts it, it throws him off headlong (ARN).

When a man is one of those who fear the Lord, no strategy will prevail against him; even if arguments are flung against him which he cannot refute, he will not succumb (Meiri).

———

RABBI ELEAZAR [BEN] HISMA SAYS: THE LAWS OF MIXED BIRD OFFERINGS AND THE KEY TO THE CALCULATIONS OF MENSTRUATION DAYS—THESE, THESE ARE THE BODY OF THE HALAKAH. EQUINOXES AND GEMATRIA ARE THE DESSERTS OF WISDOM.

THE BODY OF THE HALAKAH: That is, the core of these is the Oral Law given to Moses at Sinai (Vitry).

EQUINOXES AND GEMATRIA: In these matters complicated calculation is involved; and mathematical knowledge sharpens a man's mind (Rabbi Jonah).

Rabbi Eleazar ben Hisma wants to guide a man in his study—as did a number of sages who drew up study curricula, suggesting that one begin with a certain discipline and a certain book and then proceed systematically. Here briefly it is suggested that it is not advisable to begin with the study of science and metaphysics before one has a bellyful of meat and wine, that is to say, a knowledge of the Torah and the Talmud. . . . Only after a person has mastered the whole Talmud, from beginning to end . . . , only then let him begin with the other disciplines. Now the first studies one ought to undertake in these other disciplines have to do with the calculations of equinoxes and planets and gematria, that is, with mathematics. From this one should go on to a study of science and metaphysics (Meiri).

Chapter IV

BEN ZOMA SAYS: WHO IS A WISE MAN? HE THAT LEARNS FROM ALL MEN, AS IT IS SAID, *From all my teachers have I got understanding* (Psalm 119:99).

WHO IS A MIGHTY MAN? HE THAT SUBDUES HIS EVIL IMPULSE, AS IT IS SAID, *He that is slow to anger is better than the mighty, and he that ruleth his spirit than him that taketh a city* (Proverbs 16:32).

WHO IS A RICH MAN? HE THAT IS CONTENT WITH HIS PORTION, AS IT IS SAID, *When thou eatest the labor of thy hands happy shalt thou be and it shall be well with thee* (Psalm 128:2): *Happy shalt thou be* IN THIS WORLD, *and it shall be well with thee* IN THE WORLD TO COME.

WHO IS AN HONORABLE MAN? HE THAT HONORS MANKIND, AS IT IS SAID, *For them that honor me I will honor and they that despise me shall be lightly esteemed* (I Samuel 2:30).

A WISE MAN: It is he who is ready to learn even from his inferiors. With such readiness, if his inferior should present him with a wise view, he will not be ashamed to accept it and will not treat his words with contempt. This was characteristic of David, King of Israel, who said, ". . . I would pay attention to any man who came to teach me something" (Vitry).

The Gentile philosophers say that even if a person were to know everything [as it were], if he does not want to increase his knowledge, he is not a wise man but a fool. . . . On the other hand, one who passionately loves to increase his wisdom, may be called a wise man even if he were to know nothing. Only this way can you attain true wisdom and discover the will of God. It is to this Ben Zoma is referring when he says that the wise man is he who learns from all

153

men, that is to say, so passionately loves learning that he is ready to ask anyone when he has a question, even individuals with limited knowledge. . . . This may be compared to a man who lost a small object. Will he not hunt for it everywhere? (Rabbi Jonah).

A MIGHTY MAN: To him who subdues his evil impulse it is accounted as though he had conquered a city full of mighty men, as it is said, *A wise man scaleth the city of the mighty, and bringeth down the stronghold wherein it trusteth* (Proverbs 21:22). And the mighty are none other than the strong in Torah, as it is said, *Ye mighty in strength, that fulfil His word, hearkening unto the voice of His word* (Psalm 103:20). . . . And some say, mighty is he who makes of his enemy a friend (ARN).

The ethical philosophers say that there are three kinds of monarchs. There is a monarch over a kingdom, there is a monarch over a household, and a monarch over the body. Now then . . . a king has to govern the citizens of his kingdom with justice, punish the evildoers and strengthen the work of good men. The same applies to the master of a household in relation to the members of his house. Similarly, as regards a man's relationship to himself, he must subdue those impulses which seduce him to evil or anger or excesses and must strengthen the good impulse, and translate his intention into action (Meiri).

As to physical strength, let no man glory in it, for in this regard he is not superior to the beasts. If it is a matter of bearing heavy burdens, the ass bears more than he does; if it is a matter of might for battle, the lion is stronger than he. Indeed, sometimes a man's bodily prowess leads him to rebel against his Creator and drives him out of the world, either because he becomes guilty of oppressing others, or because of robbery, or violence, or unchastity. The man who may indeed glory in his strength, even though he is without bodily prowess to speak of, is the one who subdues his evil impulse. For the evil impulse is the enemy; and just as one's enemy destroys a man in this world, so the evil impulse ruins him for life in the world to come (Duran).

A RICH MAN: A rich man who is malcontent has no enjoyment or pleasure in his wealth. All the more so a poor man who protests against the measure meted out to him by the Holy One: he has good neither in this world nor in the world to come—none in this world, because he is poor; none in the world to come, because he is unable to receive the reward for having suffered poverty, for having borne poverty patiently. For this affliction might have served as an atonement for his iniquities, and he should have accepted his lot lovingly instead of protesting against the judgment of the Holy One (Vitry).

A hedge about wealth is contentment and avoidance of excess. He who has what is sufficient for him and does not seek superfluous things is the truly rich man, even if what he has is the result of the labor of his hands; and a person who delights in the toil of his own hands will surely attain prosperity. . . . A person who has enough for his daily needs and does not seek superfluous things, will devote his free time to service of the Lord and thus merit this world and the world to come (Meiri).

AN HONORABLE MAN: If a person honors his fellow man he is really honoring himself, not his fellow man. For when somebody is honored, if he is indeed an honorable person, the honor that is extended to him does not add to his personal merit; and if he is an unworthy person, even if he is honored by others, they cannot make him honorable. . . . Thus whenever a person honors other people he is really honoring himself because by his conduct inevitably he leads others to honor him (Rabbi Jonah).

There are some who say that because man was created in the image of God, one who honors all human beings is in effect honoring the Lord, whom we are obliged to honor (Nahmias).

———

BEN AZZAI SAYS: BE QUICK IN CARRYING OUT A MINOR COMMANDMENT AS IN THE CASE OF A MAJOR ONE, AND FLEE FROM TRANSGRESSION: FOR ONE GOOD DEED LEADS TO ANOTHER GOOD DEED AND ONE TRANSGRESSION LEADS TO ANOTHER TRANSGRESSION; FOR THE REWARD FOR A GOOD DEED IS ANOTHER GOOD DEED AND THE REWARD FOR A TRANSGRESSION IS ANOTHER TRANSGRESSION.

If thou hast carried out one commandment and dost not regret having done so, in the end it will lead to many commandments [to be carried out]; if one commits one transgression and does not regret having transgressed, in the end it leads to many transgressions (ARN).

Recoil from a light sin, so that you may recoil from a grievous sin. Hasten to overtake a good act so that calamity should not overtake you. If transgression has come your way, then do not be distressed by that transgression, but by the one coming after it. If a good deed has come your way, then do not rejoice at that good deed, but at the one coming after it (ARNB).

A MINOR COMMANDMENT: That is to say, even a commandment that seems insignificant in your sight—hasten to carry it out (Vitry).

ONE GOOD DEED LEADS TO ANOTHER GOOD DEED: It is a natural thing for a person who carries out one small commandment to find it easier afterward to carry out another, which in comparison with the first may be even more difficult—because by nature he has already grown accustomed to carrying out commandments. And if he carries out the commandments twice and three times . . . habit will govern him and he will carry out the commandments. . . . And if a person has committed one transgression and withdrawn from the service of the Lord, blessed be He, then he will commit another transgression when it comes his way, even if his evil impulse does not particularly desire it—because he has become victim to the evil impulse; though he may not desire very much to commit that sin, he will go on transgressing because his nature has grown accustomed to committing every abomination which the Lord hates (Rabbi Jonah).

THE REWARD FOR A GOOD DEED: If you carry out a minor commandment you will be rewarded by the opportunity to carry out an even greater commandment, and then you will receive a rich reward for all the commandments you carried out (Vitry).

The reward for carrying out commandments and the punishment for committing transgressions take place not in this world but in the world to come. . . . If we eagerly carry out the commandments, the Holy One, blessed be He, rewards us with prosperity. . . . And along with this reward comes the pleasure of engaging in the fulfillment of still other commandments, and then we receive rich reward in the world to come. Thus the reward for carrying out the first commandment brings leisure from worldly preoccupations, and the opportunity to carry out other commandments, which win for a person the life of the world to come. But if we commit transgressions and pursue worldly vanities then the Holy One, blessed be He, withholds prosperity . . . so that we do not get the leisure to carry out commandments. Moreover, evil decrees are decreed against us which compel us to transgress the words of the Torah. Thus it turns out that those transgressions which we committed by choice become the cause of still other transgressions (Aknin).

There are some who interpret this saying as follows: the reward for carrying out a commandment is the very commandment which the man carried out. What greater reward can a person seek in this world than to be inscribed as one whose actions shine in the splendor of the living God in the world to come? (Nahmias).

———

HE USED TO SAY: DESPISE NO MAN AND CONSIDER NOTHING IMPOSSIBLE, FOR THERE IS NO MAN WHO DOES NOT HAVE HIS HOUR AND THERE IS NO THING THAT DOES NOT HAVE ITS PLACE.

DESPISE NO MAN AND CONSIDER NOTHING IMPOSSIBLE: As it is said, *Whoso despiseth the word shall suffer thereby; but he that feareth the commandment shall be rewarded* (Proverbs 13:13) (ARN).

Do not treat with contempt even the most inferior of people (Vitry).

CONSIDER NOTHING IMPOSSIBLE: The philosophers have said: Whatever is possible will be (Duran).

THERE IS NO THING THAT DOES NOT HAVE ITS PLACE: Do not dismiss any thought out of mind until you have very carefully investigated it and found that it is indeed impossible. If, before you have examined some matter, it seems far from truth, do not hastily decide that, "Such a thing cannot be" (Aknin).

———

RABBI LEVITAS OF YAVNEH SAYS: BE OF AN EXCEEDINGLY HUMBLE SPIRIT, FOR THE END OF MAN IS THE WORM.

BE OF AN EXCEEDINGLY HUMBLE SPIRIT: In all matters a man ought to adopt a middle course. But where pride is concerned, since it is so bad a quality in the eyes of saintly people and they know what havoc it works, they have reacted against it completely and gone to the opposite extreme, towards humbleness of spirit, so that they would leave no room at all in their souls for pride. . . . The Sages, of blessed memory, have said a number of things against pride (Sotah 4b): "Any person in whom there is arrogance of spirit is like an idol-worshipper . . . is as though he had denied the root." . . . And they also say that at the Resurrection the Lord, blessed be He, will not revive those who are of a proud disposition (Maimonides).

FOR THE END OF MAN IS THE WORM: Every man is full of hopes and aspirations, but he knows that his end will be worm and maggot. Let no man therefore become arrogant: what business has he with pride! (Vitry).

   It is told that Aristotle instructed his disciple Alexander that it is unbecoming for a king to exalt himself over his people. . . . I saw the following in a book: A king once summoned one of his distinguished subjects. When the man arrived the king said to him, "What were you doing?" The subject replied, "I was considering that in comparison with the highest sphere, the planet earth is no more than a swampy pool in the great sea; and even on the earth there is no habitation everywhere but only in about one quarter of it; and even in the inhabited quarter, there is a whole northern part which is uninhabited; and even in the inhabited part of the quarter there are mountains and hills and seas and rivers and deserts and fields and vineyards; comparatively small is the inhabited part of cities; and I am in one of these innumerable cities. And in that very city there are shops and yards and market places, and I am in one spot only and am no more than a fragment of the place in which I dwell. If so small is my portion in this world, and this whole world in the sight of the Creator of all is of so little value, how shall I carry myself with pride in His presence!" . . . Note well that Rabbi Levitas commanded only that a man should be of humble spirit and not speak to others with arrogance and contempt; but he most certainly does not command a man to humiliate himself in the presence of others, for a scholar must beware of treating himself contemptuously in the presence of the *am ha-arez* (Duran).

———

RABBI JOHANAN BEN BAROKA SAYS: IF ONE PROFANES THE NAME OF HEAVEN IN SECRET HE SHALL BE PUNISHED IN BROAD DAYLIGHT: UNWITTINGLY OR WITTINGLY, IT IS ALL ONE IN PROFANING THE NAME.

IF ONE PROFANES THE NAME OF HEAVEN IN SECRET: That is to say, if a person commits a transgression in secret, which, had it been in the open, would have involved profaning the Name of God. For example: If the transgressor is a scholar—since people follow his example—he shall be punished in broad daylight so that his hypocrisy will be published abroad. . . . An example of profaning the Name: When people see a scholar doing something improper they begin to speak slanderously: "Woe to such as study the Torah, for one learns from the Torah only foul things. Note So-and-so who studied Torah, how ugly are his works." And thus because of him they come to treat the words of the Torah profanely and with contumely. That is why in regard to profaning the Name the unwitting suffers the same penalty as the witting (Vitry).

Here is the meaning of, for profaning the Name, whether it be witting or unwitting, one is punished in broad daylight: If it was a witting transgression, the sinner receives the punishment for wittingly transgressing; if it was an unwitting transgression, he receives the punishment for unwittingly transgressing. But in either case the punishment is in the open (Maimonides).

The penalty for profaning the Name is so extreme because in this instance a man sins not because he is overpowered by the evil impulse, but because he wishes to throw off the yoke and treat the Torah and commandments with contempt, and because he denies the omniscience and providence of God (Meiri).

———

RABBI ISHMAEL HIS SON SAYS: IF ONE STUDIES IN ORDER TO TEACH, IT IS GRANTED TO HIM TO STUDY AND TO TEACH; BUT IF ONE STUDIES IN ORDER TO PRACTICE, IT IS GRANTED TO HIM TO STUDY AND TO TEACH, TO OBSERVE AND TO PRACTICE.

Rabbi Ishmael says: If one studies in order to teach, it is not granted to him to study and to teach; but if one studies in order to practice, it is granted to him to study and to teach, to observe and to practice (ARNB).

STUDIES IN ORDER TO TEACH: That is, he wishes to study and teach and no more. Such a person has no intention of carrying out what he has learned, either because he is unable to do so, or, even if able to, does so only to make a reputation for himself, so that people may address him as Rabbi (Vitry).

This does not refer, God forbid, to one who studies merely in order to teach but not to practice, for to such a person it is granted neither to study nor to teach. Rather, the reference here is to one who studies merely in order to determine what is forbidden and what permitted, without taking real trouble carefully to explore whether things that are permitted might really be forbidden—he simply takes statements at their face value. For that reason no more is granted to him than to achieve what he contemplated, namely to study and to teach. "But if one studies in order to practice," that is to say, if he has in mind studying a subject profoundly in order to arrive at the truth of the matter, and he is prepared to toil away for many days and years in order to attain even a little, so that he may conduct himself according to the truth, such a person is studying in order to practice. For his thoughts have only one purpose, that his practice accord with the truth. That is why "it is granted to him to study and to teach and to practice," because everything is included in practice (Rabbi Jonah).

This is a warning and exhortation to a person who studies, that he do not study without purpose, but with the intent to adopt the ways of wisdom and influence others. This is the height of perfection. The Sage said: The beginning of wisdom is silence; the second stage is listening; the third is practice; and the fourth is study (Meiri).

We have often seen learned men who do not practice what they learned, and they are a heavy burden to the world (Duran).

———

RABBI ZADOK SAYS: DO NOT MAKE THEM A CROWN FOR SELF-EXALTATION NOR A SPADE TO DIG WITH. SO TOO HILLEL USED TO SAY: "AND HE THAT PUTS THE CROWN TO HIS OWN USE SHALL PERISH." THUS THOU DOST LEARN: HE THAT PUTS THE WORDS OF TORAH TO PERSONAL PROFIT REMOVES HIS LIFE FROM THE WORLD.

DO NOT MAKE THEM A CROWN FOR SELF-EXALTATION: That is to say, do not study the words of the Torah for self-aggrandizement and self-glorification. Study the Torah for the sake of your Creator—in the end honor will come of itself. Teach the Torah to others and take no compensation for such work. Do not regard yourself as a hired man using his axe as a source of income. As the Talmud (Nedarim 37a) explains the matter: It is written, *Behold, I have taught you statutes and ordinances, even as the Lord my God commanded me* (Deuteronomy 4:5)—even as I have taught you gratis, so should you teach others gratis. Thus we learn that it is forbidden to receive compensation for teaching the Torah. . . . Nevertheless, those who teach young children are permitted to receive compensation for their labor (Vitry).

A SPADE TO DIG WITH: I first resolved not to comment at length on this statement because it is self-explanatory. Moreover, I thought that what I had to say about it would neither please nor be feasible for most of the great scholars. Nevertheless, I do want to say certain things regardless of those who preceded me and regardless of my contemporaries. Know therefore that this statement that one should not make the Torah a spade to dig with, that is to say, that one should not treat the Torah as a source of livelihood . . . against this clear statement, many men have blinded themselves, rejected it, have paid it only the most superficial attention and not gone to the heart of the matter.— I shall give the correct explanation. Many have imposed on individuals and communities . . . have led men to think— wrongly so—that it is altogether proper, even obligatory to give financial assistance to sages, to scholars, to disciples, to all those engaged in and devoted to the study of Torah. This is entirely wrong. There is no basis at all for this in the Torah. Indeed, if we examine the words of the Sages, of blessed memory, we never find individuals seeking financial help for scholars. . . . On the contrary, in all their communities there were some scholars who were utterly poor and some who were extremely rich. And God forbid! that we say the contemporaries of those scholars were not charitable, that had a poor scholar asked for help, his contemporaries would not have filled his house with gold and diamonds! The fact is that the poor scholar refused such gifts, but preferred to be content with income from his own work, be it much or little. The scholar scorned what one can get from human hands, because the Torah forbade accepting such help. You know that Hillel the Elder was a woodchopper . . . that of Rabbi Hanina ben Dosa a heavenly voice declared,

"The whole world is nourished only for the sake of my son Hanina, while my son Hanina is content with a small portion of dried-out dates from one end of the week to the other"— he never asked anyone for charity. . . . Not one of the Sages who was poor spoke disparagingly of his contemporaries or of others that they did not make scholars rich. The Sages were true saints . . . they believed in the Lord, blessed be He, and in the Torah of Moses, that through devotion to it a man will merit the life of the world to come. They never permitted themselves this begging people for money. They saw, indeed, that this taking funds would be profaning the Name of God in the sight of the masses—because then people come to regard the study of Torah as no more than another occupation by means of which a man makes a living. Thus Torah study would become contemptible in their eyes. . . . What the Torah does permit scholars is this: they may give their money to some person for him to do business with it for them as he sees fit. A person who helps a scholar in this fashion will be rewarded. . . . The Torah also permits the merchandise of a scholar to be sold first, before anyone else's. . . . Such privileges the Lord, blessed be He, allowed, the way He set up gifts for the priest and tithes for the Levite. . . . So too the Torah has relieved scholars from various taxes . . . and this, even if the scholar happens to be a wealthy person (Maimonides).

Needless to say, when a scholar can support himself he is especially praiseworthy. . . . But if it is impossible for him to make a living from his own labors without at the same time neglecting the study of Torah, what shall he do? If he spends all his time at study, he will die of hunger; if he spends all his time trying to make a living, he will neglect the study of Torah! . . . When the Gaonim, of blessed memory, saw that unless some arrangement for the scholar's support is made, he will be compelled to worry about his livelihood, will be unable to study Torah, and the Torah will be forgotten . . . they established rules for the support of scholars, so that scholars would be free to study. Now, even though some of these scholars might be suspected of engaging in study only for the sake of the stipend, and not for the sake of study itself, nevertheless we have been taught (Sanhedrin 105b): "Let a man devote himself to the study of Torah and to the commandments even for an ulterior purpose, because from an ulterior purpose he will eventually arrive at the real purpose." By means of the stipend set aside for them, men will be drawn to study, will finally understand the Torah properly and go on studying it for the right reasons. . . . Wherever it is not possible for a scholar to survive without deriving profit from his study of Torah, let him derive profit; he is not guilty of any transgression (Aknin).

A distinguished person whom a community is in need of may receive compensation, just as it is permitted to be honored when the Torah is honored. This is not an example of exploiting the Torah for one's personal advantage. For the honoring of a scholar is the honoring of the Torah. He is not putting the Torah to his own service; he is serving it! To be sure, there were many sages who were woodchoppers, waterdrawers, humble laborers; but they adopted these occupations out of a desire for the ways of saintliness; or perhaps they did so before they were appointed heads of academies, or perhaps they simply did not wish to be a burden to the community. But there is no legal prohibition against accepting such compensation (Duran).

———

RABBI YOSE SAYS: HE WHO HONORS THE TORAH WILL HIMSELF BE HONORED BY MEN; HE WHO DISHONORS THE TORAH WILL HIMSELF BE DISHONORED BY MEN.

HE WHO HONORS THE TORAH: As it is said, *For them that honor Me I will honor, and they that despise Me shall be lightly esteemed* (I Samuel 2:30) (ARN).

A person who honors the Torah is one who teaches it to the right kind of pupil, who does not place a Torah scroll on a bed or bench, does not lay a volume of the Pentateuch on a Torah scroll, nor a volume of the Prophets and Hagiographa on top of a Pentateuch, nor a volume of the Talmud on a volume of the Prophets (Vitry).

Honoring the Torah consists in honoring its commandments by displaying an eagerness to carry out its teachings, in honoring the Sages—for they are the pillars of the Torah —and the books which they compose. Profaning the Torah is the opposite of these (Maimonides).

This is the genuine honor of the Torah: when he who studies it bears himself with meticulous conduct. Such a person will himself be honored by men. . . . As the Talmud (Yoma 86a) puts it: "Note So-and-so who studies Torah, how becoming his conduct is, how upright. Happy his father who raised him, happy the teacher who taught him Torah!" (Meiri).

———

RABBI ISHMAEL HIS SON SAYS: HE WHO REFRAINS FROM JUDGMENT RIDS HIMSELF OF ENMITY, ROBBERY, AND FALSE SWEARING. BUT HE WHO IS PRESUMPTUOUS IN RENDERING DECISION IS A FOOL, WICKED, AND ARROGANT.

REFRAINS FROM JUDGMENT: According to an interpretation I received, the statement of our Mishna does not refer to one who is a judge, for a judge must carry out his assignment. The statement refers to a litigant, and the meaning of refraining from judgment is coming to some kind of settlement with an opponent out of court. . . . But it seems to me that the statement of our Mishna might well apply to a judge. And even though a judge is under obligation to carry out his assignment, nevertheless [it is wise not to be eager for such assignments]. As the Talmud (Sanhedrin 7b) reports of a certain Sage; whenever he had to act as judge, he used to exclaim: "Here I go to my death. . . . Would that in the end I will be no worse off than in the beginning" (Vitry).

Though Scripture says, *Judges and officers shalt thou make thee in all thy gates* (Deuteronomy 16:18) and it is written, *Justice, justice shalt thou follow* (Deuteronomy 16:20)— that is to say, that one is commanded to render judgment— this applies to a situation where there is no one else to fill the role of judge. But so long as one can escape such a role, it is better for him to shift the burden to others. In this way he will be free of many doubtful matters (Rabbi Jonah).

PRESUMPTUOUS IN RENDERING DECISION: It seems to me that this refers to a person who out of arrogance rushes to render decision, as it is when a person declares, "In such and such matters I am the expert" (Vitry).

To be presumptuous in rendering decision is to render decision with arrogance, without a sense of fear and deliberation (Maimonides).

Presumption in rendering judgment involves two things: first, rushing to render decision without any sense of fear. . . . Second, having rendered a wrong decision, mulishly arguing to justify that decision in order to prevail (Meiri).

———

HE USED TO SAY: DO NOT ACT THE JUDGE'S PART BY THYSELF ALONE, FOR NONE MAY ACT THE JUDGE'S PART BY HIMSELF ALONE—SAVE ONE. AND SAY NOT: "ADOPT MY VIEW"—FOR THEY MAY SAY IT, BUT NOT THOU.

DO NOT ACT THE JUDGE'S PART BY THYSELF ALONE: Strictly speaking the Torah does permit one who is in authority to act as a judge. . . . It is a moral warning that the Sage is issuing here, not a strictly legal one (Maimonides).

FOR NONE MAY ACT THE JUDGE'S PART BY HIMSELF ALONE —SAVE ONE: That is to say the Holy One. And so too it says, *He is by Himself, who can controvert Him* (Job 23:13), that is, the Holy One acts as judge by Himself and no one dare controvert Him. But human beings should not set up a court with fewer than three judges. When there are three they will thoroughly explore the issue and then hand down a right decision. That is why, "Do not act the judge's part by thyself alone" (Vitry).

AND SAY NOT: "ADOPT MY VIEW": Never use force against anyone to come before you for trial . . . for every man is at liberty either to accept you as judge or to appear before somebody else (Vitry).

If your colleagues disagree with you in some matter do not compel them to adopt your view. They are at liberty to choose whether or not they should adopt it; you may not compel them to adopt it (Maimonides).

If something seems self-evident to you, do not say to your colleagues, "Adopt my view and disregard your own." Instead offer proofs, refute their view, and present arguments in support of your own. If you have not done this, or if you have brought proofs for your own view, but they have also presented proofs for their view, and the arguments were evenly balanced, do not say, "Adopt the view which I proposed, because I am greater than you." You are not permitted to speak this way. Only if they are willing to submit to your view and adopt it, are they to do it (Aknin).

———

RABBI JONATHAN SAYS: HE WHO FULFILLS THE TORAH IN POVERTY WILL IN THE END FULFILL IT IN RICHES; BUT HE WHO NEGLECTS THE TORAH IN RICHES WILL IN THE END NEGLECT IT IN POVERTY.

Rabbi Jonathan ben Rabbi Yose says: He who studies Torah when hard-pressed will in the end do so in ease; but he who neglects the Torah in ease will in the end neglect it because of being hard-pressed. He who studies Torah in poverty will in the end fulfill it in riches; but he who neglects the Torah in riches will in the end neglect it for reasons of poverty. He who studies Torah for his own need only will in the end forget it; and he who forgets his study in his youth, will in the end go seeking for it in his old age (ARNB).

By "fulfilling the Torah" is meant study and carrying out of the commandments (Duran).

———

RABBI MEIR SAYS: ENGAGE BUT LITTLE IN BUSINESS, AND BE BUSY WITH THE TORAH; BE OF HUMBLE SPIRIT BEFORE ALL MEN. IF THOU HAST NEGLECTED THE TORAH, THOU SHALT HAVE MANY WHO BRING THEE TO NEGLECT IT; BUT IF THOU HAST TOILED AWAY AT THE STUDY OF TORAH, THERE IS A RICH REWARD TO BE GIVEN THEE.

ENGAGE BUT LITTLE IN BUSINESS: Engage in business no more than you need for a livelihood . . . and make your chief aim study of the Torah, as it is said, *And thou shalt meditate therein day and night* (Joshua 1:8) (Aknin).

In the Midrash Kohelet (Ecclesiastes Rabba 2:18) it is reported: Rabbi Meir was an outstanding scribe and he did his work for three *sela* a week: one he spent on food, one he spent on clothing, and the third he contributed to the support of the Sages. Said his disciples to him: "Master, what are you doing in behalf of your children?" Rabbi Meir replied: "If they will be righteous, then it will be with them as David has said, *I have not seen the righteous forsaken, nor his seed begging bread* (Psalm 37:25). Otherwise, why leave what belongs to me to God's enemies?" (Duran).

BE OF HUMBLE SPIRIT BEFORE ALL MEN: That is to say, not only in the presence of those greater than yourself should you be of humble spirit, but in the presence of everyone. So that, whenever you sit with any person, speak to him and behave toward him as though he were superior to you. Such extreme conduct is recommended in order to help a man to flee from pride (Maimonides).

Even if you are successful in the study of Torah—which is the only true excellence—do not exalt yourself. Needless to say if your success is only of a material kind! (Rabbi Jonah).

IF THOU HAST NEGLECTED THE TORAH: He who is diligent over the words of the Torah is given [agents] that are diligent in his behalf; but he who neglects the words of the Torah is given over to [forces] that will make him idle—for example, wolves, lions, bears, leopards, panthers, serpents, robbers or brigands, come and surround him; and they settle accounts with him, as it is said, *God hath His chastisers on the earth* (Psalm 58:12) (ARN).

There are many things that require somebody to devote himself to them but they consume a person's time. If you do not engage in the study of Torah, you will be compelled to take care of such things (Maimonides).

THERE IS A RICH REWARD TO BE GIVEN THEE: It is the Holy One, blessed be He, Himself who will reward those engaged in the study of Torah—He, personally, and not some messenger of His or angel. By the same token, He promises all the inhabitants of the world that where punishment must be meted out, He will do so by means of His messengers, in order to make the penalty lighter. . . . To what may this be compared? To a king for whom a craftsman made a beautiful object. If the king had ordered his servants to take funds from the treasury and pay the craftsman, they would give him much less than if the king personally compensated him—for they are not as generous as is the king who enjoys an abundance of wealth and glory; they are not as generous as the king even when they make use of the king's money to pay the craftsman (Rabbi Jonah).

———

RABBI ELIEZER BEN JACOB SAYS: HE WHO CARRIES OUT ONE GOOD DEED ACQUIRES ONE ADVOCATE IN HIS OWN BEHALF, AND HE WHO COMMITS ONE TRANSGRESSION ACQUIRES ONE ACCUSER AGAINST HIMSELF. REPENTANCE AND GOOD WORKS ARE LIKE A SHIELD AGAINST CALAMITY.

HE WHO CARRIES OUT ONE GOOD DEED: This is a warning to man, that carrying out one good deed must not be of little consequence in his eyes (Meiri).

REPENTANCE AND GOOD WORKS ARE LIKE A SHIELD: Both repentance—if a person has been previously guilty of evil works—and good works in themselves keep away harm and tribulations from a man (Maimonides).

"Repentance" is mentioned before "good works" because

"the penitent stands higher than even the thoroughly righteous" (Nahmias).

———

RABBI JOHANAN HA-SANDELAR SAYS: EVERY ASSEMBLY WHICH IS FOR THE SAKE OF HEAVEN WILL IN THE END ENDURE; BUT ONE WHICH IS NOT FOR THE SAKE OF HEAVEN WILL NOT ENDURE IN THE END.

What kind of assembly was for the sake of Heaven? For example, the assembly of Israel before Mount Sinai. And what kind was not for the sake of Heaven? For example, the assembly of the Generation of Dispersion (ARN).

ASSEMBLY . . . FOR THE SAKE OF HEAVEN: That is, where men have gotten together to study and to teach (Vitry).

Any human assembly for the sake of Heaven, that is, with the aim of discovering truth and adopting the course of good and uprightness—because it is truth and goodness and uprightness that is sought—will never be broken up. For in such an assembly everybody has only one wish, to discover the truth; . . . thus they all have one object in view (Aknin).

Any assembly for the study of Torah and for the practice of good works is called an assembly for the sake of Heaven (Rabbi Jonah).

BUT ONE WHICH IS NOT FOR THE SAKE OF HEAVEN: When people get together merely to lord it over one another (Rabbi Jonah).

A person's relations with his fellow man must not be based on the desire to triumph over him. This ruins the whole relationship and is the undoing of truth. For when a person has in mind only triumph over his fellow, he strives to establish his own point of view or his own wish, regardless of whether it is true or false. . . . When in any group victory is the motive, one person does not listen to the other one, and controversy takes place (Meiri).

———

RABBI ELEAZAR BEN SHAMMUA SAYS: LET THE HONOR OF THY DISCIPLE BE AS DEAR TO THEE AS THINE OWN, AND THE HONOR OF THY COMRADE AS FEAR OF THY MASTER, AND FEAR OF THY MASTER AS FEAR OF HEAVEN.

LET THE HONOR OF THY DISCIPLE BE AS DEAR TO THEE AS THINE OWN: Where are we told that the honor of one's disciple should be as dear to him as his own honor? Let all men learn from Moses our master, who said to Joshua, *Choose us out men* (Exodus 17:9). It is not said "Choose *me* out men," but, *Choose us out men;* which teaches that Moses treated him as his equal: although he was his master and Joshua was his disciple, he treated him as his equal.

And how do we know that the honor of one's comrade should be as dear to him as his master's? For it is said, *And Aaron said to Moses: O my lord* (Numbers 12:11). Now, was not his brother younger than he? Nevertheless Aaron treated him as his master.

And how do we know that the honor of one's master should be as dear to him as the honor of Heaven? For it is said, *And Joshua the son of Nun, the minister of Moses from his youth up, answered and said: My lord Moses, shut them in* (Numbers 11:28): Joshua treated him as the equal of the Shekinah (ARN).

FEAR OF THY MASTER AS FEAR OF HEAVEN: God has put the honor of scholars on the same plane as His own honor, because by teaching him Torah and good works the scholars bring a man to life of the world to come (Aknin).

———

RABBI JUDAH SAYS: STUDY WITH CARE, FOR ERROR IN THE COURSE OF STUDY IS ACCOUNTED DELIBERATE SIN.

"Study with care" in order to learn well the detailed implications of the commandments. For if you have erred in the course of study and then rendered a wrong decision, that error will be charged against you as a deliberate transgression—you will be punished as though you had deliberately transgressed, for you should have studied carefully, and did not (Vitry).

A man must keep reviewing his study so that he will never forget, so that he may understand things thoroughly. For by nature man's understanding is limited, and forgetfulness is common to all human beings. Moreover, a person ought not to rely on the first thoughts that come to him. . . . Now, where the Torah and commandments are concerned, since error is a common thing, if a person has not taken this to heart and makes a mistake, he is not innocent but guilty, for he ought to have kept in mind that every man is prone to error, and he should have been careful not to make a mistake (Rabbi Jonah).

One's knowledge of the Law ought to be carefully organized in his mind, so that the contents of the Torah will always be accessible to help him render a decision. Otherwise, sometimes he will be asked a question about an important matter and he will render a wrong decision. Thus he will turn out to be a stumbling block to his fellow man. He may not plead that this was a mistake, for "error in the course of study is accounted deliberate sin," whoever has his mind and heart set on rendering decision must toil away at his studies until they are carefully organized in his mind (Meiri).

RABBI SIMEON SAYS: THERE ARE THREE CROWNS: THE CROWN OF TORAH, THE CROWN OF PRIESTHOOD, AND THE CROWN OF ROYALTY; BUT THE CROWN OF A GOOD NAME MUST ACCOMPANY THEM ALL.

THREE CROWNS: The crown of priesthood: What is there to be said of it? Even if one were to offer all the silver and gold in the world he cannot be given the crown of priesthood, for it is said, *And it shall be unto him, and to his seed after him, the covenant of an everlasting priesthood* (Numbers 25:13).

The crown of royalty: Even if one were to offer all the silver and gold in the world, he cannot be given the crown of royalty, for it is said, *And David My servant, shall be their prince for ever* (Ezekiel 37:25).

Not so, however, the crown of Torah: the toil of Torah, anyone who wishes to take it on can come and do so, as it is said, *Ho, everyone that thirsteth, come ye after water* (Isaiah 55:1) (ARN).

Only by virtue of the Torah did Aaron win the crown of priesthood, as it is said, *For the priest's lips should keep knowledge, and they should seek the Torah at his mouth* (Malachi 2:7). Only by virtue of the Torah did David win the crown of royalty, as it is said, *These I have had, because I have kept Thy precepts* (Psalm 119:56) (ARNB).

As regards royalty and priesthood one uses the idiom "house." Thus: "A house of royalty," as it is said, *O house of David, thus saith the Lord: Execute justice in the morning* (Jeremiah 21:12); "the house of priesthood," as it is said, *O house of Aaron, O house of Levi* (Psalm 135: 19, 20). But as regards fear of the Lord, which is the crown of the Torah, there is no special "house." Note the verse, *Ye that fear the Lord, bless ye the Lord* (Psalm 135:20). Or again, *In every place where I cause My name to be mentioned I will come unto thee and bless thee* (Exodus 20:21) (Rabbi Jonah).

These three crowns are the counterparts of the three things on which the world stands, to wit: Torah, Temple service, and acts of lovingkindness. The Torah corresponds to the crown of the Torah; Temple service corresponds to the crown of priesthood; acts of lovingkindness correspond to the crown of royalty—because by means of his wealth one has the opportunity to practice acts of lovingkindness—and so too the kings of Israel were kings filled with lovingkindness (Duran).

THE CROWN OF A GOOD NAME MUST ACCOMPANY (*Oleh Al*) THEM ALL: By means of the three crowns a man acquires a good name, if he treats them with the proper care, and if he behaves uprightly—since he has engaged in the study of Torah for the sake of Heaven, he creates for himself a good name, so that men say: "Happy the parent of such a one." "Behold the man who studied, he has fulfilled the commandments!" . . . This is an interpretation I have received. But it seems to me that the last clause of our Mishna means, "The crown of a good name excels them all." For not one of these crowns can endure if a person does not behave uprightly; and if a person does not acquire a good name everybody despises him. Thus whatever crown he may have had, is useless. And so too it is written, *A good name is better than precious oil* (Ecclesiastes 7:1) (Vitry).

A man in whom there is found knowledge of the Torah and good works is greater than a king, than a high priest, than any of the wise who have no good works to their credit (Aknin).

All the crowns require along with them the crown of a good name, and this crown is dependent upon the crown of the Torah. For in what consists a man's good name if not in study of the Torah and the carrying out of the commandments? (Rabbi Jonah).

The crown of a good name is superior to the crown of Torah. For if a man is a scholar and behaves foully, one may despise him: as we are taught in the Talmud (Moed Katan 17a), If the teacher is like an angel of the Lord of Hosts then seek Torah at his mouth; but if his relationship to human beings is bad, he is guilty of profaning the Name of

God, and if he is guilty of misconduct he is worse than an *am ha-arez.*

The crown of a good name is superior to the crown of Torah. For as the Sages of the Talmud (Baba Batra 4a) taught: It is written, *A ruler of thy people thou shalt not curse* (Exodus 22:27), that is to say, only when he acts as thy people act. . . . The upright kings of Israel were praised only for doing what is right in the sight of the Lord; the wicked ones were disgraced only for doing what is evil in the sight of the Lord.

The crown of a good name is also superior to the crown of priesthood. We are told in the Talmud (Yoma 71b) of the High Priest to whom the Sages Shemaiah and Abtalyon, who were of proselytic descent, retorted: "Welcome to descendants of heathen who act the way Aaron acted, and let there be no welcome to descendants of Aaron who do not act as Aaron acted." The High Priest had insulted the Sages because they were proselytes (Duran).

———

RABBI NEHORAI SAYS: BETAKE THYSELF TO A PLACE OF TORAH AND SAY NOT THAT IT WILL COME AFTER THEE, THAT THY COMPANIONS WILL SET IT UP FOR THEE TO MASTER; *"And lean not upon thine own understanding"* (Proverbs 3:5).

BETAKE THYSELF TO A PLACE OF TORAH: To a place where there are scholars (Vitry).

Seek out for thyself a place where study is carried on, for if you study with someone else, your study will be firmly established (Maimonides).

The Torah that a man studies with his companions is more firmly mastered than the Torah a man studies by himself, because colleagues put questions to one another, each one tries to answer the questions of his colleague, and there is a give and take until the subject is thoroughly clarified (Aknin).

This is how one of the Day of Atonement prayers goes: "And if it has been decreed that we must suffer exile, may we be led off to a place of Torah" (Duran).

SAY NOT THAT THY COMPANIONS WILL SET IT UP FOR THEE TO MASTER: Do not say that your companions who went off to study with a master will be able to set up what they have learned, for you to master, after they have returned . . . that they will be able to engage in a give and take with you. For there is no comparing what one learns directly from a teacher with what one learns from the disciple's report (Vitry).

Do not say, "I shall wait until some teacher or Sage comes along, and then I will study with him," or, "I will learn from those colleagues who have studied with the master . . . and whatever questions I have I will ask them and they will answer." Such an opportunity may not present itself to you, and every day time keeps escaping from you (Meiri).

LEAN NOT UPON THINE OWN UNDERSTANDING: Do not imagine that by your own acuteness you can discover everything (Vitry).

Do not say that you do not need the stimulation of companions and disciples (Maimonides).

Do not say, "It is enough for me if I read books." "Give me bookmen rather than books," says the maxim. For from books you will derive only what you find in them; but the bookmen will tell you also what they learned from their teachers, what they added to the tradition as a result of their own thinking, what they derived from books, and how they trained themselves in good conduct and right thinking (Nahmias).

———

RABBI YANNAI SAYS: WITHIN OUR REACH IS NEITHER THE TRANQUILLITY OF THE WICKED NOR EVEN THE SUFFERING OF THE RIGHTEOUS.

At the tranquillity of the wicked we have not arrived, the sufferings of the righteous we have not approached (ARNB).

This is the interpretation I received: It is not within our power to understand why the way of the wicked prospers and why the righteous are made to endure sufferings. But it seems to me the saying means this . . . we do not enjoy the kind of tranquillity the wicked enjoy . . . and the sufferings we endure are not like those of the righteous, but are sufferings meted out as a punishment (Vitry).

———

RABBI MATTIAH BEN HERESH SAYS: ON MEETING ANY MAN BE THE FIRST TO EXTEND GREETINGS; AND BE A TAIL TO LIONS RATHER THAN A HEAD TO JACKALS.

ANY MAN: Even on meeting a non-Jew be the first to extend greetings, inquire after his welfare (Vitry).

A TAIL TO LIONS: It is more of an honor for you to make of yourself "a tail to lions," i.e., to humble yourself so that you may be included in the company of scholars, than to be "a head to jackals," the head of inferior folk (Vitry).

It is much better and more fitting for a person to be the disciple of someone who is wiser than he, than to be the master of someone who is inferior to him. The former will lead to his improvement, the latter to his deterioration (Maimonides).

The tail of a lion is still a lion and the head of a jackal is still only a jackal. Better that one be a lion than a jackal. The lion is the strongest of the beasts; the jackal is the weakest (Duran).

———

RABBI JACOB SAYS: THIS WORLD IS LIKE A FOYER LEADING INTO THE WORLD TO COME—PREPARE THYSELF IN THE FOYER SO THAT THOU MAYEST ENTER INTO THE INNER CHAMBER.

Normally, when a man wants to enter the inner chamber of a house he first puts himself in order and then enters; so too a man must first put himself in order in this world by means of repentance and good works, so that he may merit entrance into the world to come. . . . In the world to come it is impossible to prepare oneself. For this world is like the shore, and the world to come is like the sea; this world is like the Sabbath eve, and the world to come is like the Sabbath: he who has taken the necessary pains on the Sabbath eve, will have what to eat on the Sabbath; he who has prepared food on shore, will have what to eat while at sea. If he has not taken the necessary pains and prepared food, he will not have what to eat (Vitry).

Let a man acquire in this world those virtues through which one merits the world to come—for this world is indeed no more than a thoroughfare and passageway to the other (Maimonides).

———

HE USED TO SAY: RICHER IS ONE HOUR OF REPENTANCE AND GOOD WORKS IN THIS WORLD THAN ALL OF LIFE OF THE

WORLD TO COME; AND RICHER IS ONE HOUR'S CALM OF SPIRIT IN THE WORLD TO COME THAN ALL OF LIFE OF THIS WORLD.

ONE HOUR OF REPENTANCE AND GOOD WORKS: One hour in which to repent and do good works in this world is richer than all the life in the world to come, for in the world to come it is impossible to repent or to do good works. That world exists only for the receiving of reward for what a person has carried out in this world. And one hour in the world to come provides more calm of spirit to a man than all of the life in this world; for as regards calm of spirit all of life in this world cannot compare with one hour in the world to come. For there is no perfect calm of spirit here (Vitry).

The saints of the world were eager for life so that they might continue doing good works in this world—something which they will be unable to do in the world to come (Nahmias).

———

RABBI SIMEON BEN ELEAZAR SAYS: DO NOT APPEASE THY FELLOW IN HIS HOUR OF ANGER; DO NOT COMFORT HIM WHILE THE DEAD IS STILL LAID OUT BEFORE HIM; DO NOT QUESTION HIM IN THE HOUR OF HIS VOW; AND DO NOT STRIVE TO SEE HIM IN HIS HOUR OF MISFORTUNE.

These are all statements on conduct in the improvement of human society, namely, speaking up at the proper time (Maimonides).

DO NOT APPEASE THY FELLOW IN HIS HOUR OF ANGER: It is useless, for in his hour of anger he will not accept your pacifying words. Instead, leave him alone until he calms down. Then try to placate him, and he will listen to you (Vitry).

Our Sages, of blessed memory, have said (Yebamot 65b): Even as a man is commanded to speak up when his words will be listened to, so he is commanded to hold his peace at moments when he will not be listened to (Aknin).

DO NOT COMFORT HIM WHILE THE DEAD IS STILL LAID OUT BEFORE HIM: As Maimonides, of blessed memory, put it: At such times it is madness to try to bring comfort, for who is there who can look upon a relation of his lying dead before him, and hear the voice of the mourners as they mourn, and at that moment receive comfort? (Duran).

DO NOT QUESTION HIM IN THE HOUR OF HIS VOW: Do not ask a man when he is taking a vow whether you may release him of it, because when you remind him of the vow you cause him pain. . . . Do not ask him whether you may release him of his vow until he has calmed down. I have heard still another interpretation. If you hear your fellow taking a vow, do not begin raising questions like, "Are these the terms of the vow, are those the terms of the vow?" In his temper, he may very well blurt out to you, "I have made this vow without any qualification!" You will thus turn out to be the cause of his remaining under that vow all his life. It is best, therefore, that you do not question him or begin discussing the vow with him until his rage has passed and he has calmed down (Vitry).

IN HIS HOUR OF MISFORTUNE: No man ought to go visit his fellow when he is in the midst of suffering, or when he has been seized by the government, or when he is in the midst of any misfortunes that have befallen him—because at that moment he is suffering and melancholy and is ashamed to face people (Aknin).

When some injury has befallen a person, or when he has committed some transgression, and he is suffering the torments of shame, do not at that moment go to visit him and add to his shame (Rabbi Jonah).

———

SAMUEL "THE LITTLE" SAYS: *"Rejoice not when thine enemy falleth, and let not thy heart be glad when he stumbleth; lest the Lord see it, and it displease Him and He turn away His wrath from him"* (Proverbs 24:17-18).

This saying is actually a quotation from Scripture . . . and Samuel was wont to cite it to those people who take delight in their fellows' misfortune. . . . But it is also possible to interpret as follows: The verse speaks in general terms of people who hate each other; but Samuel "the Little" applied it to scholars, that is, when they argue over some issue of the Law, one should not rejoice at his victory over the other. . . . Samuel the Little was so-called because he minimized his own importance, and when he died he was eulogized as follows: "O, the saint! O, the humble man!" In the Palestinian Talmud (J. Sotah 9:14) it is said that he was only slightly inferior to the prophet Samuel (Vitry).

Samuel was in the habit of quoting this verse because it speaks of something important and people generally fail in it. For even if one's enemy is a wicked person, it is wrong to rejoice at his misfortune. . . . The righteous should not rejoice in the downfall of the wicked; the downfall of the wicked is an occasion for rejoicing only in that Heaven's Name is thus glorified—not because one hates the wicked person (Rabbi Jonah).

ELISHA BEN ABUYAH SAYS: HE THAT STUDIES AS A CHILD, TO WHAT MAY HE BE LIKENED? TO INK WRITTEN ON FRESH PAPER. BUT HE THAT STUDIES AS AN OLD MAN, TO WHAT MAY HE BE LIKENED? TO INK WRITTEN ON WORNOUT PAPER.

ELISHA BEN ABUYAH SAYS: He that studies Torah in his youth to what may he be likened? To plaster which is poured over stones: even if all the rains come down, they cannot break it. But he that studies Torah in his old age, to what may he be likened? To plaster poured over bricks: as soon as a drop of water falls upon it, the plaster utterly disintegrates (ARNB).

He used to say: When one studies Torah as a child, the words of the Torah are absorbed by his blood and come out of his mouth distinctly. But if one studies Torah in his old age, the words of the Torah are not absorbed by his blood and do not come out of his mouth distinctly. And thus the maxim goes: "If in thy youth thou didst not desire them, how shalt thou acquire them in thine old age?" (ARN).

He that studies Torah as a child, to what may he be likened? To a heifer subdued while yet young. . . . But he that studies Torah in his old age is like a beast not subdued until its old age. . . .

He that studies Torah as a child is like a woman who kneads in hot water, but he that studies Torah in his old age is like a woman who kneads in cold water. . . .

He that studies Torah as a child is like a young man who weds a maiden: for she is suited to him and he is suited to her, and she is drawn to him and he is drawn to her. He that studies Torah in his old age, to what may he be likened? To an old man who weds a maiden: she may be suited to him but he is unsuited to her, she may be drawn to him but he withdraws from her (ARN).

In the *Mibhar Ha-Peninim* there is an epigram: He that studies Torah in his youth, to what may he be likened? To engraving on stone. He that studies Torah in old age is like engraving on sand (Rabbi Jonah).

RABBI YOSE BAR JUDAH OF KEFAR HA-BABLI SAYS: HE WHO LEARNS FROM THE YOUNG, TO WHAT MAY HE BE LIKENED? TO ONE THAT EATS UNRIPE GRAPES AND DRINKS WINE FROM THE VAT. BUT HE WHO LEARNS FROM THE OLD, TO WHAT MAY HE BE LIKENED? TO ONE THAT EATS RIPE GRAPES AND DRINKS WINE THAT'S AGED.

RABBI SAYS: DO NOT LOOK AT THE JUG BUT AT ITS CONTENTS—THERE ARE NEW JUGS FILLED WITH OLD WINE, AND OLD ONES IN WHICH THERE IS NOT EVEN NEW WINE!

DO NOT LOOK AT THE JUG: Both Rabbi Yose and Rabbi have one thing in mind really, that one should study Torah only with a scholar whose learning is clear and lucid, and not study with one whose learning is disorganized (Aknin).

RABBI ELIEZER HA-KAPPAR SAYS: ENVY, LUST, AND HANKERING FOR GLORY PUT A MAN OUT OF THE WORLD.

A man with such qualities will inevitably lose his faith in the Torah and will attain neither to intellectual nor ethical excellence (Maimonides).

The envy spoken of here refers to envying someone richer than oneself in money or social status or possessions. But if one envies a person greater than himself in wisdom, he is truly praiseworthy. For such envy will lead a man to engage in study, and his wisdom will increase (Aknin).

In the *Mibhar Ha-Peninim* there is a very nice parable about envy and excessive appetite. An envious man and a glutton were once met by Satan, who said to them: "If one of you will ask for something, it will be given to him, but his fellow will get a double portion of it." The envious one did not want to ask first, because he begrudged his companion receiving a double portion. The glutton wanted both portions, his own and the other's. So he pressed his companion to ask first. Whereupon the envious fellow asked that they gouge out one of his eyes, so that the glutton should lose both (Duran).

OUT OF THE WORLD: Out of this world and out of life in the world to come (ARNB).

———

HE USED TO SAY: THE ONES WHO WERE BORN ARE TO DIE, AND THE ONES WHO HAVE DIED ARE TO BE BROUGHT TO LIFE AGAIN, AND THE ONES WHO ARE BROUGHT TO LIFE ARE TO BE SUMMONED TO JUDGMENT—SO THAT ONE MAY KNOW, MAKE KNOWN, AND HAVE THE KNOWLEDGE THAT HE IS GOD, HE IS THE DESIGNER, HE IS THE CREATOR, HE IS THE DISCERNER, HE IS THE JUDGE, HE THE WITNESS, HE THE PLAINTIFF, AND HE WILL SUMMON TO JUDGMENT: BLESSED BE HE, IN WHOSE PRESENCE IS NEITHER INIQUITY, NOR FORGETFULNESS, NOR RESPECT OF PERSONS, NOR TAKING OF BRIBES—FOR EVERYTHING IS HIS. KNOW THOU THAT EVERYTHING IS ACCORDING TO THE RECKONING.

AND LET NOT THINE IMPULSE GIVE THEE REASSURANCES THAT THE NETHERWORLD WILL PROVE A REFUGE TO THEE— FOR AGAINST THY WILL ART THOU FORMED, AGAINST THY WILL ART THOU BORN, AGAINST THY WILL DOST THOU LIVE, AGAINST THY WILL DIE, AND AGAINST THY WILL SHALT THOU GIVE ACCOUNT AND RECKONING BEFORE THE KING OF KINGS OF KINGS, THE HOLY ONE, BLESSED BE HE.

THE ONES WHO WERE BORN ARE TO DIE: Since in the end all those who were born have to die, are alive today and in the grave tomorrow, they must reflect on their ways and repent (Rabbi Jonah).

THE ONES WHO HAVE DIED ARE TO BE BROUGHT TO LIFE AGAIN: For the Lord will revive them in the age to come, as it is said, *And many of them that sleep in the dust of the earth shall awake, some to everlasting life, and some to reproaches and everlasting abhorrence* (Daniel 12:2). That is why a man ought to do whatever he can to be of those who will be part of life and not of those who will be an everlasting abhorrence (Rabbi Jonah).

THE ONES WHO ARE BROUGHT TO LIFE ARE TO BE SUMMONED TO JUDGMENT: The ones who will be resurrected will be brought to judgment when the Day of Judgment in the Valley of Jehoshaphat arrives (Vitry).

Although the ultimate punishment will take place in the world to come, even in this world all those who have been alive will receive part of the punishment coming to them (Meiri).

KNOW, MAKE KNOWN, AND HAVE THE KNOWLEDGE: By the verb "know" is meant that all the nations of the world may know. . . ; by the verb "make known" is meant that they make known to others, that they teach their children; by the expression to "have the knowledge" is meant that the truth will be made manifest to all the nations so that they may be in awe before God (Vitry).

The idiom here refers to three groups, those who will be born, those who have been born, and those who will be resurrected after death (Maimonides).

By the verb "know" is meant that one learns from others who teach him; by the verb "make known" is meant that one teaches others in this world; by the expression "have the knowledge" is meant that in the world to come one will receive the knowledge of himself, without anyone teaching him, as it is said, *And they shall teach no more every man his neighbor, and every man his brother, saying: 'Know the Lord'; for they shall all know Me, from the least of them unto the greatest of them* (Jeremiah 31:34) (Rabbi Jonah).

HE IS THE DESIGNER . . . HE IS THE DISCERNER: He is the Creator who created man in His image, according to His likeness, and He knows what are men's most secret thoughts; for He made all men and it is impossible to hide anything from Him, and He discerns all their doings, as it is written, *He that fashioneth the hearts of them all, that considereth all their doings* (Psalm 33:15) (Vitry).

HE IS THE JUDGE . . . HE WILL SUMMON TO JUDGMENT: That is to say, He now passes sentence upon everyone for life or death and all other matters. And in the future, He will also sentence to either reward or punishment those who are resurrected for the world to come (Maimonides).

HE THE WITNESS, HE THE PLAINTIFF: As it is written, *And I will come near to you to judgment; and I will be a swift witness* (Malachi 3:5). . . . And He Himself will be the plaintiff, making charges against man to bring him to judgment (Vitry).

IN WHOSE PRESENCE IS NEITHER INIQUITY . . . NOR TAKING OF BRIBES: This idiom is derived from the verse in Chronicles in connection with Jehoshaphat: *For there is no iniquity with the Lord our God, nor respect of persons, nor taking of bribes* (II Chronicles 19:7) (Vitry).

THE NETHERWORLD: Let not your impulse give you reassurances that you have in the netherworld a resting place (ARNB).

AGAINST THY WILL: Even as you were born against your will and continue in life at all times, in travail and vanity, against your will and in spite of yourself—for many are the times that you have wished to die and were unable to; or again, when the time to die comes you will be unable to escape or elude it—so too in the future, will you have to give account and reckoning for everything you have done (Vitry).

Take careful note of this statement which mentions things that come to pass by nature, over which a man has no choice. . . . The Mishna did not say against thy will dost thou sin, or transgress, or walk, or stand still and such like matters. These latter are within man's power and he is coerced into none of them (Maimonides).

Chapter V

BY TEN UTTERANCES WAS THE WORLD CREATED. AND WHAT DOES THIS TEACH? SURELY IT COULD HAVE BEEN CREATED BY ONE UTTERANCE! BUT THIS WAS SO THAT THE WICKED BE PUNISHED, FOR THEY DESTROY A WORLD CREATED BY TEN UTTERANCES; AND THAT THE RIGHTEOUS BE RICHLY REWARDED, FOR THEY SUSTAIN A WORLD CREATED BY TEN UTTERANCES.

TEN UTTERANCES: To wit: *And God said: Let there be light* (Genesis 1:3). *And God said: Let there be a firmament* (Genesis 1:6). *And God said: Let the waters be gathered together* (Genesis 1:9). *And God said: Let the earth put forth grass* (Genesis 1:11). *And God said: Let there be lights* (Genesis 1:14). *And God said: Let the waters swarm* (Genesis 1:20). *And God said: Behold I have given* (Genesis 1:29). *And God said: Let us make man* (Genesis 1:26). *And God said: It is not good that the man should be alone,* etc. (Genesis 2:18). Rabbi Jeremiah used to include, *And God created the great sea-monsters. . . . And God blessed them saying* (Genesis 1:21, 22), and exclude the verse, *And God said: It is not good that the man should be alone* (ARNB).

In the Talmud (Rosh Hashana 32a) the TEN utterances are specified as: nine occurrences of "and God said" in the first chapter of Genesis, and the word, "Bereshit" (*In the beginning*) which is itself an utterance, as it is written, *By the word of the Lord were the heavens made* (Psalm 33:6) (Vitry).

WHAT DOES THIS TEACH? This is to teach thee that he who puts one commandment into practice and he who keeps one Sabbath and he who sustains one soul is accounted by Scripture as though he had sustained a whole world which was created by TEN words; but he who commits one transgression and he who profanes one Sabbath and he who destroys one soul is accounted by Scripture as though he had destroyed a whole world which was created by TEN words.

For thus we find of Cain who killed his brother Abel, as it is said, *The voice of thy brother's blood crieth unto Me* (Genesis 4:10): though he shed the blood of one, it is said *damim* ("bloods") in the plural. Which teaches that the blood of Abel's children and children's children and all his descendants to the end of all generations destined to come forth from him, all of them stood crying out before the Holy One, blessed be He.

Thus thou dost learn that one man's life is equal to all the work of Creation (ARN).

There was a separate utterance for each act of creation in order to make known the greatness of everything that exists and the beauty of its order; so that he who wrecks it wrecks a great thing, while he who improves it is improving a great thing. By this I mean to say: he is either wrecking his own soul and remains imperfect or he improves his own soul which is in his power either to improve or to wreck, and that is, as it were, the ultimate goal of all existence (Maimonides).

If a person has studied the sciences and grown in wisdom, and if he engages in good and upright works, and walks in the ways of the Lord, why then, he has improved his soul which learns to desire fear of the Lord and those things assigned to the soul from the moment of its creation. But if a person turns to idleness and worldly vanities, neither studies nor practices good, but follows after the evil desires of his heart, then he has ruined it and cut it off from life in the world to come and its pleasures (Aknin).

TEN GENERATIONS FROM ADAM TO NOAH—TO MAKE KNOWN WHAT LONG-SUFFERING WAS HIS: FOR ALL THESE GENERATIONS KEPT ON PROVOKING HIM UNTIL HE BROUGHT UPON THEM THE WATERS OF THE FLOOD.

TEN GENERATIONS FROM ADAM TO NOAH: This is to teach thee that although all the generations went on provoking Him, He did not [at once] bring upon them the waters of the flood —because of the righteous and saints in their midst. And some say: so long as Methuselah was alive the flood did not come down on the world; and even when Methuselah died, it was still withheld from them for seven days after his death. ... What purpose was served by these seven days? They were the seven days of mourning for Methuselah the righteous, which prevented the calamity from coming upon the world (ARN).

The TEN generations from Adam to Noah are: Adam, Seth, Enosh, Kenan, Mahalalel, Jared, Enoch, Methuselah, Lamech, Noah. And why TEN? To correspond to the TEN utterances by which the world was created (Vitry).

Observe: all the generations between Adam and Noah provoked God by their evil works; yet He restrained His wrath during all these generations. But in the end He brought upon them the waters of the flood—for not forever will He exercise long-suffering! So too think of our state of exile brought about by the "Romans." Say not, "Note how many days and years has He held back His wrath from the 'Roman Empire,' and we are still in exile. Will He forever exercise long-suffering towards them because He is a God of long-suffering?" Know of a certainty that in the end He will requite them according to their deeds and the work of their hands, and He will redeem and save us (Rabbi Jonah).

TEN GENERATIONS FROM NOAH TO ABRAHAM—TO MAKE KNOWN WHAT LONG-SUFFERING WAS HIS: FOR ALL THE GENERATIONS KEPT ON PROVOKING HIM UNTIL ABRAHAM APPEARED, AND HE RECEIVED THE REWARD OF ALL OF THEM.

TEN GENERATIONS FROM NOAH TO ABRAHAM: This is to teach that all those generations kept provoking Him and there was not one of them that walked in the ways of the Holy One, blessed be He, until Abraham our father came and walked in the ways of the Holy One, blessed be He. ... Moreover, Abraham our father would first practice charity and then justice. ... When two litigants would come before Abraham our father for judgment and one would say of his fellow, "He owes me a *mina,*" Abraham our father would take out a *mina* of his own, give it to him, and say to them: "Draw up your claims before me." Then each would draw up his claims. In the event that the defendant was found owing the other a *mina,* Abraham would say to the one with the *mina:* "Give the *mina* to thy fellow." But if it was not so, he would say to them: "Divide the sum between you and depart in peace" (ARN).

The TEN generations from Noah to Abraham are: Shem, Arpachshad, Shelah, Eber, Peleg, Reu, Serug, Nahor, Terah, Abraham. . . . Abraham instructed the whole world in the ways of righteousness, and thus saved all mankind; and the Holy One rewarded him for his having saved them all for life, for the Holy One does not delight in the death of the wicked. And Abraham taught them the ways of repentance (Vitry).

ABRAHAM APPEARED, AND HE RECEIVED THE REWARD: As we often say: the Holy One, blessed be He, rewards lavishly that righteous man who comes after wicked generations that preceded him, and does not adopt the ways of those wicked people in whose midst he lives, but on the contrary, independently understands the truth and turns to wisdom and walks in the ways of the Lord. . . . Now, that reward which those generations would have deserved had they been righteous, the Holy One, blessed be He, gives to that individual who comes after all of them. For all men were created only for the purpose of understanding the Creator and acquiring wisdom and engaging in good works. This is the meaning of "until Abraham our father appeared and he received the reward of all of them," that is, the reward that they would have deserved to receive had they been righteous. It was therefore only right to give a rich reward to this man who came after all the generations of wickedness and lived among them, because they did not deflect him from the ways of the Lord (Aknin).

————

WITH TEN TRIALS WAS ABRAHAM OUR FATHER (MAY HE REST IN PEACE) TRIED, AND HE WITHSTOOD THEM ALL—TO MAKE KNOWN HOW GREAT WAS THE LOVE OF ABRAHAM OUR FATHER, MAY HE REST IN PEACE.

TEN TRIALS:

Twice, when ordered to move on (Genesis 12:1 f., 12:10);
Twice, in connection with his two sons (Genesis 21:10, 22:1 ff.);
Twice, in connection with his two wives (Genesis 12:11 ff., 21:10);
Once, on the occasion of his war with the kings (Genesis 14:13 ff.);
Once, at the [covenant] between the pieces (Genesis 15);
Once, in Ur of the Chaldees [when he was thrown into a fire furnace by Nimrod];

And once, at the covenant of circumcision (Genesis 17: 9 ff.)

Now, what was the reason for all this? So that when Abraham our father comes to take his reward, the peoples of the world shall say: "More than all of us, more than everyone, is Abraham worthy of getting his reward!" (ARN).

The various Midrashim do not agree exactly in what the TEN were, although all of them are unanimous that there were TEN trials (Duran).

Why was Abraham tried with TEN trials, no more no less? These trials correspond to the TEN utterances by which the world was created. Abraham, who was tried with TEN trials and was found steadfast, was worthy to sustain the world which was created by TEN utterances (Vitry).

The TEN trials with which Abraham was tried are mentioned here to teach us that when one of us is put to the test, he should not grieve over it; let this not seem evil in his sight; let him not say, "Why bother acquiring wisdom and good works, seeing that troubles come upon me? I might as well pursue my heart's desires for worldly delights, and not labor in vain." Lo, there was Abraham our father, may he rest in peace, this grandee of the universe, the lover of the Lord, of whom it is written, *The seed of Abraham who loved me* (Isaiah 41:8)—God tested him many times! All the more therefore should I, of the least in the world, accept trouble with cheer and love and not regard it as evil. Now, why are trials brought upon the righteous? In order to make them known in the world as lovers of the Most High whose hearts are steadfast before Him, as it is written, *That He might afflict thee, to prove thee, to know what was in thy heart, whether thou wouldst keep His commandments, or no* (Deuteronomy 8:2)—that is, to make known to the inhabitants of the world what is in your heart, for before Him it is revealed and well known; and in order to give you double reward, as it is written, *To do thee good at thy latter end* (Deuteronomy 8:16) (Aknin).

TEN MIRACLES WERE WROUGHT FOR OUR ANCESTORS IN EGYPT AND TEN AT THE SEA.

TEN PLAGUES THE HOLY ONE, BLESSED BE HE, VISITED ON THE EGYPTIANS IN EGYPT, AND TEN AT THE SEA.

TEN MIRACLES: Corresponding to the TEN trials with which Abraham our father was tried and in all of which he was found steadfast, the Holy One, blessed be He, performed TEN miracles for his children in Egypt. Corresponding to those trials, the Holy One, blessed be He, brought TEN plagues on the Egyptians in Egypt. Corresponding to those, TEN miracles were wrought for Israel at the Red Sea. Corresponding to those, TEN plagues were brought upon the Egyptians in the Sea (ARN).

TEN miracles were wrought for our ancestors in Egypt and TEN at the Sea to make known His love of Israel. TEN plagues the Holy One, blessed be He, brought upon the Egyptians in Egypt and TEN at the Sea, to make known the might of God (ARNB).

The TEN miracles wrought for our ancestors in Egypt were their being spared from the TEN plagues visited on the Egyptians (Maimonides).

TEN AT THE SEA: When our ancestors stood at the Red Sea, Moses said to them: "Rise, go across!"

"We shall not go across," they declared, "until tunnels are made in the sea."

Moses took his rod and smote the sea, and tunnels were made in it, as it is said, *Thou hast stricken through with rods the head of his rulers* (Habakkuk 3:14).

Said Moses to them: "Rise, go across!"

"We shall not go across," they declared, "until the sea is turned into a valley before us."

Moses took the rod and smote the sea, and it became a valley before them, as it is said, *He made a valley of the sea, and caused them to pass through* (Psalm 78:13), and it is said, *As the cattle that go down into the valley, so didst Thou lead Thy people* (Isaiah 63:14).

Said Moses to them: "Rise, go across!"

"We shall not go across," they declared, "until it is cut asunder before us."

Moses took the rod and smote the sea, and it was cut asunder before them, as it is said, *To Him who divided the Red Sea in sunder* (Psalm 136:13).

Said Moses to them: "Rise, go across!"

"We shall not go across," they declared, "until it is turned into clay for our benefit."

Moses took the rod and smote the sea, and it became clay,

as it is said, *Thou hast trodden the sea with Thy horses, through the clay of mighty waters* (Habakkuk 3:15).

Said Moses to them: "Rise, go across!"

"We shall not go across," they declared, "until it is made into a wilderness before us."

Moses took the rod and smote the sea, and it became a wilderness, as it is said, *And He led them through the depths as through a wilderness* (Psalm 106:9).

Said Moses to them: "Rise, go across!"

"We shall not go across," they declared, "until it is broken into many pieces before us."

Moses took the rod and smote the sea, and it was broken into many pieces, as it is said, *Thou didst break the sea in pieces by Thy strength* (Psalm 74:13).

Said Moses to them: "Rise, go across!"

"We shall not go across," they declared, "unless it is turned into rocks before us."

Moses took the rod and smote the sea, and it turned into rocks, as it is said, *Thou didst shatter the heads of the sea-monsters on the waters* (*ibid.*). Now on what are the heads of sea-monsters dashed? Say surely, the heads of sea-monsters would not be dashed save on rocks!

Said Moses to them: "Rise, go across!"

"We shall not go across," they declared, "until it is turned into dry land for us."

Moses took the rod and smote the sea, and it turned into dry land, as it is said, *He turned the sea into dry land* (Psalm 66:6); it also says, *But the children of Israel walked upon dry land in the midst of the sea* (Exodus 14:29).

Said Moses to them: "Rise, go across!"

"We shall not go across," they declared, "unless it is turned into walls before us."

Moses took the rod and smote the sea, and it turned into walls, as it is said, *And the waters were a wall unto them, on their right hand, and on their left* (*ibid.*).

Said Moses to them: "Rise, go across!"

"We shall not go across," they declared, "unless it is turned flask-shaped before us."

Moses took the rod and smote the sea, and it turned flask-shaped, as it is said, [*The waters*] *stood upright like flasks containing liquids* (Exodus 15:8).—

As for the waters between the sundered paths, a fire came down and lapped them up, as it is said, *When fire caused that which melts to disappear, and the fire lapped up the waters;*

to make Thy name known to Thine adversaries (Isaiah 64:1).—

And the flasks released oil and honey into the mouths of the babes and of this they took suck, as it is said, *And He made him to suck honey out of the crag* (Deuteronomy 32:13).

Some say: Fresh water came forth for them from the sea, and this they drank in the midst of the sundered paths—for the waters of the sea are salty—for it is said *flowing streams,* and "flowing streams" are none other than sweet waters, as it is said, *A well of living waters, and flowing streams from Lebanon* (Canticles 4:15).

With the clouds of glory over them lest the sun overpower them, Israel crossed so as not to be discomfited.

Rabbi Eliezer and Rabbi Simeon say: The upper and lower waters tossed the Egyptians up and down, as it is said, *And the Lord tossed the Egyptians up and down in the midst of the sea* (Exodus 14:27) (ARN).

TEN PLAGUES: These are the TEN plagues: *Blood* (Exodus 7:17 ff.), *frogs* (Exodus 7:27 ff.), *gnats* (Exodus 8:12 ff.), *swarms* (Exodus 8:17 ff.), *murrain* (Exodus 9:2 ff.), *boils* (Exodus 9:8 ff.), *hail* (Exodus 9:18 ff.), *locust* (Exodus 10:4 ff.), *darkness* (Exodus 10:21 ff.), *death of the first born* (Exodus 11:4 ff.) (ARNB).

TEN AT THE SEA: These are the plagues they were smitten with at the Sea: *The horse and his rider hath He thrown into the Sea* (Exodus 15:1); *Pharaoh's chariots and his host hath He cast into the Sea* (Exodus 15:4a); *And his chosen captains are sunk in the Red Sea* (Exodus 15:4b); *Thou overthrowest them that rise up against Thee* (Exodus 15:7a); *Thou sendest forth Thy wrath* (Exodus 15:7b); *They sank as lead in the mighty waters* (Exodus 15:10b); *And with the blast of Thy nostrils the waters were piled up* (Exodus 15:8) (ARNB).

These are the TEN plagues at the Sea, TEN kinds of death described by TEN different verbs in the fifteenth chapter of Exodus: *hath He thrown* (15:2); *hath He cast* (15:4); *deeps cover them* (15:5); *they went down into the depths* (15:5); *dashes in pieces the enemy* (15:6); *Thou overthrowest them that rise up against Thee* (15:7); *it consumeth them as stubble* (15:7); *the waters were piled up, the floods stood upright as a heap* (15:8)—for the waters were made into a heap, piled high, against which the Egyptians broke their heads; *they sank as lead* (15:10) (Vitry).

Mention is made here of the TEN plagues which the Holy One, blessed be He, brought upon Israel's enemies, and the trials He put them through, in order to stir scholars to study and practice, and in order to make known to them that the Holy One, blessed be He, will for their sake bring to pass miracles and wonders if they study Torah for the right reasons, and that He will punish their enemies—even as He did for their ancestors (Aknin).

———

WITH TEN TRIALS OUR ANCESTORS TRIED GOD, BLESSED BE HE, IN THE WILDERNESS, AS IT IS SAID, *They have put Me to proof these ten times, and have not hearkened to My voice* (Numbers 14:22).

TEN TRIALS: To wit, *In the wilderness, at Arabah, over against Suph, in the neighborhood of Paran and Tophel, and Laban, and Hazeroth, and Di-zahab* (Deuteronomy 1:1).

In the wilderness, where they made the golden calf, as it is said, *They made a calf in Horeb* (Psalm 106:19).

At Arabah, where they clamored for water, as it is said, *And the people thirsted there for water* (Exodus 17:3). Some say: This refers to the idol of Micah.

Over against Suph is a reference to their being rebellious at the Red Sea. Rabbi Judah says: They were rebellious at the sea, they were rebellious in the sea, as it is said, *But they were rebellious at the sea, even in the Red Sea* (Psalm 106:7).

In the neighborhood of Paran refers to the incident of the spies, as it is said, *And Moses sent them from the wilderness of Paran* (Numbers 13:3).

And Tophel refers to the slanderous words which they uttered over the manna.

And Laban refers to the controversy of Korah.

And Hazeroth refers to the incident of the quail.

These are seven. And elsewhere it says, *And at Taberah, and at Massah, and at Kibroth-Hattavah ye made the Lord wroth* (Deuteronomy 9:22).

And Di-zahab: Said Aaron to them: "Enough for you is the sin of the gold which you brought for the calf!"

Rabbi Eliezer ben Jacob says: For this iniquity there is enough to punish Israel from now until the dead are resurrected (ARN).

———

TEN MIRACLES WERE WROUGHT FOR OUR ANCESTORS IN THE TEMPLE:

NO WOMAN EVER MISCARRIED BECAUSE OF THE SMELL OF THE SACRED FLESH;

THE SACRED FLESH NEVER WENT BAD;

NEVER WAS A FLY SEEN IN THE SLAUGHTERHOUSE;

NEVER DID THE HIGH PRIEST SUFFER UNCLEANNESS ON THE DAY OF ATONEMENT;

NEVER DID THE RAINS EXTINGUISH THE FIRE OF THE WOODPILE [ON THE ALTAR];

NO WIND PREVAILED OVER THE PILLAR OF SMOKE;

NEVER WAS A DEFECT FOUND IN THE OMER OR IN THE TWO LOAVES OR IN THE SHOWBREAD;

THE PEOPLE STOOD PRESSED TOGETHER YET BOWED DOWN AND HAD ROOM ENOUGH;

NEVER DID A SERPENT OR SCORPION HARM ANYONE IN JERUSALEM;

NO MAN EVER SAID TO HIS FELLOW: "TOO CONGESTED IS THE PLACE FOR ME THAT I SHOULD LODGE IN JERUSALEM."

TEN MIRACLES WERE WROUGHT FOR OUR ANCESTORS IN THE TEMPLE: This Mishna informs us of the miracles that were wrought, in the sacrifices, in the furnishings for the sacrifices, in behalf of those who offered the sacrifices, in the Temple and its environs, and of God's love for the Temple service (Aknin).

THE SACRED FLESH NEVER WENT BAD: Even though the climate of the Land of Israel is very hot (Nahmias).

NEVER WAS A FLY SEEN IN THE SLAUGHTERHOUSE: Neither were reptiles found there, nor did birds fly over it (ARNB).

NEVER DID THE HIGH PRIEST SUFFER UNCLEANNESS ON THE DAY OF ATONEMENT: Excepting Rabbi Ishmael ben Kimhit: He went out to converse with a certain *hegemon*, and spittle flew from the *hegemon*'s mouth and landed on Ishmael's clothes; so his brother came in and served as High Priest in his place. Their mother thus beheld them both on that day High Priests. When the Sages saw her, they asked: "What merit was thine?" And she replied: "Never did the rafters of my house see the hair of my head" (ARN).

NO WIND PREVAILED OVER THE PILLAR OF SMOKE: When the pillar of smoke rose from the altar of the burnt-offering, it rose straight upward like a staff until it reached the heavens; and when the pillar of incense rose from the golden altar, it entered straightway into the chamber of the Holy of Holies (ARN).

THE OMER: It is brought on Passover, as it is written, *Ye shall bring the omer of the first fruits of your harvest unto the priest* (Leviticus 23:10) (Aknin).

THE TWO LOAVES: They are brought on the festival of Pentecost, as it is written, *Ye shall bring out of your dwellings two wave loaves of two tenth parts of an ephah* (Leviticus 23:17) (Aknin).

THE SHOWBREAD: Of which it is said: *Every Sabbath day he shall set it in order before the Lord continually* (Leviticus 24:8) (Vitry).

The showbread was as fresh on the day it was removed from the table as on the day it was first put there, even as it is said, *Bread hot on the day of its being taken away* (I Samuel 21:7) (Rabbi Jonah).

THE PEOPLE STOOD PRESSED TOGETHER YET BOWED DOWN AND HAD ROOM ENOUGH: On the occasion when Israel went up to worship their Father who is in heaven, while they were sitting, they sat crowded together and no one could force a finger between them; yet when they bowed down, they bowed down and had room enough.

The greatest miracle of all was this: Even if a hundred men bowed down at one time, the minister of the synagogue did not need to call out and say: "Make room for your brethren!"

Miracles were wrought in the Temple-Court: Even if all Israel entered the Temple-Court, the Temple-Court held them.

The greatest miracle of all was this: While Israel was standing up for the Prayer, they were crowded together and no one could force a finger between them; yet when they bowed down, space was formed between them of fully a man's height.

Rabban Simeon ben Gamaliel says: In the future Jerusalem will be the gathering place of all the nations and all the kingdoms, as it is said, *And all the nations shall be gathered unto it, to the name of the Lord, to Jerusalem* (Jeremiah 3:17). Now elsewhere it says, *Let the waters under the heaven be gathered unto one place* (Genesis 1:9). Even as the gathering spoken of in the latter instance refers to the assembling of all the waters of Creation in one place, so the gathering spoken of here refers to the assembling of all the nations and kingdoms in one place, as it is said, *And all the nations shall be gathered unto it* (ARN).

NEVER DID A SERPENT OR SCORPION HARM ANYONE IN JERUSALEM: Never was a man attacked [by demons] in Jerusalem; no man was ever harmed or met with an accident in the Temple (ARN).

Whoever met with an accident outside of Jerusalem would be healed as soon as he looked at the walls of Jerusalem (ARNB).

NO MAN EVER SAID TO HIS FELLOW: "TOO CONGESTED IS THE PLACE FOR ME THAT I SHOULD LODGE IN JERUSALEM": No payment for a bed is accepted there—Rabbi Judah says: Not even payment for beds [and] coverings.

The hides of the sacrificial beasts are not for sale there. What was done with them? Rabban Simeon ben Gamaliel says: They were given to the innkeepers. The guests would stay indoors and the innkeepers out of doors. The guests resorted to an evasion by buying painted sheep whose hides were worth four to five *sela,* and these were left as compensation for the men of Jerusalem (ARN).

No man ever said to his fellow, "I am pressed for time, for I haven't sufficient means and I am unable to remain or lodge in Jerusalem." For the Holy One provides with a livelihood all those who dwell in Jerusalem, so that they need not quit it. This is an interpretation I have received. But it seems to me that the statement refers actually to the pilgrimage festivals when all Israel gathered in Jerusalem and the upkeep was enormous. . . . And no man ever spoke to his fellow as people on such occasion are wont to complain and grumble, "The place is too crowded for me to spend the night here," either because a night's lodging was not available, or because one could not get what he needed in the city (Vitry).

I have been told that the Jerusalem synagogue is filled to capacity when all the residents of the community come into it. During the pilgrimage festivals more than three hundred people come up to the city from the communities round about. And yet all of them are able to get into the synagogue without difficulty. The holiness of the place still clings to it! (Duran).

TEN THINGS WERE CREATED ON THE [FIRST] SABBATH EVE
AT TWILIGHT, TO WIT: THE MOUTH OF THE EARTH, THE
MOUTH OF THE WELL [IN THE WILDERNESS], THE ASS'S
POWER OF SPEECH, THE RAINBOW, THE MANNA, THE ROD
[OF MOSES], THE SHAMIR, THE LETTERS, THE WRITING, AND
THE TABLES OF THE COMMANDMENTS.

SOME SAY: ALSO THE DEMONS, THE BURIAL PLACE OF
MOSES, AND THE RAM OFFERED UP BY ABRAHAM OUR
FATHER.

AND SOME SAY: ALSO THE TONGS MADE WITH TONGS.

TEN THINGS WERE CREATED: From the very beginning of
Creation, God included in the nature of every created thing
whatever He was going to do with it—whether it would always behave uniformly and hence in accordance with the
laws of nature, or act extraordinarily, that is, be a miracle.
That is why the Sage says that on the sixth day it was ordained
for the earth to swallow Korah, and for the rock to bring forth
water, for the ass to speak, and so on (Maimonides).

All the ancient signs and wonders performed by the prophets, and whatever is destined to be in the future, all were
created in the first six days of Creation. . . . The Holy One,
blessed be He, simply informs the prophet of the time and the
occasion when He will perform the wondrous act the like of
which had not come to pass before (Aknin).

According to my view, it is not because the things mentioned in our Mishna were miracles that it is said of them
that they were created at twilight and at that time was their
existence decreed; rather, they are said to have been created
at twilight because they are unlike the other works of Creation, their creation is not reported [in Scripture], nor were
they created after the first six days of Creation, for it is said,
There is nothing new under the sun (Ecclesiastes 1:9); therefore they must have been created at twilight [of the first
Sabbath eve] (Duran).

AT TWILIGHT: Until twilight of the first Sabbath eve the
Holy One, blessed be He, was occupied with the works described in the first chapter of Genesis. . . . After having made
all those things, He made these [spoken of in our Mishna]
(Vitry).

Each of the things listed in our Mishna was created in the
twilight of the day of its creation. For example, the rainbow,
the manna, the tongs . . . the mouth of the earth . . . the

stone tables of the commandments, the burial place of Moses, were created on the twilight of the first day of Creation. The mouth of the well . . . was created on the twilight of the second day of Creation. . . (Aknin).

THE MOUTH OF THE EARTH: As it is said, *And the earth opened her mouth, and swallowed them up, and their households, and all the men that appertained unto Korah, and all their goods* (Numbers 16:32) (Vitry).

THE MOUTH OF THE WELL: Of which Israel sang, "*Spring up, O well* (Numbers 22:17), Spring up, O well," and it would appear immediately and follow them in their journey through the wilderness (Vitry).

THE ASS'S POWER OF SPEECH: As the verse says, *And the Lord opened the mouth of the ass* (Numbers 22:28) (Vitry).

THE RAINBOW: As it is said, *I have set My bow in the cloud* (Genesis 9:13) (Vitry).

THE MANNA: Which served Israel as food in the wilderness (Vitry).

THE ROD [OF MOSES]: With which Moses split the [Red] Sea. There was nothing like it in the world, for on it was engraved the ineffable Name of God. This rod Adam handed on to Seth, and it was handed on from one generation to the next until Jacob, our father, went down to Egypt and handed it on to Joseph. Now, when Joseph died Pharaoh's servants searched through everything in his house, and they deposited the rod in Pharaoh's treasury. In Pharaoh's household was Jethro, the father-in-law of Moses; Jethro was one of Pharaoh's astrologers and he learned of the importance of this rod by means of astrology. He took it and planted it in his garden, and it took root in the earth. By means of astrology Jethro discovered that whoever would be able to uproot this rod, would be the savior of Israel. He therefore used to put people to the test, and when Moses came to his household and then rose and uprooted it, Jethro threw him into the dungeon he had in his courtyard. Zippora fell in love with Moses and demanded from her father that he be given her as husband. Thereupon Jethro married her off to Moses. Another interpretation we have come upon is this: that "the rod" refers to Aaron's rod which [put forth buds and] bore ripe almonds (Numbers 17:23) . . . and it was decreed that by means of it should Moses achieve all the signs and wonders (Vitry).

THE SHAMIR: According to a tradition I received, it was a kind of worm and by means of it [miraculously] the names of the tribes of Israel were engraved on the stones of the ephod and High Priest's breastplate, as is explained in the Talmud (Sotah 48b): the name would be outlined on the stones, the shamir would then be drawn along the stone over the outline of the letter, and the engraving would take place on the stone wherever the shamir moved (Vitry).

The shamir is a small crawling thing which cleaves large stones when it crawls over them. With its help Solomon built the Temple (Maimonides).

THE WRITING: That is, the stylus with which the Tables of the Commandments were engraved (Vitry).

The Divine Writing which was inscribed on the Tables of the Commandments, as it is said, *And the writing was the writing of God, graven upon the tables* (Exodus 32:16) (Maimonides).

THE TABLES OF THE COMMANDMENTS: For they were the handiwork of God (Exodus 32:16) (Vitry).

THE BURIAL PLACE OF MOSES: As it is said, *And no man knoweth of his sepulchre unto this day* (Deuteronomy 34:6) (Vitry).

THE RAM OFFERED UP BY ABRAHAM OUR FATHER: As it is said, *And behold, long before him a ram caught in the thicket by his horns* (Genesis 22:13), that is, from the very beginning the ram had been appointed (Vitry).

TONGS MADE WITH TONGS: For the way to make tongs is by means of other tongs. The first tongs, therefore, who made them? Perforce you must say that they were created by Heaven (Vitry).

⅂EVEN QUALITIES CHARACTERIZE THE CLOD AND SEVEN THE WISE MAN: THE WISE MAN DOES NOT SPEAK BEFORE HIM THAT IS GREATER THAN HE IN WISDOM; HE DOES NOT BREAK INTO HIS FELLOW'S SPEECH; HE IS NOT IN A RUSH TO REPLY; HE ASKS WHAT IS RELEVANT AND REPLIES TO THE POINT; HE SPEAKS OF FIRST THINGS FIRST AND OF LAST THINGS LAST; OF WHAT HE HAS NOT HEARD HE SAYS: "I HAVE NOT HEARD"; AND HE ACKNOWLEDGES WHAT IS TRUE.

AND THE OPPOSITES APPLY TO THE CLOD.

SEVEN THINGS: After lists involving the number TEN, begin statements involving the number SEVEN (Duran).

THE CLOD ... THE WISE MAN: A person without perception and intelligence is called a clod, for he is like an object that has not been completely finished (Vitry).

As we have explained earlier in our work: A boor is a man in whom are neither intellectual nor moral virtues, that is to say, neither learning nor moral conduct—even evil qualities he does not acquire; he is naked, as it were, of all good and evil. That is why he is called a boor, he is like earth which can grow nothing. . . . The *am ha-arez* is a person in whom are to be found moral virtues but no intellectual ones, that is to say, he is characterized by moral behavior but not by learning. And he is called *am ha-arez* ("worldly person"), that is, he is valuable for social and civic purposes, because he does have those qualities which benefit social intercourse. Now, a clod is a person in whom are to be found moral and intellectual virtues, but in a state of incompleteness, and not functioning properly, but in a state of confusion and complete disorganization, and with deficiencies. That is why he is called a clod; he is like an implement beginning to take shape in the hands of the craftsman but still lacking completion. . . . The wise man is a person in whom the two virtues, the intellectual and the moral are developed perfectly, and as they should be. . . .

Now, the Mishna tells us that a wise man will be characterized by the seven qualities it lists. These are basic characteristics, and that is why the Mishna directs attention to them since by means of these learning and study are improved. Four of these characteristics belong to the ethical virtues, namely, a person not speaking before him that is wiser than he; not breaking into his fellow's speech, but waiting until he has heard what his fellow has to say; and not sounding off on subjects he knows nothing about: and this is what the Mishna is referring to by the statement "of what he has not heard he says, 'I have not heard,'" and not being perverse in argument, but acknowledging what is true when he hears it; even if it is possible for him to contradict and persist in his own arguments and to triumph over his fellow—this does not seem right to him. It is to this the Mishna refers in the statement "and he acknowledges what is true."

As to the three characteristics which belong to the intellectual virtues—if in debate some sophist tries to mislead him by the tricks of sophistry, let him not grow flustered and confused in his reply and remain in doubt about the truth of the matter; instead, let him immediately feel where the error lies, and explain it. It is to this that the Mishna refers in its statement "he is not in a rush (i.e., confused) to reply." And this can indeed be done by diligent and perceptive attention to the sophist's argument, and a knowledge of the terms used. A second intellectual virtue is asking what is relevant to the subject—not demanding metaphysical proofs in the study of nature or natural arguments in metaphysical studies, and such like confusions. And so too if a person is asked a question, let him answer what is relevant to the question . . . and this is what is meant by the statement "he asks what is relevant and replies to the point." This capacity is developed only after very much learning. The third characteristic is this, that he organizes his learning, and what should come first he puts first and what should come last he puts last. This way of study is really excellent (Maimonides).

THE WISE MAN DOES NOT SPEAK BEFORE HIM THAT IS GREATER THAN HE IN WISDOM: Or in age. Such a wise man was Moses. For it says, *And Aaron spoke all the words which the Lord had spoken unto Moses, and did the signs in the sight of the people* (Exodus 4:30). Who indeed was qualified to speak, Moses or Aaron? Surely Moses! For Moses heard [the words] from the mouth of the Almighty, while Aaron heard them [only] from the mouth of Moses. But thus thought Moses: Shall I then speak while my older brother is standing by? He therefore said to Aaron: "Speak thou." That is why it is said, *And Aaron spoke all the words which the Lord had spoken unto Moses* (ARN).

HE DOES NOT BREAK INTO HIS FELLOW'S SPEECH: Such was Aaron. For it is said, *Then Aaron spoke . . . Behold, this day have they offered their sin-offering, and their burnt-offering . . . and there have befallen me such things as these* (Leviticus 10:19): He kept quiet until Moses finished what he wanted to say, and Aaron did not say to him: "Cut thy words short." Only afterwards did he say to Moses: *"Behold, this day they have brought their offerings,* although we are in mourning!" (ARN).

When Abraham was praying in behalf of the Men of Sodom, the Holy One, blessed be He, said to him: *If I find in Sodom fifty righteous . . . then I will forgive all the place for their sake* (Genesis 18:26). It was manifest and foreknown to Him that spake and the world came into being that had there been present in Sodom three or five righteous men, iniquity would not have affected it. Yet the Holy One, blessed be He, waited until Abraham finished what he wanted to say, and only then answered him; as it is said, *And the Lord went His way when He had left off speaking to Abraham* (Genesis 18:33): God, as it were, said to him: "Now, I shall depart"; as it is said, *And the Lord went His way . . . then Abraham returned unto his place* (*ibid.*) (ARN).

If the Holy One, blessed be He, to whom belongs the universe and everything in it, did not wish to break into the words of Abraham our father, how much the more should man, who is dust, worm, and maggot, not break into the speech of his fellow (ARNB).

HE IS NOT IN A RUSH TO REPLY: Such was Elihu ben Barachel the Buzite. For it is said, *I am young, and ye are very old; wherefore I held back, and durst not declare you mine opinion. I said: Days should speak, and multitude of years should teach wisdom* (Job 32:6 f.). This teaches that Job's friends sat and kept quiet in the presence of Job. When he stood up, they stood up; when he sat down, they sat down; when he ate, they ate; when he drank, they drank. Finally he asked their permission and spoke up, cursing his day, as it is said, *After this opened Job his mouth and cursed his day . . . and said: Let the day perish when I was born, and the night wherein it was said: A man-child is brought forth* (Job 3:1 ff.). . . .

And how do we know that they did not respond out of turn? For it is said, *Then Job answered and said* (Job 3:2 and *passim*); *Then answered Eliphaz the Temanite, and said* (Job 4:1, etc.); *Then answered Bildad the Shuhite, and said* (Job 8:1, etc.); *Then answered Zophar the Naamathite, and said* (Job 11:1, etc.); *Then Elihu the son of Barachel the Buzite answered, and said* (Job 32:1). Scripture arranged them one by one only in order to make known to all the inhabitants of the world that the wise man does not speak before him that is greater than he in wisdom, does not break into his fellow's speech, and is not in a rush to reply (ARN).

HE ASKS WHAT IS RELEVANT: Such was Judah who said, *I will be surety for him* (Genesis 43:9). Asking what is not relevant was Reuben. For it is said, *And Reuben said unto his father: Thou shalt slay my two sons* (Genesis 42:37) (ARN).

HE SPEAKS OF FIRST THINGS FIRST AND OF LAST THINGS LAST: Such was Rebecca, the daughter of Bethuel, as it is said, *He said: Whose daughter art thou? tell me, I pray thee. Is there room in thy father's house for us to lodge in? And she said unto him: I am the daughter of Bethuel the son of Milcah, whom she bore unto Nahor. She said moreover unto him: We have both straw and provender enough, and room to lodge in* (Genesis 24:23-25) (ARNB).

It is a characteristic of childishness [to answer first things last and last things first] (Vitry).

OF WHAT HE HAS NOT HEARD HE SAYS: "I HAVE NOT HEARD": He is not ashamed to say I have not heard. Such a person was Moses, as it is said, *And Moses said unto him: Stay ye, that I may hear what the Lord will command concerning you* (Numbers 9:8) (ARNB).

We have been taught in the Talmud (Berakot 4a), "Teach your tongue to say 'I don't know' lest you be caught in error" (Vitry).

When a person has not heard something from his teacher, let him say, "The following view I have not heard from my teacher." If he has an opinion of his own in the matter, let him give it, but let him add, "So it seems to me" (Rabbi Jonah).

HE ACKNOWLEDGES WHAT IS TRUE: Such was Moses, for it is said, *And the Lord said unto me: They have well said that which they have spoken* (Deuteronomy 18:17). So too the Holy One, blessed be He, acknowledged what is true, as it is said, *And the Lord spoke unto Moses, saying: The daughters of Zelophehad speak right* (Numbers 27:6 f.) (ARN).

AND THE OPPOSITES APPLY TO THE CLOD: He is in a rush to speak; he breaks into his fellow's speech; he speaks in the presence of those who are greater than he; he is in a rush to reply; he asks what is not proper and replies irrelevantly; of things that are first he says that they are last, and of last things that they are first; he does not acknowledge the truth; he is ashamed to learn and ashamed to say, "I have not heard" (ARNB).

SEVEN KINDS OF CALAMITY COME UPON THE WORLD FOR SEVEN CLASSES OF TRANSGRESSION:

IF SOME TITHE AND SOME DO NOT, FAMINE AS A RESULT

OF DROUGHT COMES—SOME GO HUNGRY AND [ONLY] SOME HAVE ENOUGH TO EAT;

IF [ALL] DETERMINE NOT TO TITHE, A FAMINE AS A RESULT OF TUMULT AND OF DROUGHT COMES;

AND IF [THEY RESOLVED] NOT TO SET ASIDE THE DOUGH-OFFERING, AN ALL-CONSUMING FAMINE COMES.

SEVEN KINDS OF CALAMITY: The purpose of this saying is this: Let a man review his works meticulously and take thought over every calamity that befalls him. Perhaps it is a punishment (Meiri).

IF SOME TITHE AND SOME DO NOT, FAMINE AS A RESULT OF DROUGHT COMES: As it is said, *Therefore over you the Heaven hath kept back, so that there is no dew* (Haggai 1:10) (ARNB).

For neglect of heave-offerings and tithes the Heavens are held back from bringing down dew and rain, and the people are handed over to the government (ARN).

IF [ALL] DETERMINE NOT TO TITHE: If all determine not to tithe, they hold back the Heavens from bringing down dew and rain and men toil but cannot provide for themselves (ARN).

If all determined not to tithe at all, an all-consuming famine would come upon the world, as it is said, *And ye shall eat the flesh of your sons, and the flesh of your daughters shall ye eat* (Leviticus 26:29). Said the Holy One, blessed be He, to them: "I gave you fruits in abundance so that you set aside tithes for Me, but you did not wish to do so. I shall therefore give you something which is exempt of tithes!" (ARNB).

AND IF [THEY RESOLVED] NOT TO SET ASIDE THE DOUGH-OFFERING: For the neglect of the dough-offering no blessing comes upon the fruits, and men toil but cannot provide for themselves (ARN).

Said the Holy One, blessed be He, to them: "I gave you loaves in abundance so that you set aside the dough-offering for Me. But you did not wish to do so. I shall therefore give you something which is exempt of dough offering. And what is that? The flesh of your sons and daughters!" (ARNB).

DROUGHT . . . TUMULT . . . ALL-CONSUMING FAMINE: When in a few places only a little rain falls in the course of the year and in some place there is no rain at all, and where it does rain, it rains only little—that is a famine of drought. As for an all-consuming famine—men are distraught by wars and calamities and evil happenings constantly befalling them, so that lands become barren and there is no sowing in the sowing season because of the turmoil in the world. And a famine because of tumult is this: No rain at all falls, and the streams and the rivers run utterly dry, and it is as Scripture says, *And thy heaven that is over thy head shall be brass, and the earth that is under thee shall be iron* (Deuteronomy 28:23) (Maimonides).

———

PESTILENCE COMES UPON THE WORLD FOR CRIMES PUNISHABLE BY DEATH ACCORDING TO THE TORAH WHICH HAVE NOT BEEN TURNED OVER TO THE COURT, AND FOR NEGLECT OF THE LAW REGARDING THE EARTH'S FRUITS IN THE SABBATICAL YEAR.

PESTILENCE: Pestilence comes upon the world for neglect of the laws of harvest-gleanings, the forgotten sheaf, the corner of the field, and poor man's tithe.

There was once a [poor] woman who dwelt in the neighborhood of a landowner. Her two sons went out to gather gleanings, but the landowner did not let them take any. Their mother kept saying: "When will my sons come back from the field; perhaps I shall find that they have brought something to eat." And they kept saying: "When shall we go back to our mother; perhaps we shall discover that she has found something to eat."

She found that they had nothing and they found that she had nothing to eat. So they laid their heads on their mother's lap and the three of them died in one day.

Said the Holy One, blessed be He, "Their very existence you take away from them! By your life! I shall make you too pay for it with your very existence!"

And so indeed it says, *Rob not the weak, because he is weak, neither crush the poor in the gate; for the Lord will plead their cause, and despoil of life those that despoil them* (Proverbs 22:22 f.) (ARN).

CRIMES PUNISHABLE BY DEATH ACCORDING TO THE TORAH: That is to say, crimes punishable by death at the hand of Heaven. Namely, if people have gotten into the habit of committing transgressions for which the sentence is not death at the hand of the courts, but death at the hand of Heaven, then the Holy One brings a pestilence upon the world and exacts punishment from men; and this is what is meant by death at the hand of Heaven (Vitry).

Our statement means this: Since the courts did not punish with death those guilty of this penalty, the Holy One, blessed be He, slays them by means of pestilence and wipes them out of the world (Aknin).

[Pestilence comes] when the courts have not sentenced a person with the death penalty he deserved. And this is a kind of measure for measure. In this penalty are included also those guilty of neglect of the law regarding the earth's fruits in the sabbatical year: that is, he who does not make such fruits free to all, is the cause of death to the poor who have nothing to eat; for in the seventh year men have not sown, and the poor have therefore no hope of tithes or poor-man's gifts. For this reason pestilence comes upon the world, a kind of measure for measure (Meiri).

NEGLECT OF THE LAW REGARDING THE EARTH'S FRUITS IN THE SABBATICAL YEAR: Through such neglect the poor are robbed of what is their due (Vitry).

Neglect of this law consists in not removing such fruits from the house, but engaging in trade with them; and this is forbidden (Rabbi Jonah).

———

THE SWORD COMES UPON THE WORLD FOR THE DELAY OF JUSTICE, FOR THE PERVERSION OF JUSTICE, AND BECAUSE OF THOSE THAT TEACH THE TORAH NOT IN ACCORDANCE WITH THE HALAKAH.

THE SWORD COMES UPON THE WORLD: Now when Rabban Simeon ben Gamaliel and Rabbi Ishmael were taken off to be slain, Rabban Simeon ben Gamaliel kept turning the matter over in his mind, saying: "Woe unto us that we are being slain like Sabbath-breakers, like idol-worshippers, like the unchaste, and like bloodshedders!"

Said Rabbi Ishmael ben Elisha to him: "By thy leave, may I say something before thee?"

"Speak," he replied.

Said Rabbi Ishmael: "Perhaps when thou didst settle down to dinner, poor folk came and stood at thy door, and thou didst not let them come in and eat?"

"By Heaven!" Rabban Simeon protested, "I did not act that way. On the contrary, I had doormen sitting at the entrance: when the poor came, the doormen would bring them in to me and the poor used to eat and drink with me and recite a blessing in the name of Heaven."

"Perhaps," Rabbi Ishmael asked him, "when thou didst sit holding a discourse on the Temple-mount and all the hosts of Israel sat before thee, thy thoughts puffed up with pride?"

"Ishmael my brother," he replied, "a person must be prepared to receive his punishment."

Now they both kept appealing to the executioner. Rabbi Ishmael said to him: "I am a priest, son of a High Priest; kill me first and let me not behold the death of my fellow."

And Rabban Simeon said: "I am a prince, son of a prince; kill me first and let me not behold the death of my fellow."

Said the executioner to them: "Cast lots."

So they cast lots and the lot fell upon Rabban Simeon ben Gamaliel [to die first]. Whereupon the executioner took his sword and cut off Rabban Simeon's head.

Rabbi Ishmael ben Elisha took hold of it and held it to his breast, and kept weeping and crying out, "O holy mouth, O faithful mouth! O mouth that uttered beautiful gems and precious stones and pearls! Who hath laid thee in the dust! Who hath filled thy tongue with dust and ashes! Of thee the verse says, *Awake, O sword, against My shepherd, and against the man that is near unto Me"* (Zechariah 13:7).

Before he could finish his lament, the executioner took the sword and cut off his head. And of them the verse said, *My wrath shall wax hot, and I will kill you with the sword; and your wives shall be widows, and your children fatherless* (Exodus 22:23).

Since the verse says, *And I will kill you with the sword,* do I not know that the wives will become widows? But [Scripture here tells us that] they will be widows and yet not widows: for no witnesses shall be found for them to permit them to rewed—as in Bettar, from which not a soul escaped to testify that the married women might now remarry.

And since the verse says, *And your wives shall be widows,* do I not know that the children will be fatherless? But [Scripture implies that] they will be fatherless and yet not fatherless: for their property shall remain under title of their fathers, and the children will not be permitted to take possession, or to transact business with it (ARN).

DELAY OF JUSTICE: That is, the judge keeps putting off one day and then another the judgment of the person on trial, and instead turns to other cases; in the meantime the person on trial is filled with suffering and worry, for he is kept waiting and he does not know whether he will be found guilty or not (Vitry).

Delaying justice is putting off sentence and postponing it for a long time although the outcome is clear to the judge (Maimonides).

PERVERSION OF JUSTICE: Of perversion of justice the Sages have said (Baba Kamma 119a): He who robs his fellow has taken his soul from him, as it were. . . . And the perverter of justice is he who takes the wealth of one person and gives it to another unjustly (Vitry).

Perversion of justice is rendering a decision contrary to what it should be (Maimonides).

TEACH THE TORAH NOT IN ACCORDANCE WITH THE HALAKAH: That is, not rendering a proper decision . . . for example, a disciple not yet qualified to render decisions, doing so (Vitry).

To "teach the Torah not in accordance with the Halakah" is to say of the forbidden that it is permitted and of the permitted that it is forbidden (Rabbi Jonah).

EVIL BEASTS COME UPON THE WORLD FOR THE TAKING OF FALSE OATHS AND FOR PROFANING THE NAME.

EVIL BEASTS COME UPON THE WORLD: For the sin of false swearing and false testimony and profaning the Name there is a letting loose of evil beasts upon the world; the cattle perish and human population dwindles and the highways are made desolate, as it is said, *And I will send the beast of the field among you, which shall rob you of your children, and destroy your cattle, and make you few in number; and your ways shall become desolate* (Leviticus 26:22) (ARNB).

The difference between humankind and beasts is in speech, and by the power of speech we rule over the animal kingdom. That is why he who does not take the necessary precaution with the honor due his Creator deserves to be trampled by the beasts. . . . For it is proper that beasts should rule over such men as profane the Glory (Rabbi Jonah).

Profaning the Name [of God] is to commit transgressions in defiance and broad daylight (Duran).

EXILE COMES UPON THE WORLD FOR IDOLATROUS WORSHIP, FOR UNCHASTITY, FOR BLOODSHED, AND FOR NEGLECT OF THE YEAR OF RELEASE OF THE LAND.

EXILE COMES UPON THE WORLD: For idolatry, as it is said, *And I will destroy your high places . . . and you will I scatter among the nations* (Leviticus 26:30, 33). Said the Holy One, blessed be He, to Israel: "Since you desire idolatry, I shall indeed exile you to a place where there is idolatry!" That is why it is said, *And I will destroy your high places . . . and you will I scatter among the nations.*

FOR UNCHASTITY, why is that? Said Rabbi Ishmael, son of Rabbi Yose: So long as Israel abandon themselves to unchastity, the Shekinah withdraws from their midst. For it is said, *That He see no unseemly thing in thee, and turn away from thee* (Deuteronomy 23:15).

<FOR BLOODSHED, why is that? For it is said, *So ye shall not pollute the land wherein ye are; for blood, it polluteth the land* (Numbers 35:33).>

FOR NEGLECT OF THE YEAR OF RELEASE OF THE LAND, how do we know that? For it is said, *Then shall the land be paid her sabbaths* (Leviticus 26:34). Said the Holy One, blessed be He, to Israel: "Since you did not release the land, it will release you; the number of months which you did not release it, it will release itself." That is why it is said, *Even then shall the land rest, and repay her sabbaths. As long as it lieth desolate it shall have rest; even the rest which it had not in your sabbaths, when ye dwelt upon it* (Numbers 35:35) (ARN).

The three commandments against idolatry, unchastity, and bloodshed are the gravest of all the commandments in the Torah. If at a time when there is no persecution, and there is no intention of compelling him to apostasize, a person is told, "Commit a transgression and your life will be spared," he may transgress in order not to be slain—but not if it involves these three transgressions! If he is told to commit one of these transgressions, he must die rather than transgress. And when men wittingly commit these transgressions, the Holy One, blessed be He, punishes them with exile, which is captivity. For there is no harsher punishment than this, because then a man is under the domination of others and is without any trace of independence (Aknin).

AT FOUR PERIODS PESTILENCE IS ON THE INCREASE: IN THE FOURTH YEAR, IN THE SEVENTH, AT THE DEPARTURE OF THE SEVENTH, AND ANNUALLY AT THE DEPARTURE OF THE FEAST—

"IN THE FOURTH," FOR NEGLECTING THE POOR MAN'S TITHE IN THE THIRD; "IN THE SEVENTH," FOR NEGLECTING THE POOR MAN'S TITHE IN THE SIXTH YEAR; "AT THE DEPARTURE OF THE SEVENTH YEAR," FOR NEGLECTING THE COMMANDMENT TO RELEASE THE FRUITS OF THE EARTH IN THE SEVENTH YEAR; "ANNUALLY, AT THE DEPARTURE OF THE FEAST," FOR ROBBING THE POOR OF THEIR GIFTS.

AT FOUR PERIODS: After listing statements introduced by the number SEVEN, the Mishna presents statements involving the number FOUR (Duran).

PESTILENCE IS ON THE INCREASE: The Sages (Baba Kamma 119a) teach us: The verse says, *Rob not the impoverished because he is impoverished; for the Lord will plead their cause, and despoil of life those that despoil them* (Proverbs 22:22–23). But does the poor have anything for anybody to rob him of? However, the verse is referring to the gifts due the poor man; that is to say, that he who withholds these gifts and does not give them to the poor, deprives the poor man of his life, as it were. And to what does *And despoil of life those that despoil them* refer? To the robber's own life. For the grasping hand of the robber condemns him to death. Thus we learn that he who robs the poor of their gifts, or withholds the gifts from them, deserves to die (Vitry).

THE FOURTH YEAR: For of the third year it is said, *At the end of every three years, even in the same year, thou shalt bring forth all the tithe of thine increase, and shalt lay it up within thy gates. And the Levite, because he hath no portion nor inheritance with thee, and the stranger, and the fatherless, and the widow, that are within thy gates, shall come, and shall eat and be satisfied* (Deuteronomy 14:28–29). . . . Now, this is the order for the giving of tithes: in the first and second years [of the Sabbatical cycle] the First Tithe [is given to the Levite] and the Second Tithe [is set aside to be eaten in Jerusalem]; in the third year the First and <Poor Man's>

Tithes are set aside; and so too in the fourth and fifth years the First and Second Tithes are set aside, in the sixth year the First and Poor Man's Tithes are set aside (Vitry).

THE DEPARTURE OF THE SEVENTH YEAR: The eighth year is called the departure of the seventh (Vitry).

ANNUALLY, AT THE DEPARTURE OF THE FEAST: The season for ingathering the harvest is in the Feast of Booths, and that is why this holiday is called Feast of Ingathering, that is to say, the feast that comes at the time of ingathering. And when the poor are robbed of their gifts, that is, if the field owners do not leave for them harvest gleanings, the forgotten sheaf, and the corner of the field, the Holy One punishes the owners immediately after they have brought in the harvest (Vitry).

———

THERE ARE FOUR TYPES OF MEN:
  ONE WHO SAYS, "MINE IS MINE AND THINE IS THINE" —THIS IS THE COMMONPLACE TYPE. SOME SAY: THAT IS THE SODOM TYPE.
  "MINE IS THINE AND THINE IS MINE"—THE *Am Ha-Arez*.
  "MINE IS THINE AND THINE IS THINE"—THE SAINT.
  "MINE IS MINE AND THINE IS MINE"—THE WICKED.

"MINE IS MINE AND THINE IS THINE": It is impossible to say that such a person is "the commonplace type" if he refrains altogether from giving charity. Why, that's absolutely wicked! . . . What we are dealing with here is a person who gives charity only out of fear of the Lord, but by nature is really uncharitable. Since he does after all lend a helping hand to the poor and the needy, what difference does his nature make to us? Such behavior is commonplace (Rabbi Jonah).

THE SODOM TYPE: The men of Sodom did not want to take anything from anybody, but they also did not want any poor man to benefit from their possessions, as it is written, *Behold, this was the iniquity of thy sister Sodom: pride, fullness of bread, and careless ease was in her and in her daughters; neither did she strengthen the hand of the poor and needy* (Ezekiel 16:49) (Vitry).

The ones who say that this is the Sodom type are not in controversy with the first view, but make an additional point, namely, that such an attitude [of mine is mine and thine is thine] is very close to the behavior of Sodom. . . . A person who lets no one enjoy of what he has, once he gets into such a habit, will eventually refuse to let people enjoy even of what costs him nothing (Duran).

"MINE IS THINE AND THINE IS MINE": That is to say, he does want his neighbor to derive some benefit from him but he also wants to derive benefit from his neighbor . . . and this attitude is fairly common to most people. . . . However, there are certain commentators who insist that in describing the attitude "mine is thine and thine is mine" as characteristic of the *am ha-arez*, dispraise is intended, that is, that such an attitude reflects deficiency in a man's character even though he is not altogether wicked. I do not think this is so. Nevertheless, even according to this interpretation, it seems to me we can say that such a person, while not so wicked as to rob and indulge in violence, is nevertheless deficient in his character. And this deficiency will lead him to covet the wealth of other people, even though he cannot find it in himself to rob others, since he is not entirely wicked. But because of his coveting he is always thinking in his heart that the next person's wealth is greater than his own. . . . O how many people there are in whom you can find this affliction! It is almost impossible to find even two brothers or two partners who have taken their respective shares, not jealous of each other's portion (Aknin).

THERE ARE FOUR KINDS OF TEMPERAMENT:

EASILY ANGERED AND EASILY APPEASED—HIS GAIN IS CANCELED BY HIS LOSS.

HARD TO ANGER AND HARD TO APPEASE—HIS LOSS IS CANCELED BY HIS GAIN.

HARD TO ANGER AND EASY TO APPEASE—THE SAINT.

EASILY ANGERED BUT HARD TO APPEASE—THE WICKED.

THERE ARE FOUR KINDS OF TEMPERAMENT: Actually these temperaments are in man's power either to improve or to make worse. Otherwise you could not call a man a saint for the one temperament and wicked for the other (Duran).

Note well that the Mishna describes as a saint the person who is extremely long-suffering, to the point where he is free of all stirrings of anger; while the person who has the fault of proneness to anger is called wicked (Maimonides).

The difference between characteristics and temperaments is this: characteristics are within a man's power. For example, saying "mine is mine" and so on. Temperaments, on the other hand, are something implanted in man's nature. But it is possible for a person to control them by the teachings of wisdom, until a complete change of heart takes place in you (Aknin).

It is not necessary that a person should never grow angry—for there are times when a man needs to get angry for the sake of the Lord, as was Phineas. That is why the Mishna uses the expression "hard to anger": that is to say, there are times when it may be necessary for a person by all means to get angry, when he is not permitted to be without anger; but the anger should come with difficulty. It is of this that the ethical philosophers have said, "Do not be sweet, lest you be swallowed up" (Rabbi Jonah).

EASILY ANGERED AND EASILY APPEASED: His loss is canceled by his gain . . . and contrariwise a person who is hard to anger and hard to appease, his gain is canceled by his loss (Aknin, who adopts the following variant reading in the Mishna: "Easily angered and easily appeased—his loss is canceled by his gain. Hard to anger and hard to appease—his gain is canceled by his loss").

———

THERE ARE FOUR TYPES OF DISCIPLES:

QUICK TO UNDERSTAND BUT QUICK TO FORGET—HIS GAIN IS CANCELED BY HIS LOSS.

UNDERSTANDS WITH DIFFICULTY BUT FORGETS WITH DIFFICULTY—HIS LOSS IS CANCELED BY HIS GAIN.

QUICK TO UNDERSTAND AND FORGETS WITH DIFFICULTY—THE WISE.

UNDERSTANDS WITH DIFFICULTY AND QUICK TO FORGET—THIS IS AN EVIL LOT!

On the subject of disciples Rabban Gamaliel the Elder spoke of FOUR kinds: The unclean fish, the clean fish, the fish from the Jordan, the fish from the Great Sea.

The unclean fish: who is that? A poor youth who studies Scripture and Mishna, Halakah and Agada, and is without understanding.

The clean fish: who is that? That's a rich youth who studies

Scripture and Mishna, Halakah and Agada and has understanding.

The fish from the Jordan: who is that? That's a scholar who studies Scripture and Mishna, Midrash, Halakah, and Agada, and is without the talent for give and take.

The fish from the Great Sea: who is that? That's a scholar who studies Scripture and Mishna, Midrash, Halakah, and Agada, and has the talent for give and take (ARN).

There are FOUR types of disciples:

One wishes that he might study and that others might study too—the liberal.

[One wishes] that he might study but not others—the grudging.

[One wishes] that others should study but not he—the commonplace type.

Some say: that's the Sodom type.

[One wishes] that neither he nor others should study—that's the thoroughly wicked (ARN).

If one says, "I shall go and study Torah, for such is my obligation," he is a worthy person. Inferior to him is one who says, "I shall go and study Torah, perhaps others will see me at it." A middling person is one who says, "I shall go and study Torah; perhaps I can learn something and then come and teach it to everyone else." If one says, "I shall go and study Torah so that I may be called a disciple of the wise," he is trash (ARNB).

Note well that the Mishna does not call the intelligent person with a good memory a saint, because this is an intellectual capacity. Therefore it calls him a wise man. Nor has the Mishna called a person who has difficulty understanding and suffers from a bad memory wicked, because this is not within his power. Such abilities are not within a person's power to acquire (Maimonides).

The Sages of the Talmud (Niddah 70b) say: What should a man do in order to become wise? Let him study diligently. But many have acted in this way and it did not help! In that event, let a person plead for mercy from Him to whom belong wisdom and perception, as it is said, *For the Lord giveth wisdom, out of His mouth cometh knowledge and discernment* (Proverbs 2:6) (Nahmias).

———

THERE ARE FOUR TYPES OF CHARITY GIVERS:

HE WHO WISHES TO GIVE BUT THAT OTHERS SHOULD NOT GIVE—BEGRUDGES WHAT BELONGS TO OTHERS.

THAT OTHERS SHOULD GIVE BUT NOT HE—BEGRUDGES WHAT BELONGS TO HIMSELF.

THAT HE SHOULD GIVE AND OTHERS TOO—THE SAINT.

THAT NEITHER HE NOR OTHERS GIVE—THE WICKED.

Three things were said of men: One gives charity; may blessing come upon him! Superior to him is one who lends his funds. Superior to all is one [who forms a partnership with the poor] on terms of one half the profits [for each] or on terms of sharing what remains (ARN).

Note well: the Mishna calls a man of great compassion— who is not content merely to show compassion himself, but wants others also to join him in this—a saint, and the heartless person it calls wicked (Maimonides).

The sages are right in saying that charity may be of three kinds: there is charity that is like gold, there is charity like silver, there is charity like brass. The kind of charity that is like gold is the charity a man practices in secret. . . . Charity that is like silver is hardly a credit to a man—it is the kind a man gives when he is in trouble, or when he has a favorite son who is sick, or when his wife is giving birth with difficulty, or when he is on board ship at sea and storms come up. . . . Charity that is like brass is the following: the man is totally hostile to it, that is to say, he is grudging and will not give charity at all. But when his time is up and he must depart from the world, he realizes his end is at hand, that there is no escape; then he puts his mind to it and orders the members of his household to use his wealth for charitable purposes, imagining that the charity will deliver him from death (David the Prince).

BEGRUDGES WHAT BELONGS TO OTHERS: He does not want others to practice charity, lest thereby their wealth increase; nor does he want them to enjoy a good name (Vitry).

———

THERE ARE FOUR TYPES AMONG THOSE THAT FREQUENT THE STUDY-HOUSE: THERE IS ONE WHO ATTENDS BUT DOES NOT PUT TO PRACTICE—HE RECEIVES THE REWARD FOR ATTENDANCE.

THERE IS ONE WHO PUTS TO PRACTICE BUT DOES NOT ATTEND—HE RECEIVES THE REWARD FOR PRACTICE.

THERE IS ONE WHO ATTENDS AND PUTS TO PRACTICE—THE SAINT.

NEITHER ATTENDS NOR PUTS TO PRACTICE—THE WICKED.

THERE ARE FOUR TYPES AMONG THOSE THAT FREQUENT THE STUDY-HOUSE: One takes his place close to [the sage], and is rewarded; one takes his place close to [the sage], and is not rewarded. One takes his place at a distance [from the sage], and is rewarded; one takes his place at a distance, and is not rewarded.

One engages in discussion, and is rewarded; one engages in discussion, and is not rewarded. One sits and keeps quiet, and is rewarded; one sits and keeps quiet, and is not rewarded.

If one takes his place close to [the sage] in order to listen and learn, he is rewarded.

If one takes his place close to [the sage] so that men may say "There's So-and-so drawing close to and sitting down before a sage," he is not rewarded.

If one takes his place at a distance so that he may honor someone greater than he, he is rewarded.

If one takes his place at a distance so that men may say "So-and-so has no need of a sage," he is not rewarded.

If one engages in discussion in order to understand and learn, he is rewarded.

If one engages in discussion so that men may say "So-and-so engages in discussion in the presence of sages," he is not rewarded.

If one sits and keeps quiet in order to listen and learn, he is rewarded.

If one sits and keeps quiet so that men may say "There's So-and-so sitting quietly in the presence of sages," he is not rewarded (ARN).

Note that the Mishna calls one who more and more acquires good qualities a saint, and one who neglects to acquire them, wicked (Maimonides).

ONE WHO ATTENDS BUT DOES NOT PUT TO PRACTICE: This does not mean that the person does not at all put to practice what he has learned in the study-house; why, even a person who simply refrains from carrying out the commandments is thoroughly wicked, even if he does not commit transgressions outright. But the meaning is this: he does not go out of his way to carry out the commandments; he puts them to practice only by chance if the opportunity happens to present itself to him. Putting to practice and not attending is not attending the study-house to find out the detailed implications of the commandments, so that one may be most meticulous with them; the person who does not attend simply carries them out in accordance with his own limited knowledge. For such practice he will receive some [limited] reward (Rabbi Jonah).

Attending and not putting to practice, that is, the person is constantly on the move from one place of Torah to another and does not achieve results. In other words, he does not prosper in his study and does not master it. Nevertheless he receives the reward for attendance. Putting to practice and not attending refers to a person who does not take the trouble to go to a place where Torah is taught, but engages in study at home; he succeeds at his study, although, had he attended a place of Torah he would have mastered more and more of it. Nevertheless he receives the reward for achievement (Meiri).

It is possible to interpret "attends but does not put to practice" as engaged in the study of Torah but not in acts of lovingkindness (Duran).

THERE ARE FOUR TYPES AMONG THOSE THAT SIT IN THE PRESENCE OF THE SAGES: THE SPONGE, THE FUNNEL, THE STRAINER, AND THE SIFTER.

THE SPONGE SOAKS UP EVERYTHING.

THE FUNNEL TAKES IN AT ONE EAR AND LETS OUT AT THE OTHER.

THE STRAINER LETS PASS THE WINE AND RETAINS THE LEES.

THE SIFTER HOLDS BACK THE COARSE AND COLLECTS THE FINE FLOUR.

FOUR TYPES AMONG THOSE THAT SIT IN THE PRESENCE OF THE SAGES: One is like a sponge: For example, the staunch disciple who sits before the Sages and studies Scripture and Mishna, Midrash, Halakah, and Agada. Even as the sponge soaks up everything, so he soaks up everything.

One is like a sifter: For example, the bright disciple who sits before the scholars and studies Scripture and Mishna, Midrash, Halakah, and Agada. Even as the sifter holds back the coarse flour and collects the fine flour, so he holds back the bad and collects the good.

One is like a funnel: For example, the witless disciple who sits before the scholars and studies Scripture and Mishna, Midrash, Halakah, and Agada. Even as the funnel takes in at one end and lets out at the other, so does he—everything which comes to him goes in one ear and out the other: one after another slips through and is gone.

One is like a strainer: For example, the wicked disciple who sits before a sage and studies Scripture and Mishna, Midrash, Halakah, and Agada. Even as the strainer lets pass the wine and retains the lees, so he lets pass the good and retains the bad (ARN).

One may well describe these FOUR types in our Mishna as follows: The first is a simpleton; the second is a fool; the third has an evil portion; and the fourth is wise (Aknin).

Like the strainer, there are disciples who retain the lees, that is to say, such interpretations and traditions and legends as are only of a playful kind; and they forget what is of chief importance. This is characteristic of the mass of people. . . . Like the sifter, there are disciples who study and retain the heart of the matter and forget the chaff. And this is the best kind of disciple. Such a person is called learned and acute. And in *Abot de-Rabbi Natan* a disciple of this sort is described as "mighty and armed." And it is of such disciples that it is said, they are fit to render decision on all matters (Meiri).

IF LOVE DEPENDS ON SOME SELFISH END, WHEN THE END FAILS, LOVE FAILS; BUT IF IT DOES NOT DEPEND ON A SELFISH END, IT WILL NEVER FAIL. AN EXAMPLE OF LOVE WHICH DEPENDED ON A SELFISH END? THAT WAS THE LOVE OF AMNON FOR TAMAR. AN EXAMPLE OF LOVE WHICH DID NOT DEPEND ON A SELFISH END? THAT WAS THE LOVE OF DAVID AND JONATHAN.

Since in the preceding statements the distinction between the saintly and the wicked was described, the Mishna now presents several statements describing the difference between things undertaken for the sake of Heaven and those not for the sake of Heaven, between things that endure and those that do not (Duran).

You will find no kind of love in the world that is evil except the love of women (ARNB).

SELFISH END: What is a vain end? For example, an appetite for worldly things, e.g., loving a woman, or loving one's friend for his wealth. If the woman falls sick and loses her beauty, gone is his love for her; if his friend's generosity comes to a halt, gone is his love for him. And the same is true of all things that have to do with bodily needs: a love based on such things is bound to disappear; when the cause is gone, the object is gone. But where love is for the sake of Heaven, as, for example, when a disciple loves his master in order to be able to learn from him, or as it is when scholars who love the truth assemble to study, then the love never vanishes, because the cause—namely, wisdom—endures forever. And that is why the effect—namely, love—will never vanish (Aknin).

———

EVERY CONTROVERSY WHICH IS FOR THE SAKE OF HEAVEN WILL IN THE END ENDURE; BUT ONE WHICH IS NOT FOR THE SAKE OF HEAVEN WILL NOT ENDURE IN THE END. A CONTROVERSY FOR THE SAKE OF HEAVEN? SUCH WAS THE CONTROVERSY OF HILLEL AND SHAMMAI. AND ONE WHICH WAS NOT FOR THE SAKE OF HEAVEN? SUCH WAS THE CONTROVERSY OF KORAH AND ALL HIS COMPANY.

FOR THE SAKE OF HEAVEN: That is, to establish truth, or to upbraid human beings because of their transgression—and not out of a passion for lording it over others or building up a reputation or self-glorification at the expense of others (Vitry).

If one debates with his fellow not out of low motives, but out of a desire to seek the truth, his words will endure and not come to an end. So too, if one puts men on the straight path, the Lord, blessed be He, will reward him in that He will keep him from sin. But he who leads men astray will be punished by the Lord, blessed be He, in that He will deprive him of the opportunity to repent (Maimonides).

CONTROVERSY . . . FOR THE SAKE OF HEAVEN WILL . . . ENDURE: The meaning is this: Those engaged in such debate will endure forever. Today they will argue about one subject, on the morrow about another subject, and the give and take between them will continue all their lives. What is more, these intellectual tussles will add length of days and years to their lives. But controversy "which is not for the sake of Heaven, will not endure in the end"; on the contrary, the disputants will perish in the very first controversy, as in the instance of Korah (Rabbi Jonah).

THE CONTROVERSY OF HILLEL AND SHAMMAI: In their debates one of them would render a decision and the other would argue against it, out of a desire to discover the truth, not out of cantankerousness or out of the wish to prevail over his fellow. That is why when he was right, the words of the person who disagreed, endured. A controversy not for the sake of Heaven was the controversy of Korah and his company; for they came to undermine Moses, our master, may he rest in peace, and his position, out of envy and contentiousness and ambition for victory (Meiri).

IF ONE LEADS THE MULTITUDES TO VIRTUE, THROUGH HIM SHALL NO SIN COME; BUT ONE WHO CAUSES THE MULTITUDES TO SIN SHALL BE GIVEN NO OPPORTUNITY TO REPENT. MOSES WAS HIMSELF VIRTUOUS AND LED THE MULTITUDES TO VIRTUE; THEREFORE THE MERIT OF THE MANY IS LINKED TO HIM, AS IT IS SAID, *He achieved the righteousness of the Lord, and his ordinances are with Israel* (Deuteronomy 33:21). JEROBOAM HIMSELF SINNED AND CAUSED THE MULTITUDES TO SIN; THEREFORE THE SIN OF THE MANY IS LINKED TO HIM, AS IT IS SAID, *For the sins of Jeroboam which he sinned, and wherewith he made Israel to sin* (I Kings 15:30).

If one leads the multitudes to virtue, through him transgression shall not come to pass, lest his disciples inherit the world to come and he go down to Sheol; as it is said, *For thou wilt not abandon my soul to the netherworld* (Psalm 16:10). But one who causes the multitudes to sin shall be given no opportunity to repent, lest his disciples go down to Sheol and he inherit the world to come; as it is said, *A man that is laden with the blood of any person shall hasten his [own] steps unto the pit* (Proverbs 28:17) (ARN).

ONE LEADS THE MULTITUDES TO VIRTUE: That is, he directs them along the right course by means of which they acquire merit (Vitry).

HE WHO HAS TO HIS CREDIT THE FOLLOWING THREE THINGS
IS OF THE DISCIPLES OF ABRAHAM OUR FATHER; BUT IF THREE
OTHER THINGS, IS OF THE DISCIPLES OF THE WICKED BALAAM:

A LIBERAL OUTLOOK, A HUMBLE SPIRIT, AND A MODEST
APPETITE—OF THE DISCIPLES OF ABRAHAM OUR FATHER.

A GRUDGING EYE, AN ARROGANT SPIRIT, AND LIMITLESS
APPETITE—OF THE DISCIPLES OF THE WICKED BALAAM.

WHAT DISTINGUISHES THE DISCIPLES OF ABRAHAM OUR
FATHER FROM THE DISCIPLES OF THE WICKED BALAAM? THE
DISCIPLES OF ABRAHAM OUR FATHER ENJOY THIS WORLD
AND INHERIT THE WORLD TO COME, AS IT IS SAID, *That I
may cause those that love me to inherit substance and that
I may fill their treasuries* (Proverbs 8:21). BUT AS TO THE
DISCIPLES OF THE WICKED BALAAM, THEIR PORTION IS
GEHENNA AND THEY GO DOWN TO THE PIT OF DESTRUCTION,
AS IT IS SAID, *But thou, O God, wilt bring them down into the
nethermost pit; men of blood and deceit shall not live out
half their days; but as for me, I will trust in Thee* (Psalm
55:24).

The disciples of Abraham are characterized by a liberal outlook, a humble spirit, and a modest appetite. How do we
know about "the liberal outlook"? For it is said, *And Abraham ran unto the herd, and fetched a calf tender and good*
(Genesis 18:17). *Calf,* that is to say, one animal of three
years of age, *tender,* that is to say, one animal of two years of
age, and *good,* that is to say, one animal a year old. [Though
he spoke originally of fetching only *a morsel of bread,* Abraham prepared so lavish a feast for his guests.]

How do we know about "the humble spirit"? For it is
said, *I am a stranger and a sojourner with you* (Genesis 23:4).

How do we know about "the modest appetite"? For it is
said, *And Abraham answered and said . . . I am but dust and
ashes* (Genesis 18:27).

The opposites of these qualities are characteristic of the
disciples of Balaam: a grudging eye, an arrogant spirit, and a
limitless appetite. How do we know about "the grudging
eye"? For before Israel went out of Egypt, all the nations in
the world used to come consulting Balaam; after Israel went
out of Egypt, even a maidservant in Israel was wiser than he.
He began therefore to cast a grudging eye on Israel, as it is
said, *Behold, there is a people come out from Egypt* (Num-

bers 22:5); and so too it says, *And they abide over against me. Come now . . . curse me this people,* etc. (*ibid*).

As to "the arrogant spirit," note the verse, *For the Lord refuseth to give me leave to go with you* (Numbers 22:13)— that is to say, shall I go with the like of you? I will go only with those greater than you! And the end of the matter was that, *Balak sent yet again princes, more, and more honorable than they* (Numbers 22:15).

How do we know about "the limitless appetite"? For it is said, *If Balak would give me his house full of silver and gold,* etc. (Numbers 22:18) (ARNB).

THAT I MAY CAUSE THOSE THAT LOVE ME TO INHERIT SUBSTANCE: This verse speaks of Abraham, for it is written, *The seed of Abraham who loves Me* (Isaiah 41:8) (Vitry).

THEIR PORTION IS GEHENNA: In this instance Gehenna refers to worldly misfortunes, for by way of metaphor most of the misfortunes in this world may be called Gehenna (Meiri).

JUDAH BEN TEMA SAYS: BE STRONG AS THE LEOPARD, SWIFT AS THE EAGLE, FLEET AS THE GAZELLE, AND BRAVE AS THE LION, TO DO THE WILL OF THY FATHER WHO IS IN HEAVEN.

He used to say: Do thou love Heaven, be in awe of Heaven, tremble and rejoice at all the commandments (ARN).

With all your might and all your powers strive to serve your Creator. And in those matters where strength is needed, let a man be strong as the leopard; where promptness is needed, let him be swift as the eagle; where a stout heart and courage are needed, let him be brave as the lion; and let him be fleet as the gazelle to do the will of his Father in heaven (Meiri).

BE STRONG AS THE LEOPARD: Use your powers to engage in the study of Torah with all your might. . . . The idiom "swift as the eagle" and "brave as the lion" is a Biblical one, as David said of Saul and Jonathan, *They were swifter than eagles, they were stronger than lions* (II Samuel 1:23) (Vitry).

A student ought to be "strong as the leopard" and not be ashamed to ask questions in the course of study. If he has not understood something, let him not say, "I have understood"; or, if his teacher taught him something once, twice and three times, and he still did not understand, let him say to his master, "Teach it to me once again"—until he understands the matter. And even if his teacher gets angry at him, let the student not be shamed into silence. If a leopard, a creature of no intelligence, uses all his daring to seize his prey, to get food, how much the more should man, a creature of intelligence, use all his daring to acquire life for his soul in the world to come (Aknin).

One should be "strong as the leopard" to upbraid those who transgress and to study Torah (Rabbi Jonah).

SWIFT AS THE EAGLE: One ought to be "swift as the eagle" in the company of sages to honor them, to minister to their needs. . . . The image of the eagle is to teach us that even as the eagle soars on high but also swoops down, so must scholars be: though they may be acute and brilliant, they must not puff themselves up in the presence of their teachers; [they must listen humbly] so that they may learn something (Aknin).

In carrying out the commandments a man should not be sedate and slow, but prompt and swift, like an eagle (Rabbi David the Prince).

FLEET AS THE GAZELLE: That is to say, let men hasten, like the gazelle, and not grow weary. In general when people run, they get tired out; but if they run to carry out a commandment, they will not weary (Rabbi Jonah).

It is possible that a man may refrain from carrying out a commandment because of a natural laziness and little strength to run. That is why the Mishna declares, be quick about carrying out a commandment, like a gazelle, for the gazelle is the swiftest of all the animals (Rabbi David the Prince).

A man ought to travel from one place to the next, from one country to another, from city to city [in order to be in a place of Torah] (Aknin).

BRAVE AS THE LION: A man ought to save his strength so that he will be able to get up at night and engage in study. . . . Let him not say: "I have studied much Scripture and I have studied much Mishna, I can indulge in ease." On the contrary, he can be sure of one thing, that the things he has not studied exceed by far the things that he has. Let him not ruin his days in idleness. Let him always envy the person greater than he in wisdom; let him not set his sights on those who are inferior to him in wisdom and say, "I know enough, I am greater than that one." And where bodily needs and his own comforts are concerned, let his conduct be the reverse, that is, let him take note of those who are more hard-pressed than he, and let him say, "I am more fortunate than that person.". . . He should not envy those who enjoy wealth and honor, grumbling, "Woe is me, I am not like So-and-so! He lives in such comfort!" He ought to know that the Torah is to be found only among those who wear themselves out in study. Let his diet be bread with salt, let the floor be his bed . . . for the Torah is to be found only among those who slay themselves for its sake. And the image of the lion teaches this: with all his might a man should devote himself to the labors of the Torah only, for this is the soul's source of life (Aknin).

All of a man's thoughts and all his activities should have one objective: fulfilling the will of the Father in heaven (Rabbi Jonah).

HE USED TO SAY: THE ARROGANT IS HEADED FOR GEHENNA, THE BLUSHING FOR THE GARDEN OF EDEN.

[He used to say:] If thou hast done thy fellow a slight wrong, let it be a serious matter in thine eyes; but if thou hast done thy fellow much good, let it be a trifle in thine eyes. And if thy fellow hath done thee a slight favor, let it be a great thing in thine eyes; if thy fellow hath done thee a great evil, let it be a little thing in thine eyes (ARN).

THE ARROGANT IS HEADED FOR GEHENNA: This statement is brought here because in the preceding statement the Mishna had taught that one ought to be aggressive in heavenly matters. Now the Mishna says, in worldly matters, affecting your relations with other men, beware of all manner of arrogance (Aknin).

THE BLUSHING FOR THE GARDEN OF EDEN: So the Sages have noted (Yebamot 79a): It is one of the distinguishing signs of the seed of Abraham that they are of the blushing and compassionate, and they engage in acts of mercy (Maimonides).

MAY IT BE THY WILL, O LORD OUR GOD, TO REBUILD THY CITY SPEEDILY IN OUR DAYS, AND SET OUR PORTION IN THE STUDYING OF THY TORAH.

MAY IT BE THY WILL: After having spoken of the virtue of blushing, the Mishna utters a prayer: O our God, even as in Thy grace Thou hast bestowed upon us this virtue, so be gracious unto us and have Thy city rebuilt speedily in our days (Maimonides).

This sentence may have been the concluding words of our treatise originally and the subsequent statements may have been added later (Meiri).

———

HE USED TO SAY:
> AT FIVE YEARS OF AGE THE STUDY OF SCRIPTURE;
> AT TEN, THE STUDY OF MISHNA;
> AT THIRTEEN, SUBJECT TO THE COMMANDMENTS;
> AT FIFTEEN, THE STUDY OF TALMUD;
> AT EIGHTEEN, MARRIAGE;
> AT TWENTY, PURSUIT [OF LIVELIHOOD];
> AT THIRTY, THE PEAK OF STRENGTH;
> AT FORTY, WISDOM;
> AT FIFTY, ABLE TO GIVE COUNSEL;
> AT SIXTY, OLD AGE CREEPING ON;
> AT SEVENTY, FULLNESS OF YEARS;
> AT EIGHTY, THE AGE OF "STRENGTH";
> AT NINETY, BODY BENT;
> AT ONE HUNDRED, AS GOOD AS DEAD AND GONE COMPLETELY OUT OF THE WORLD.

The purpose of this statement is to outline the life of man, as a stimulus to parents to teach their children the right subject at the right time (Meiri).

AT THIRTEEN, SUBJECT TO THE COMMANDMENTS: For at thirteen the signs of one's puberty appear, and he is legally adult (Vitry).

AT EIGHTEEN, MARRIAGE: Although it is proper for a man to marry early, it is not right to hurry and take a wife before this age, for then a man will find he has a millstone round his neck and is unable to study Torah. Instead, let him study Talmud for three years, and then take a wife (Vitry).

AT TWENTY, PURSUIT: In the interpretation I received, this refers to pursuit of livelihood, for the support of one's wife and children. . . . But to me it seems that "pursuit" refers to military service as practiced in the Land of Israel . . . as is borne out by the verse in the beginning of the Book of Numbers (1:3), *From twenty years old and upward, all that are able to go forth to war in Israel* (Vitry).

AT THIRTY, THE PEAK OF STRENGTH: That is, then a man has his full bodily strength, and he should watch out lest he squander it on anything save the service of the Lord (Meiri).

AT FIFTY, ABLE TO GIVE COUNSEL: That is to say, then the counsel a man gives is indeed valuable. For proper counsel depends on two things: first, the man's natural intelligence; second, the experience he has gone through in the course of time. As the ethical philosophers put it, "Time will test wisdom." And by the time a man has reached his fiftieth year, he has had many experiences, and at that age he is in the full strength of his intelligence, that is, his thinking faculties have not begun to decline. His counsel then is tested on both scores (Meiri).

AT EIGHTY, THE AGE OF "STRENGTH": As it is said, *The days of our years are threescore years and ten, or even by reason of strength fourscore years* (Psalm 90:10) (Vitry).

AT NINETY, BODY BENT: The story is told of a certain philosopher who said when he saw his hair growing white: "These are the messengers of death" (Duran).

———

BEN BAG BAG SAYS: TURN IT THIS WAY, TURN IT THAT WAY, EVERYTHING IS IN IT; KEEP THINE EYE ON IT, GROW OLD AND AGED OVER IT, AND FROM IT DO NOT STIR—FOR THOU HAST NO BETTER PORTION THAN IT.

Again and again review the words of the Torah, for everything is in it. For all the wisdom in the world is included in the Torah, as the Sages have said (Erubin 54b) in interpretation of the verse (Proverbs 5:19) *Let her breasts satisfy thee at all times*: Even as the infant sucking at its mother's breast is nourished thereby, so man, so long as he is engaged in the study of Torah, finds nourishment. And one can learn from the words of the Torah worldly matters and wisdom (Vitry).

EVERYTHING IS IN IT: Ben Bag Bag comes to warn man not to be content with superficial reading of the Torah; on the contrary, let him go over it and over it, that is to say, any number of times; for if he will act thus he will ultimately find the answer to whatever doubts he has. And this is the meaning of "everything is in it." So too man is warned not to depend on his memory and first understanding, but to be always reviewing, growing old and aged over this labor, and never departing from it. As the Sages in the Talmud (Hagigah 9b) teach us: One who studies his text one hundred times cannot be compared with him who studies it one hundred and one times (Meiri).

You will find everything in the Torah, and each time you study, you will discover new insights (Duran).

KEEP THINE EYE ON IT: That is to say, in the Torah you will see the truth; therefore keep a penetrating eye on it (Maimonides).

By the light of the Torah you will be enlightened, and the darkness of folly will be rolled away from your heart, and God will open wide the eye of your intelligence (Aknin).

GROW OLD AND AGED OVER IT: Even if in your youth you have studied Torah, hold fast to the Torah of God in your old age also (Vitry).

THOU HAST NO BETTER PORTION THAN IT: That is to say, you will find nothing like the Torah whose fruits you can enjoy in this world while the stock is laid up for you in the world to come: you will find no investment like this investment (Aknin).

It is said (Proverbs 4:2), *For I give you good doctrine; forsake ye not My Torah.* And it says (Psalm 119:72), *The Torah of Thy mouth is better unto me than thousands of gold and silver* (Nahmias).

———

BEN HE HE SAYS: ACCORDING TO THE PAINSTAKING, THE REWARD.

Once Hillel the Elder was walking along the road and met men carrying wheat. "At how much a *seah*?" he asked them.

"Two *denar*," they replied.

Then he met others; he asked them: "At how much a *seah*?"

"Three *denar*," they said.

"But the former said two!" he protested.

"Stupid Babylonian!" they retorted, "knowest thou not that 'according to the painstaking is the reward'!"

"Wretched fools!" he answered, "is this the way you retort to my question?"

What did Hillel the Elder do with them? He brought them to a correct understanding (ARN).

Both the statements of Ben Bag Bag and Ben He He are given in Aramaic, the vernacular, because these sayings are like folk sayings (Vitry).

Wisdom is firmly acquired only when you labor at your study and respond with awe in the presence of your teacher; but light reading and casual study produce nothing permanent, and there is little use to it (Maimonides).

We do not understand why the statements of Ben Bag Bag and Ben He He were given in Aramaic. Perhaps these two sages came from Babylonia, as did Hillel (Duran).

Chapter VI

THE SAGES HAVE TAUGHT IN THE IDIOM OF THE MISHNA: BLESSED BE HE WHO CHOSE THEM AND THEIR MISHNA.

RABBI MEIR SAYS: HE WHO STUDIES THE TORAH FOR ITS OWN SAKE MERITS MANY THINGS; NOT ONLY THAT, BUT HE IS WORTH THE WHOLE WORLD, ALL OF IT. HE IS CALLED BELOVED FRIEND; HE LOVES GOD, HE LOVES MANKIND, HE IS A JOY TO GOD AND A JOY TO MAN. AND THE TORAH CLOTHES HIM WITH HUMILITY AND REVERENCE, EQUIPS HIM TO BE RIGHTEOUS AND SAINTLY AND UPRIGHT AND TRUSTWORTHY; IT KEEPS HIM FAR FROM SIN AND DRAWS HIM TO VIRTUE; AND MEN PROFIT FROM HIS COUNSEL AND WISDOM, UNDERSTANDING AND STRENGTH; AS IT IS SAID, *Counsel is Mine, and sound wisdom; I am understanding, power is Mine* (Proverbs 8:14). AND IT BESTOWS UPON HIM ROYALTY AND DOMINION AND ACUTENESS OF JUDGMENT. TO HIM ARE REVEALED THE SECRETS OF TORAH, AND HE BECOMES AS IT WERE AN EVER-FLOWING SPRING, A RIVER OF UNCEASING STREAMS; HE BECOMES MODEST, LONG-SUFFERING, FORGIVING OF INSULT; AND IT MAGNIFIES HIM AND EXALTS HIM OVER EVERYTHING.

It is the practice everywhere in Israel to study the treatise *Abot* on the Sabbaths between Passover and Pentecost, every Sabbath one chapter. Now, since between Passover and Pentecost there are six Sabbaths, and the treatise *Abot* has only five chapters, statements akin to the content of *Abot* were collected from the *baraitot* and made into a chapter, called *Kinyan Torah* ("On Acquiring the Torah"), and this is studied on the sixth Sabbath, the one before Pentecost. And it is because the Torah was given [to Moses and Israel] on Pentecost, that the practice developed to study these chapters between Passover and Pentecost (Nahmias).

THE IDIOM OF THE MISHNA: The chapter begins with "The Sages have taught in the idiom of the Mishna," because this chapter is a *baraita*, but it is composed in the language of the Mishna, for a *baraita* may also be called Mishna (Vitry).

HE IS WORTH: That is, he is sufficient reason for the creation of the whole world (Vitry).

COUNSEL IS MINE: The wise Solomon has the Torah say this [of itself] (Vitry).

SECRETS OF TORAH: For example, the Creation Account and the Chariot Account and the contents of the *Book of Creation* —and certainly the other themes of the Torah (Vitry).

———

RABBI JOSHUA BEN LEVI SAID: EVERY SINGLE DAY A *Bat Kol* GOES FORTH FROM MOUNT HOREB, PROCLAIMING AS FOLLOWS: "WOE TO MANKIND FOR THEIR CONTEMPT OF THE TORAH!" FOR HE WHO DOES NOT STUDY THE TORAH IS CALLED *Nazuf* (REPROBATE), AS IT IS SAID, *As a ring of gold in a swine's snout, so is a fair woman that turneth aside from discretion* (Proverbs 11:22). AND IT SAYS, *And the tables were the work of God, and the writing was the writing of God, graven upon the tables* (Exodus 32:16). READ NOT *"harut"* (graven) BUT *"herut"* (freedom), FOR THOU WILT FIND NO FREE MAN SAVE HIM WHO IS ENGAGED IN THE STUDY OF TORAH. BUT HE WHO IS ALWAYS PREOCCUPIED WITH THE TORAH IS SURELY EXALTED, AS IT IS SAID, *And from the gift, his heritage is God, and from the heritage of God, he is raised to high places* (Numbers 21:19).

BAT KOL: A *Bat Kol* is not an angel, but a kind of sound. For example, when the wind blows, it can be heard as a distinct thing. Rabbi Saadia explained it as a kind of echo: when one calls out in the mountains, a sound is thrown back from the crags or the mountain caves (Vitry).

MOUNT HOREB: Where the Torah was given. That is why the *Bat Kol* is heard from there (Vitry).

"WOE TO MANKIND FOR THEIR CONTEMPT OF THE TORAH!": Included in this reproof is also he who has books and neglects to study, who treats his books like things that are to be put out of sight. Woe, woe to him! And let not such a half-wit think that the contempt affects the Torah [God forbid]. It is he who is the disgraceful one, he who is the contemptible one (Rabbi David the Prince).

Since the Torah was given at Mount Horeb, that is Mount Sinai, and it was there that all Israel took an oath to study it day and night, therefore when Israel do not study the Torah, a person should feel as though Mount Horeb itself were crying out in protest, "Woe to mankind for their contempt of the Torah!" (Midrash Shemuel).

NAZUF (REPROBATE): This is a notarikon for "ring of gold in a snout" (Nezem Zahab be-aF) (Vitry).

A FAIR WOMAN THAT TURNETH ASIDE FROM DISCRETION: Although the verse speaks of a "woman," it refers to the Torah (Vitry).

THE GIFT: The Torah was given to man as a gift (Vitry).

———

HE WHO LEARNS FROM HIS FELLOW ONE CHAPTER, OR ONE LAW, OR ONE VERSE, OR ONE WORD, EVEN ONE LETTER—IS OBLIGED TO TREAT HIM WITH HONOR. FOR THUS WE FIND CONCERNING DAVID, KING OF ISRAEL. HE LEARNED FROM AHITOPHEL NO MORE THAN TWO THINGS, YET HE ADDRESSED HIM AS HIS MASTER, HIS GUIDE, HIS BELOVED, AS IT IS SAID, *But it was thou, a man mine equal, my guide, my beloved* (Psalm 55:14). NOW IS THERE NOT AN INFERENCE TO BE DRAWN FROM THIS? IF DAVID, KING OF ISRAEL, WHO LEARNED FROM AHITOPHEL NO MORE THAN TWO THINGS, ADDRESSED HIM AS HIS MASTER, HIS GUIDE, AND HIS BELOVED, ALL THE MORE MUST HE WHO LEARNS FROM HIS FELLOW ONE CHAPTER OR ONE LAW OR ONE VERSE OR ONE WORD, EVEN ONE LETTER, TREAT HIM WITH HONOR! AND HONOR APPLIES TO NAUGHT SAVE TORAH, AS IT IS SAID, *It is honor that sages inherit* (Proverbs 3:35); *and the wholehearted shall inherit good* (Proverbs 28:10): AND THE *good* IS NAUGHT BUT TORAH, AS IT IS SAID, *For I give you good doctrine, forsake ye not My Torah* (Proverbs 4:2).

DAVID . . . LEARNED FROM AHITOPHEL NO MORE THAN TWO THINGS: For we find that Ahitophel said to David: *We took sweet counsel together, in the house of God we walked with the throng* (Psalm 55:15). From Ahitophel's retort you can learn David's answer. For once Ahitophel found David sitting and studying by himself. "What are you doing?" he said to him. "Has it not been written, *A sword is upon the boasters, and they shall become fools* (Jeremiah 50:36), that is to say (Berakot 63b), a sword upon those scholars who sit by themselves studying Torah. Moreover. they become fools. . . ." Whereupon David replied: *"Let us take sweet counsel together,* that is, let us study Torah together, you and I."

On another occasion Ahitophel found David walking alone to the study-house at a leisurely pace. "What are you doing?" he asked him. "Is it not written, *In the multitude of people is the king's glory*"? (Proverbs 14:28). "What shall I do?" David asked him. Ahitophel replied: *"To the house of God let us walk with eagerness* (Psalm 55:15), that is, with eagerness let us go, you and I" (Vitry).

THOU, A MAN MINE EQUAL: David thus sang the praises of Ahitophel, making him his equal and on a par with himself, even more important than himself, "my guide and my beloved, my sage and master" (Vitry).

HONOR APPLIES TO NAUGHT SAVE TORAH: No man is worthy of being honored more than a person who devotes himself to the Torah (Vitry).

———

THIS IS THE HIGHWAY TO THE TORAH—A SALTY CRUST FOR FOOD, WATER IN RATION FOR DRINK, THE GROUND THY BED, THY LIFE A LIFE OF PRIVATION, AND THY LABORS IN THE TORAH. IF THOU DOEST THUS, *Happy shalt thou be and it shall be well with thee* (Psalm 128:2): *Happy shalt thou be* IN THIS WORLD; *And it shall be well with thee* IN THE WORLD TO COME.

SEEK NOT GREATNESS FOR THYSELF, COVET NOT HONOR; PRACTICE MORE THAN THOU LEARNEST. AND YEARN NOT FOR THE TABLE OF KINGS, FOR THY TABLE IS GREATER THAN THEIR TABLE, AND THY CROWN GREATER THAN THEIR CROWN. "AND FAITHFUL IS THY TASKMASTER TO PAY THEE THE REWARD OF THY LABOR."

THIS IS THE HIGHWAY TO THE TORAH: Even if you find yourself in the extremes of poverty, where you have no more to eat than a crust of bread dipped in salt and have no more to drink than water in rations, and have nothing other than the ground to lie on, and your life is a life of privation, even then toil away in the Torah. But this Mishna does *not* say that those who study Torah will have nothing to eat save a crust of bread dipped in salt, and so on. Lo, Scripture says, *Its ways are ways of pleasantness and all its paths are peace* (Proverbs 3:17). . . . Though Gentile monks may cultivate a sackcloth habit and a diet of bread and water, this is not the way for those who study the Torah. On the contrary, they conduct themselves in ways of pleasantness and in paths of peace, that is, do not indulge excessively but do not afflict themselves excessively. . . . Do not get into the habit of afflicting yourself excessively (Nahmias).

SEEK NOT GREATNESS FOR THYSELF: Even when you have attained to the station of the learned, do not exalt yourself over other men (Nahmias).

COVET NOT HONOR: Do not seek honor out of thy learning (Vitry), say not "I shall study so that I may be addressed as Rabbi, so that I may be addressed as Your Honor" (Nahmias).

THY TASKMASTER: The Holy One, whose work you are doing (Vitry).

GREATER IS LEARNING [TORAH] THAN PRIESTHOOD AND THAN ROYALTY, FOR ROYALTY IS ACQUIRED BY THIRTY STAGES, PRIESTHOOD BY TWENTY-FOUR: BUT THE TORAH IS ACQUIRED BY FORTY-EIGHT THINGS—BY STUDY, BY DILIGENT ATTENTION, BY PROPER SPEECH, BY AN UNDERSTANDING HEART, BY A PERCEPTIVE HEART, BY AWE, BY FEAR, BY HUMILITY, BY JOY, BY ATTENDANCE UPON SAGES, BY CRITICAL GIVE AND TAKE WITH FELLOWS, BY ACUTE EXCHANGES AMONG DISCIPLES, BY CLEAR THINKING, BY STUDY OF SCRIPTURE, BY STUDY OF MISHNA, BY A MINIMUM OF SLEEP, BY A MINIMUM OF CHATTER, BY A MINIMUM PURSUIT OF PLEASURE, BY A MINIMUM OF FRIVOLITY, BY A MINIMUM PREOCCUPATION WITH WORLDLY MATTERS, BY LONG-SUFFERING, BY GENEROSITY, BY FAITH IN THE SAGES, BY ACCEPTANCE OF SUFFERING.

ROYALTY IS ACQUIRED BY THIRTY STAGES: Some of these are listed in Scripture, and some in the Mishna of the treatise Sanhedrin (18a). They are the following: The king does not try cases, nor is he brought to trial; he does not perform *halizah* (Deuteronomy 25:7–10) nor is the *halizah* ceremony performed for his wife; he does not take a woman in levirate marriage, nor may his wife be taken in levirate marriage; none may wed his widow; even if a relation of his died, the king does not go out of his palace [to accompany the dead]; [if a death has occurred in the king's family,] when the king is comforted everyone sits on the ground, and he reclines on a couch. . . ; he may break through private property to make a highway for himself, and none may prevent it; when the nation brings back booty, they place it before him and he takes his share first; he may take no more than eighteen wives; he may have no more horses than what he requires for his chariot, nor may he heap up silver and gold for himself excessively, beyond the needs of his household entertainment; he has a Torah scroll written specially for him, and it is with him in battle, in the city, when on a journey, when at rest; none may sit on his throne, none may ride on his horse, none may handle his scepter, none may behold him naked or when his hair is being trimmed. . . . The king is one *whom the Lord thy God shall choose* (Deuteronomy 17:15), by the mouth of a prophet, *one from among thy brethren* (*ibid.*) and not from outside the Land; he is *thy brother* (*ibid.*) and not of foreign stock. . . ; and even if a Jew he is disqualified if he is a slave or a bastard. . . .

It is however, possible that the thirty conditions are instead those the prophet Samuel referred to, *This will be the manner of the king that shall reign over you: he will take your sons, and appoint them unto him, for his chariots, and to be his horsemen; and they shall run before his chariots. And he will appoint them unto him for captains of thousands and captains of fifties; and to plow his ground, and to reap his harvest, and to make his instruments of war, and the instruments of his chariots. And he will take your daughters to be perfumers, and to be cooks, and to be bakers. And he will take your fields and your vineyards, and your oliveyards, even the best of them. . . . And he will take the tenth of your seed, and of your vineyards. . . . And he will take your manservants, and your maidservants, and your goodliest young men, and your asses. . . . He will take the tenth of your flocks; and ye shall be his servants* (I Samuel 8:11–17). Here you have twenty-three from Scripture. To this add the following: *Thou shalt set a king over thee whom the Lord thy God shall choose; one from among thy brethren shalt thou set king over thee.* . . (Deuteronomy 17:15). You must be in awe of him; *he shall write him a copy of the Torah* (Deuteronomy 17:19). This is a total of thirty (Vitry).

PRIESTHOOD BY TWENTY-FOUR: To wit: holiness, purity, fine linen clothing, trimming of the hair of one's head and beard every thirty days and of the High Priest every seven days, *There shall none defile himself for the dead among his people* (Leviticus 21:1), *they shall not make baldness upon their head, neither shall they shave off the corners of their beard, nor make any cuttings in their flesh* (Leviticus 21:5), *they shall not take a woman that is a harlot, or profaned, neither shall they take a woman put away from her husband* (Leviticus 21:7), *for whatsoever man he be that hath a blemish, he shall not approach: a blind man, or a lame, or he that hath anything maimed, or anything too long* (Leviticus 21:18), nor may he be *brokenhanded,* nor *brokenfooted* (Leviticus 21:19), nor *crook-backed* (Leviticus 21:20), nor *a dwarf* (Leviticus 21:20), nor with *eye overspread* (Leviticus 21:20), nor *scabbed,* nor one with *scurvy,* nor one with *stones crushed* (Leviticus 21:20), nor may he have any affliction: he must rid himself of every affliction and disfigurement, and he must be holy. . . (Vitry).

BY STUDY: That is, one should learn from teachers rather than from books (Nahmias).

BY AWE, BY FEAR: By "awe" is meant awe towards Heaven, a person putting his mind to it not to err. By "fear" is meant fear in the presence of one's master, that is, not behaving frivolously in his presence (Vitry).

BY HUMILITY: As it is written, *Seek righteousness, seek humility* (Zephaniah 2:3). Now, our Sages have said, "The shamefaced man will not learn"; that is why a person must be humble and ask his teacher when he needs to ask, and not regard himself as a great man (Vitry).

BY JOY: For when a person studies with joy, then whatever he learns is a pleasure to him; and that is why we say in our prayer, "O Lord our God, make the words of thy Torah sweet in our mouths" (Nahmias).

BY ATTENDANCE UPON SAGES: That is, one must wait upon the Sages and do their work in order to learn from them how to study and how to reason. As we are told in the Talmud (Berakot 7b), Even greater than study of the Torah is attendance upon the Sages. Moreover, the Sages have said (Berakot 47b), Who is an *am ha-arez?* He who has studied

Scripture and has studied Mishna but has not attended upon scholars (Vitry).

CRITICAL GIVE AND TAKE WITH FELLOWS: The Sages put it this way (Taanit 7a) by way of parable: Fellows engaged in the study of Torah, to what may they be likened? To a wood fire burning with increasing strength: one log keeps kindling the other. So are fellows engaged in the study of Torah: one asks and the other replies, one raises problems and the other solves them—thus all of them "inflame" one another (Nahmias).

BY ACUTE EXCHANGES AMONG DISCIPLES: As Rabbi said (Makkot 10a): "From my disciples I have learned more than from everyone else" (Vitry).

BY FAITH IN THE SAGES: That is, by believing what they teach and not being like the Sadducees and the Boethusians (Vitry).

BY ACCEPTANCE OF SUFFERING: If sufferings come upon a person, let him receive them lovingly and not rise up in revolt against them. Let him not plan in his heart to neglect the Torah, to rebel against God and say that he is toiling in vain since the Torah does not protect him from sufferings. For there is no such thing in this world as reward for the commandments (Vitry).

———

[LEARNING IS ACQUIRED ALSO BY HIM] WHO KNOWS HIS PLACE, WHO IS CONTENT WITH HIS PORTION, WHO MAKES A HEDGE ABOUT HIS WORDS, WHO TAKES NO CREDIT TO HIMSELF, WHO IS BELOVED, WHO LOVES GOD, LOVES MANKIND, LOVES ACTS OF CHARITY, LOVES REPROOF, LOVES RECTITUDE, KEEPS FAR FROM HONORS, IS NOT PUFFED UP WITH HIS LEARNING, DOES NOT DELIGHT IN HANDING DOWN DECISIONS, BEARS THE YOKE ALONG WITH HIS FELLOW, JUDGES HIM WITH THE SCALES WEIGHTED IN HIS FAVOR, LEADS HIM ON TO THE TRUTH, LEADS HIM ON TO PEACE, CONCENTRATES ON HIS STUDY, IS CAPABLE OF INTELLECTUAL GIVE AND TAKE, IS CAPABLE OF ADDING TO WHAT HE HAS LEARNED, STUDIES IN ORDER TO TEACH, AND STUDIES IN ORDER TO PRACTICE, MAKES HIS TEACHER WISER, IS EXACT IN WHAT HE HAS LEARNED, AND QUOTES HIS SOURCE. THUS THOU DOST LEARN THAT WHOEVER QUOTES HIS SOURCE BRINGS

DELIVERANCE TO THE WORLD, AS IT IS SAID, *And Esther told the King thereof in Mordecai's name* (Esther 2:22).

KNOWS HIS PLACE: That is, he who comes early to the study-house (Vitry).

He has a true estimate of his worth (Rabbi David the Prince).

"He knows his place," even as it is said, *Glorify not thyself in the presence of the King, and stand not in the place of great men* (Proverbs 25:6). Another interpretation: He knows his place in the study-house, for because of his frequent visits, he has a permanent place there (Nahmias).

TAKES NO CREDIT TO HIMSELF: That is, he does not swell up with pride over what he has learned; instead he says to himself that what he has learned was his obligation to learn, indeed he has not studied enough (Vitry).

As was said above: "If thou hast studied much Torah, take no credit to thyself, for to this end wast thou created" (Nahmias).

IS BELOVED: That is, he is a person with whom men are delighted and they love him because of his good works (Nahmias).

LOVES GOD: As it is said, *And thou shalt love the Lord thy God* (Deuteronomy 6:5) (Nahmias).

LOVES MANKIND: In that way the Torah is honored and becomes precious in the sight of men; all follow it eagerly, and they strengthen his hand in the study thereof (Vitry).

As it is said, *Thou shalt love thy neighbor as thyself* (Leviticus 19:18) (Nahmias).

LOVES ACTS OF CHARITY: As it is said, *Charity, charity shalt thou follow* (Deuteronomy 16:20) (Nahmias).

LOVES REPROOF: That is, he loves him who reproves him, and he loves also to give reproof to a person who requires it: for all Israel are responsible the one for the other (Nahmias).

LOVES RECTITUDE: That is, he loves to be an upright person, carries on with people in a gentle way, so that folks say of him: "How fortunate is So-and-So who studied Torah, how fortunate his father who taught him!" (Nahmias).

IS NOT PUFFED UP WITH HIS LEARNING: As it is said in the Talmud (Erubin 55a): The Torah is not in the heavens, that is to say, it is not to be found among the high-and-mighty (Nahmias).

BEARS THE YOKE ALONG WITH HIS FELLOW: Even in such matters as royal imposts, although he personally may be exempt (Vitry).

It is said, *And if thy brother be waxen poor, and his means fail with thee; then thou shalt uphold him* (Leviticus 25:35). Included in this principle is also sharing in the suffering of one's fellow, grieving with him in his grief, and rejoicing with him in his joy (Nahmias).

LEADS HIM ON TO THE TRUTH: If his fellow asked him a question about some matter, he gives him the truthful answer (Nahmias).

LEADS HIM ON TO PEACE: As it is said, *But to the counselors of peace is joy* (Proverbs 12:20). And the bringing of peace between man and his fellow man is one of those things the fruits of which one enjoys in this world while its stock is laid up for him in the world to come (Nahmias).

STUDIES IN ORDER TO TEACH: As it is said, *Thou shalt teach them diligently unto thy children* (Deuteronomy 6:7). And it says, *But make them known unto thy children and thy children's children* (Deuteronomy 4:9). . . . *And the Lord commanded me at that time to teach you statutes and ordinances* (Deuteronomy 4:14) (Nahmias).

STUDIES IN ORDER TO PRACTICE: As it is said, *That ye may learn them, and observe to do them* (Deuteronomy 5:1); and it says, *Hear therefore, O Israel, and observe to do it* (Deuteronomy 6:3). And "not study is the principal thing, but action" (Nahmias).

MAKES HIS TEACHER WISER: Thus . . . his teacher can say of him, "I have learned most from my disciples" (Nahmias).

IS EXACT IN WHAT HE HAS LEARNED: That is, he is most meticulous not to add to the statement he has received nor to subtract from it (Vitry).

QUOTES HIS SOURCE: That is, he does not attribute what he learned from his master, to himself (Vitry).

From this positive statement you can derive the negative implication, that he who does not quote his source causes the Shekinah to withdraw from Israel; for there is no deliverance when there is no Shekinah, and when there is deliverance, the Shekinah dwells in the midst of Israel (Nahmias).

———

HOW GRAND IS TORAH, FOR TO THOSE WHO ENGAGE IN IT, IT GIVES LIFE IN THIS WORLD AND THE WORLD TO COME! AS IT IS SAID, *For they are life unto those that find them, and health to all their flesh* (Proverbs 4:22). AND IT SAYS, *It shall be health to thy navel, and marrow to thy bones* (Proverbs 3:8). AND IT SAYS, *She is a tree of life to them that lay hold upon it, and happy is everyone that holdeth her fast* (Proverbs 3:18). AND IT SAYS, *For they shall be a chaplet of grace unto thy head, and chains about thy neck* (Proverbs 1:9). AND IT SAYS, *She will give to thy head a chaplet of grace: a crown of glory will she bestow on thee* (Proverbs 4:9). AND IT SAYS, *Length of days is in her right hand; in her left hand are riches and honor* (Proverbs 3:16). AND IT SAYS, *For length of days, and years of life, and peace, will they add to thee* (Proverbs 3:2).

SHE IS A TREE OF LIFE TO THEM THAT LAY HOLD UPON IT: Perhaps the reason the verse says, *To them that lay hold upon it,* is this: The words of the Torah require reinforcement, that is, one must review them every single day. . . . And successive reviewing is indeed study of Torah for its own sake. For, the first time a man studies for the sake of understanding; from then on what he studies he studies in order to learn well (Nahmias).

———

RABBI SIMEON BEN MENASIA SAYS IN THE NAME OF RABBI SIMEON BEN YOHAI: BEAUTY, STRENGTH, RICHES, HONOR, WISDOM, OLD AGE, FULLNESS OF YEARS, AND CHILDREN ARE BECOMING TO THE RIGHTEOUS AND BECOMING TO THE WORLD. AS IT IS SAID, *The hoary head is a crown of glory, it is found in the way of righteousness* (Proverbs 16:31). AND IT SAYS, *the crown of the wise is their riches* (Proverbs 14:24). AND IT SAYS, *Children's children are the crown of old men; and the glory of children are their fathers* (Proverbs 17:6). AND IT SAYS, *The glory of young men is their strength; and the beauty of old men is the hoary head* (Proverbs 20:29). AND IT SAYS, *Then the moon shall be confounded and the sun ashamed; for the Lord of Hosts will reign in Mount Zion and in Jerusalem, and before His elders shall be glory* (Isaiah 24:23).

RABBI SIMEON BEN MENASIA SAYS: THESE SEVEN ITEMS WHICH THE SAGES LISTED FOR THE RIGHTEOUS, WERE ALL OF THEM FULFILLED IN RABBI AND HIS SONS.

BEAUTY: That is, a beautiful face; for through the beauty of his face he gets to look like an angel, and his words are listened to (Vitry).

STRENGTH: That is, people stand in awe of him (Vitry).

BECOMING TO THE WORLD: For that is a handsome generation in which there are such people (Vitry).

RABBI: That is, Rabbi Judah the Saint, Rabbi Judah the Prince (Vitry).

Rabbi was called by three names, "Rabbi," "Rabbi Judah the Prince," and "our Master the Saint." He was called "Rabbi," because he was the master of Israel and taught them the Torah; he was called "Rabbi Judah the Prince," because he was elevated and made the prince and most honored of Israel, and his name was Rabbi Judah; and he was called "our Master the Saint," because his body was as pure as the soul in his body. And the ancients told of him that on the day he departed from this world he stretched his ten fingers towards the heavens and said, "Master of the universe, before Thee it is revealed and known, that at no time in my life did I take advantage of the pleasures of this world by as much as my little finger. I beseech Thee, O my God, that this behavior of mine find pleasure in Thy sight, and that my death may be in peace" (Rabbi David the Prince).

SAID RABBI YOSE BEN KISMA: ONE TIME AS I WAS WALKING ON THE HIGHWAY A CERTAIN MAN MET ME AND GREETED ME. I RETURNED HIS GREETING.

HE SAID TO ME: "RABBI, FROM WHAT PLACE ART THOU?"

I SAID TO HIM: "FROM A GREAT CITY OF SAGES AND TEACHERS AM I."

HE SAID TO ME: "RABBI, WOULDST THOU LIKE TO DWELL WITH US IN OUR PLACE? I WOULD GIVE THEE ONE THOUSAND THOUSAND *denar* AND PRECIOUS STONES AND PEARLS."

I SAID TO HIM: "MY SON, EVEN IF THOU WERT TO GIVE ME ALL THE SILVER AND GOLD AND PRECIOUS STONES AND

PEARLS IN THE WORLD, I WOULD DWELL NOWHERE SAVE IN
A PLACE OF TORAH—FOR IN THE HOUR OF A MAN'S DE-
PARTURE, NEITHER SILVER NOR GOLD NOR PRECIOUS STONES
AND PEARLS ACCOMPANY THE MAN, ONLY TORAH AND GOOD
WORKS, AS IT IS SAID, *When thou walkest it shall lead thee,
when thou liest down, it shall watch over thee: and when
thou awakest, it shall talk with thee* (Proverbs 6:22): *When
thou walkest, it shall lead thee,* IN THIS WORLD; *When thou
liest down, it shall watch over thee,* IN THE GRAVE; *And
when thou awakest, it shall talk with thee,* IN THE WORLD TO
COME. AND SO TOO IT IS WRITTEN IN THE BOOK OF PSALMS
BY DAVID, KING OF ISRAEL, *The law of Thy mouth is better
unto me than thousands of gold and silver* (Psalm 119:72).
AND IT SAYS, *Mine is the silver, and Mine the gold, saith the
Lord of Hosts"* (Haggai 2:8).

WHEN THOU WALKEST IT SHALL LEAD THEE: That is, it
will speak up in your behalf (Vitry).

FIVE POSSESSIONS DID THE HOLY ONE, BLESSED BE HE, SET
ASIDE FOR HIMSELF IN THIS WORLD, TO WIT: TORAH, ONE
POSSESSION; THE HEAVENS AND THE EARTH, ANOTHER
POSSESSION; ABRAHAM, ANOTHER POSSESSION; ISRAEL, AN-
OTHER POSSESSION; THE TEMPLE, ANOTHER POSSESSION.

HOW DO WE KNOW THAT TORAH IS ONE POSSESSION?
FOR IT IS WRITTEN, *The Lord made me as the beginning of
His way, the first of His works of old* (Proverbs 8:22).

HOW DO WE KNOW THAT THE HEAVENS AND THE EARTH
ARE ONE OF HIS POSSESSIONS? FOR IT IS SAID, *Thus saith the
Lord: The heaven is My throne, and the earth is My footstool;
where is the house that ye may build unto Me? And where
is the place that may be My resting-place* (Isaiah 66:1)? AND
IT SAYS, *How manifold are Thy works, O Lord! In wisdom hast
Thou made them all; the earth is full of Thy possessions*
(Psalm 104:24).

HOW DO WE KNOW THAT ABRAHAM IS ONE OF HIS
POSSESSIONS? FOR IT IS WRITTEN, *And He blessed him, and
said*: *Blessed be Abram of God most high, possessor of
heaven and earth* (Genesis 14:19).

HOW DO WE KNOW THAT ISRAEL IS ONE OF HIS POS-

SESSIONS? FOR IT IS WRITTEN, *Till Thy people pass over, O Lord, till the people pass over that Thou hast gotten* (Exodus 15:16). AND IT SAYS, *As for the holy that are in the earth, they are excellent in whom is all My delight* (Psalm 16:3).

HOW DO WE KNOW THAT THE TEMPLE IS ONE OF HIS POSSESSIONS? FOR IT IS SAID, *The sanctuary, O Lord, which Thy hands have established* (Exodus 15:17). AND IT SAYS, *And He brought them to His holy border, to the mountain, which His right hand had gotten* (Psalm 78:54).

———

WHATSOEVER THE HOLY ONE, BLESSED BE HE, CREATED IN HIS WORLD, HE CREATED FOR HIS OWN GLORY ONLY, AS IT IS SAID, *Every one that is called by My name, him I created for My glory, I have formed him, yea, I have made him* (Isaiah 43:7). IT SAYS ALSO, *The Lord shall reign for ever and ever* (Exodus 15:18).

———

SAID RABBI HANANIAH BEN AKASHYA: IT PLEASED THE HOLY ONE, BLESSED BE HE, TO GRANT MERIT TO ISRAEL; THAT IS WHY HE GAVE THEM TORAH AND COMMANDMENTS IN ABUNDANCE, AS IT IS SAID, *The Lord was pleased for His righteousness' sake, to make Torah great and glorious* (Isaiah 42:21).

SAID RABBI HANANIAH: This saying is not part of the treatise *Abot*, but the conclusion of the treatise *Makkot*. But since it makes a beautiful peroration the people have made a habit of reading it at the conclusion of each chapter of the treatise *Abot* (Vitry).

A Note and Acknowledgments

Some comment on text and procedure may be useful, since in a volume of this kind critical annotations and footnote references would be out of place. For the *Abot* text underlying the translation, I have used (with some minor departures) the version in the Mishna being prepared by Albeck and Yallon. But along with this text I consulted at all times the *Meleket Shelomo* of Rabbi Shelomo Adani (1567-1624) and C. Taylor's *Sayings of the Jewish Fathers* (Cambridge, 1897 and 1900).

The principal commentaries I have drawn on are:

Abot de-Rabbi Natan, Versions A and B, ed. S. Schechter, Vienna, 1887 (the Version A passages are quoted from the translation, *The Fathers According to Rabbi Nathan,* Yale Judaica Series, Yale University Press, 1955).

Machsor Vitry, ed. S. Hurwitz, Nürnberg, 1923.

Maimonides' *Commentary* (as printed in the Vilna editions of the Talmud, with the corrections of E. Baneth in *Festschrift zu Israel Lewy's Siebzigstem Geburtstag,* ed. Brann and El-bogen, Breslau, 1911, pp. 76–103; see also *idem* in *Jubelschrift . . . Israel Hildesheimer,* Berlin, 1890, pp. 57–76).

Sepher Musar of Joseph ben Judah ibn Aknin, ed. W. Bacher, Berlin, 1910.

Commentary of Rabbenu Jonah ben Abraham Gerondi (as printed in the Vilna editions of the Talmud).

Bet Ha-Behirah on *Abot* by Rabbi Menahem ben Solomon Ha-Meiri, ed. Z. Stern, Vienna, 1855.

Commentary by Rabbi Joseph Nahmias, ed. M. L. Bamberger, Berlin, 1907.

Magen Abot of Rabbi Simeon ben Zemah Duran, Leipzig, 1855.

Although I have not drawn very much from the following, nevertheless they too were constantly consulted:

Midrash David of Rabbenu David Ha-Nagid in the Hebrew translation of Ben Zion Krynfiss, Jerusalem, 5704 (1944).

Midrash Shemuel of Samuel ben Isaac of Uçeda, New York, 5705 (1945) (since this edition is bound together with *Yarim Mosheh* of Rabbi Moses Alshik and *Hasde Abot* of Rabbi Hayyim Joseph David Azulai, I have consulted these commentaries too, though I have not quoted them).

The *Commentary* of Rabbi Obadiah Bertinoro (as printed in the regular editions of the Mishna).

So too, although I have not cited them, I have found the commentaries *Tosafot Yom Tob* and *Tiferet Yisrael* most instructive and helpful.

What I have tried to present in the translation of *Abot*, and in the translation of selections from its classical commentators, is the *peshat* (plain meaning), and such *derush*, homiletical interpretations, as are very close to the *peshat*, offered by the *Rishonim*, the earliest Talmud commentators. In one or two instances I have frankly presented interpretations which are far from the *peshat*, because the interpretations preserved rather interesting notions. Generally, a comment is quoted from the earliest source. But I have occasionally cited the commentary as it appears in a later authority, if the idiom in the latter is clearer or fuller or more succinct than in the first source. Similarly, for the most part the commentators are cited in chronological order; I have sometimes departed from this order if, in my opinion, a different order would make more vivid what the commentators themselves were trying to reveal of the meaning of the *Abot* maxims. Finally, the *Rishonim* often cite Talmudic statements and offer them as their own comment. In such cases I cite the *Rishonim*, since by citation they have made the Talmudic statement an integral part of their interpretation.

Much, much more than is quoted in this little book could be quoted from the *Rishonim*, who have preserved for us extremely valuable traditions and insights. But this book had to be of a specified, limited size; I had therefore to omit much that I would have loved to include. Perhaps these representative selections may nonetheless serve as an example of the real riches in the works of the early Talmud commentators and of the vitality and relevance they always found in the Talmudic texts they studied and taught. That the Talmud is a living work, not just an archaeological curiosity, is principally the achievement of these *Rishonim*.

Biblical citations are from the Jewish Publication Society version, except where exegetical treatment required otherwise. A more formal idiom was adopted in the translation of *Abot*, in order to distinguish it from the comments. The same formality recurs in the *Abot de-Rabbi Natan* (Version A) passages because these are cited from the translation of that work where "thees" and "thous" are retained. I want to thank the Yale University Press for permission to use that translation liberally.

The translation of the Talmudic passages in the essay is, quite frankly, an attempt to capture in English the very cadence of the Hebrew and Aramaic original. The opaqueness of the Talmudic style can of course be eliminated by extensive paraphrase—but then one is no longer translating but deciding that it is futile to try conveying the flavor of Talmudic material.

Talmudists know what complex problems lie hidden in—and even on the surface of—every Talmudic sentence. That fear and hesitancy have not paralyzed me into giving up is a result of the good fortune of close association with Talmudists and Rabbinics scholars of first magnitude whose instruction, by their writings and their Oral Torah, has been an illumination and shield. The works of the late Professor Louis Ginzberg continue to teach me at every reading. Since my undergraduate days Professor Louis Finkelstein has taught and prodded and sustained me, drawing me to the Torah and especially to whatever is related to *Pirke Abot*. My debt to Professor Saul Lieberman, *princeps* in Talmudica and Rabbinica, is enormous: I steal from his writings without letup and seldom care to move in my studies without his guidance and disciplining but open hand.

I am under particular obligation to my wonderful colleague, Professor Hayyim Zalman Dimitrovsky, who, among other things, checked my translation of the halakic passages and the essay with affectionate, thoroughgoing care, and protected me from Heaven knows how many pitfalls. Another close colleague, Professor Abraham Schreiber, has given me many opportunities to discuss halakic problems with him, and from these discussions I have always profited.

Grace Goldin's suggestions are incorporated in many pages of this book. The terribly complicated typescript of this volume is the work of my devoted secretary, Ruth S. Stern, who has assisted me in this work from the first draft through the last stages of proofreading. Finally, to have had Marc Jaffe as my editor has been a delight from beginning to end.

List of Commentators

Aknin = Commentary of Joseph ben Judah ibn Aknin (*c.*1160–1226)

ARN = Abot de-Rabbi Natan, Version A

ARNB = Abot de-Rabbi Natan, Version B

Bertinoro = Rabbi Obadiah ben Abraham Bertinoro (*c.*1470–1520)

Rabbi David the Prince = Commentary of Rabbi David Ha-Nagid (1223–1300), the grandson of Maimonides

Duran = Commentary of Simeon ben Zemah Duran (1361–1444)

Rabbi Jonah = Commentary of Rabbi Jonah ben Abraham (d.1263)

Maimonides = Commentary of Rabbi Moses ben Maimon (1135–1204)

Meiri = Commentary of Rabbi Menahem ben Solomon Ha-Meiri (1249–1306)

Midrash Shemuel = Commentary of Rabbi Samuel ben Isaac of Uçeda (16th cent.)

Nahmias = Commentary of Rabbi Joseph ben Joseph Nahmias (14th cent.)

Vitry = Machsor Vitry, 11th and 12th centuries (the work of pupils of Rashi, 1040–1105)

Index of Sages

244

From the Mentor Record of Readings from *The Living Talmud:* "The Language of *The Wisdom of the Fathers*," by E. Y. Kutscher and Judah Goldin.

(Note: These comments, prepared especially for the Mentor Record described at the front of the book, are included here to give the reader further insight into the Talmud and its relation to the Bible. E. Y. Kutscher is a member of the Department of Hebrew Language and Literature, Hebrew University, Jerusalem.)

The language of *Pirke Abot, The Wisdom of the Fathers,* is Hebrew, which means, of course, that it is the language the books of the Holy Scriptures are written in, the language of what is generally called the Old Testament. Indeed, if you can read the Bible in the original Hebrew you will find in *Pirke Abot* quite a number of words which you can translate easily. But if you knew only Biblical Hebrew, as you began reading *Pirke Abot* you would quickly discover that there are many words whose meaning you did not know; you would discover words you knew but which in their present context evidently mean something else; and what is more, you would be puzzled very frequently by the sentence structure, even when the words individually did make sense. This can be exasperating. You say to yourself: I know what each word in the clause means, but it all sounds strange. Why? How is it that though I know Biblical Hebrew, I feel like a stranger in *Pirke Abot*.

The answer is really very simple, and paradoxical as it may seem, the phenomenon is not a strange one—if we keep in mind what happens with every language in the course of time. Just as the English language has been radically transformed since the days of King Alfred the Great in the ninth century, so Hebrew developed and changed profoundly in the course of centuries. And just as if Alfred the Great tried to hold a conversation with Hemingway, they would have difficulty understanding each other, so if Isaiah tried to talk with Rabbi Judah the Prince, they might very well not understand each other at all. A millennium separates the Prophet Isaiah from Rabbi Judah the Prince, and in a thousand years very many things happen to a language. No living language stands still.

Biblical Hebrew and post-Biblical Hebrew, then, are both Hebrew, but they are not the same. And the Hebrew of *Pirke Abot* is post-Biblical; it is—to give it its proper designation—Mishnaic Hebrew.

There are a number of differences between Biblical and Mishnaic Hebrew, but the chief difference lies in the behavior of verbs. In Biblical Hebrew the complicated system of tenses has only a hazy relationship to time. For example, in Biblical Hebrew there is a perfect tense and what is called an imperfect tense, which, among other purposes, serves also as future. In other words in Biblical Hebrew the same form of the verb may mean: He speaks, he spoke, he was speaking, or, he will speak. The present tense practically does not exist at all. If you want to say: He is speaking, or, he speaks, what you do is sometimes use the perfect, sometimes the imperfect. What it amounts to therefore is that the two tenses, the perfect and the imperfect, are very elusive—you might almost say slippery—in their conduct, and do not make clear-cut distinctions in time. Sometimes when you read a Biblical passage, especially in the Prophets, you are not sure whether the verb is reporting what has happened, or what is happening now, or what will happen in the future. Remarkable effects can be achieved poetically that way, and story-telling becomes extraordinarily vivid. Thus a prophet foretelling what will happen in the days to come can speak of the forthcoming event as though it were an actuality, virtually consummated now, in the immediate present.

But the fact is that such a system of verbs is hardly suitable for the needs of societies as they grow more complex. Such a system of verbs as we have in Biblical Hebrew is especially difficult to operate with, probably, when you want to define the innumerable subtleties of law, when you want categorically to make clear what people should do or should not do in a great variety of contingencies. When you get to Mishnaic Hebrew, the Biblical verb system therefore changes in the most radical way. Here you receive a genuine sense of time, the verbs clearly register time past and time future and time present. There is no mistaking the tense, and the language as a result takes on greater precision. What was, was; what is, is; what will be, will be—Mishnaic Hebrew leaves no doubt about it.

There is still another important distinction between Biblical

246

Hebrew and Mishnaic Hebrew, the Hebrew of *Pirke Abot,* and this has to do with vocabulary. In the thousand years between Isaiah and Judah the Prince many old words disappeared, and many new words were added. In this respect too Hebrew is no different from any other living language, especially if the language has a long known history. Now, many of the new words which entered the Hebrew language came from cultures and languages with which the Jews were brought into contact. Sometimes Hebrew was affected not only by the new words of the other language, but by the very grammatical patterns of that language. Thus, for example, many Aramaic words were absorbed by Hebrew, and the spirit of Aramaic penetrated late Biblical and then post-Biblical Hebrew almost down to the very roots—as a philologian might put it—in phonology and phonetics and accidence and syntax and lexicography. Aramaic, by the way, had this effect at one time not only on Hebrew but on the spoken and literary language of the whole Near East from India to Southern Egypt.

Again, after the death of Alexander the Great, when Judaism came under Hellenistic influences, Hebrew began to borrow a large number of Greek words to enrich its own vocabulary. These Greek loan-words reflect virtually the whole range of Hellenistic culture. Now we begin to meet Jewish sages with names like Antigonus; we find Hebrew sources using words like Sanhedrin to describe Jewish institutions. We come upon Greek terms adopted to express specific situations of the Hellenistic-Roman age, situations for which there is no perfect equivalent in the older Hebrew vocabulary. New terms are created in Hebrew for phenomena first encountered in the Hellenistic world. In short, Greek loan-words are appropriated and even Hebraized, as it were. Nor is it only with Greek that this happened. To a lesser extent the same took place with Latin. And we find also that ancient Hebrew words change their meaning, as they adjust to ever widening horizons of experience and new concepts become necessary. In this way the language adapts itself to the needs of the people, and in turn enlarges the capacity of the people to express itself.

Mishnaic Hebrew, the language of *Pirke Abot,* is thus the offspring of the language of the Prophets, but it has its own character, it reverberates with its own echoes, and carries its own message too. Its vocabulary and structure added a new dimension to the ancient words of the Law and the Prophets and the Holy Writings, and that vocabulary and structure made possible the creation of the second authoritative classic of Judaism, the Mishnah.

SIGNET and MENTOR Books of Related Interest

(0451)

☐ **THE STORY BIBLE: VOLUME I by Pearl S. Buck.** The winner of the Nobel and Pulitzer Prizes retells the Greatest Story Ever Told in the living language of our times. In VOLUME I the immortal stories of the Old Testament are brought to life with a power and immediacy for the modern reader. (119460—$2.95)

☐ **THE STORY BIBLE: VOLUME II by Pearl S. Buck.** This superlative rendering of the New Testament brings the crowning achievement of Pearl Buck's career, THE STORY BIBLE, to a triumphant conclusion. Here, adding relevance to its wisdom and freshness to its beauty, is the story of the birth, life, death and resurrection of Jesus. (126947—$2.95)

☐ **WHAT JESUS SAID ABOUT IT by K.H. Koestline.** In these pages, Jesus speaks to you about faith, love, healing, marriage, passion, discipleship, forgiveness—every milestone on your path to true spiritual freedom. (121961—$2.25)

☐ **THE CONFESSIONS OF ST. AUGUSTINE translated by Rex Warner.** The classic autobiography of the man who journeyed from sin to sainthood, from heresy to the highest theological insight, from the darkness of worldly ambition to the changeless light of grace. (621883—$3.95)

Buy them at your local bookstore or use this convenient coupon for ordering.

THE NEW AMERICAN LIBRARY, INC.,
P.O. Box 999, Bergenfield, New Jersey 07621

Please send me the books I have checked above. I am enclosing $_____
(please add $1.00 to this order to cover postage and handling). Send check or money order—no cash or C.O.D.'s. Prices and numbers are subject to change without notice.

Name_____

Address_____

City _____ State _____ Zip Code _____

Allow 4-6 weeks for delivery.
This offer is subject to withdrawal without notice.